Piers
the Plowman

LITERARY RELATIONS
OF THE A AND B TEXTS

By David C. Fowler

University of Washington Press
SEATTLE : 1961

To James Root Hulbert

PREFACE

Piers the Plowman is an English alliterative poem written in the second half of the fourteenth century. It exists in three distinct versions, customarily called the A, B, and C texts. The earliest form of the poem, the A-text, is the shortest of the three, having about 2,500 lines. The B-text is more than 7,000 lines long. The main reason for this greater length is that there is in B a continuation of some 4,000 lines added to the original poem. The C-text, although it is about the same length as B, is distinguished by a rather complex rearrangement of various passages. There are also some omissions, and a certain amount of new material is added in this third and final version.

The present book represents an effort to define the literary relations of the A and B texts of *Piers the Plowman*. It should perhaps be pointed out that there is a certain ambiguity in my use of the words "literary relations" in the title, for I am really referring to two things at once: first, the actual literary relationship of the two versions of the poem, and, second, the relation of the B-continuation itself to literary tradition. Chapter 1 is concerned exclusively with the A-text, and concentrates primarily on the latter part, the *Vita*, an understanding of which is especially important in an analysis of the relationship of A and B. Chapter 2 defines the literary traditions with which the reader must be acquainted in order to understand the structure of the B-continuation. Then chapters 3, 4, and 5 offer my analysis of the B-continuation. The literary relations of the A and B texts are a fundamental part of these chapters, although, as the title indicates, chapter 3 contains the most important discussion of this complicated matter. Chapter 6 returns to the A-text, but this time for the purpose of revealing the significance of the changes made in the B-poet's revision. The last chapter presents such evidence as I have been able to uncover concerning the identity of the author of the B-text.

The order of presentation just outlined may seem a bit perverse, but I believe it can be justified. It is of course difficult to say exactly what the poet's procedure was in making his revision. But my study of the B-text has led me to believe that we cannot understand the B-revision of A without first grasping the nature and purpose of the B-continuation. The poet must have at least conceived the main outlines of his continuation before he began to remake and remold the existing A-text. This is my conclusion. The reader will have to judge for himself. My only excuse for relegating discussion of the author to the last chapter is that the evidence which I offer concerning him emerged from my literary analysis. I began my study of the poem without the faintest notion concerning his identity.

So much has been done on *Piers the Plowman* in the last fifty years that it might be well to indicate briefly the position of this study in relation to the work of others. One of the most notorious features of *Piers Plowman* criticism, I suppose, is the energy that has been expended on the problem of authorship. This controversy began early in the present century, and has continued sporadically ever since. One immediate benefit of it was the realization by all concerned that new editions of the texts were sorely needed. An edition of all three texts is now being prepared,* but the only visible advance that has been made so far is an edition of the A-version by the late Professor Thomas A. Knott and the present writer, pub-

---

* The first volume has just been published: George Kane (ed.), *Piers Plowman, The A Version* (University of London: Athlone Press, 1960).

lished in 1952. This text is used in the following pages for A, but for B I have had to rely on the nineteenth-century edition of W. W. Skeat. Actually, Skeat's edition of the B-text is unusually good, and it is therefore unlikely that a new edition of it will require as many changes as did his edition of A.

Although it was recognized that new editions of the three versions of *Piers* were urgently needed, scholars very wisely did not wait for these to appear before undertaking studies of the poem. As a result, much has been done to advance our understanding of all three versions. There is not space here for a review of this scholarship, but I would like at least to mention those whose work I have found most helpful in the preparation of the present book. T. P. Dunning (A-text), D. W. Robertson, Jr., and B. F. Huppé (B-text), and E. T. Donaldson (C-text), though they vary considerably in their methods of approaching the poem, have all been of great value. Particularly stimulating to me has been the book by R. W. Frank, Jr., *Piers Plowman and the Scheme of Salvation,* published in 1957. Many other studies to which I am indebted are mentioned in the course of my analysis and in the footnotes.

There are two ways, however, in which I believe my work differs fundamentally from that of my predecessors. First of all, most recent *Piers Plowman* criticism is based on the assumption that the three texts of the poem are the product of a single mind. My analysis is based on no such assumption, and I make no apology for this. Our understanding of *Piers the Plowman* is helped, I believe, rather than hindered, by the existence of studies based on differing assumptions about its authorship. On the other hand, although I am a member of the multiple authorship "school," I make no attempt to argue this question in my analysis of the texts, nor should my criticism of the "biographical" method of reading the poem be construed as such an argument. My paraphrases of the meaning of the B-text in particular may seem at times to assume multiple authorship, but this cannot be avoided, since I am trying to represent the "tone" of the author, and the "tone" of B is often that of a conversation with A. In such cases, adherents of single authorship should read these "conversations" between authors as internal monologues in which the B-poet looks back on himself, the poet of the A-text, almost as if the latter were a separate individual.

The other way in which the present work differs to a considerable extent from earlier criticism is its emphasis on literary tradition. The studies mentioned above deal primarily with ideological influences such as scholasticism, scriptural tradition (especially in its relation to doctrine), and what might be called main currents of medieval thought. Without the benefit of these studies I am sure that this book could never have been written. But it does differ from them in its attempt to point out the literary traditions which combine to determine the structure of the poem, and which help explain the texture and meaning of its parts.

In the preparation of this study I have profited greatly from the advice and assistance of many individuals. I wish to thank especially members of the staff of the University of Washington Library for their many kindnesses, and their patience with my frequent requests. During my recent stay in England I enjoyed the unqualified cooperation of the librarians and assistants of the British Museum, the Public Record Office, Museum of the Royal Institution of Cornwall, the Morrab Library, and the libraries of Queen's College and the Bodleian at Oxford. To all these, and to many individuals both at home and abroad, I express my deepest gratitude. I am indebted also to colleagues who have heard me patiently and contributed valuable suggestions, and to graduate students whose specialized researches have been of great help in the preparation of this book. In particular I extend my warmest thanks to Professor Porter Perrin for reading the manuscript and providing incisive comments on its style, although I must of course take the responsibility for its final form. Publication of this book has been made possible by grants from the Agnes H. Anderson Fund of the Graduate School, University of Washington, and from the American Council of Learned Societies. For this support I am very grateful. Although I have not been able to thank individually all of those to whom I am indebted, I cannot resist at least mentioning my wife, Mary Gene Fowler, who, with an unparalleled selflessness, and a grace superior to both clergie and kind wit, literally made the writing of this book possible.

DAVID C. FOWLER

CONTENTS

Piers the Plowman:

Literary Relations of the A and B Texts

One

VITA DE DO-WEL, DO-BET, & DO-BEST IN THE A-TEXT

———◆•••◆———

In the last twenty years much has been accomplished in *Piers Plowman* scholarship. Books by Dunning, Robertson and Huppé, and Donaldson represent marked advances in our understanding, respectively, of the A, B, and C texts of the poem.[1] What is especially encouraging about these studies is that each concentrates on a single version, thus reducing that speculative tendency which too often hinders the critic who would deal with "the poem," meaning all three texts seen as one. Of course the ultimate goal should and must be a synoptic interpretation. But differences concerning proper methods of literary analysis must first be resolved, agreement must be reached on the nature of the allegorical structure in all versions, and then all the texts will need to be re-examined.

Meanwhile, I wish to offer, in the present chapter, an interpretation of the *Vita de Do-wel, Do-bet, & Do-best* of the A-text. This particular unit of *Piers the Plowman* constitutes, I believe, a pronounced challenge to anyone who would understand the nature of its allegory, its literary form, and its meaning. Yet it has been largely neglected. Students of the A-text have been interested primarily in the *Visio*, which has, certainly, an immediate and brilliant appeal; but the *Vita*, I hold, is a worthy companion to the *Visio*, and, when correctly understood, requires no apologies for its existence. Furthermore, if we are ever to arrive at a valid synoptic interpretation of

Piers the Plowman, we must first be firmly in control of the meaning of the *Vita* as it stands in the A-text. R. W. Frank, Jr., in a recent and important book, *Piers Plowman and the Scheme of Salvation,* gives the following as his reason for choosing the B-text as a basis for analysis: "I shall study the B-text version rather than the relatively neglected C-text, because the B-text, it is generally agreed, preceded the C-text, and because I believe one faces fewer problems working from an understanding of B to an understanding of C than one does working in the reverse order." [2] This seems to me an eminently sensible statement, to which I would merely add that it is likewise important to work from an understanding of A—all of it— to an understanding of B.

Before we can come to a direct analysis of the *Vita,* we will need to consider certain important preliminary matters. One of these is the problem of the exact form of the text itself. Another is the extent to which existing criticism of the *Vita* has advanced our understanding of it. A third very crucial matter concerns the genesis of the *Vita,* the way in which it grows out of the ending of the *Visio;* this will require an examination of the famous pardon scene in passus 8. Finally, we will need to consider the nature and function of allegory as it exists in the *Vita.* When these matters are dealt with, we will then be ready for a direct analysis of the text. And this analysis will reveal, I believe, that the *Vita de Do-wel, Do-bet, & Do-best* is a poem of remarkable penetration and power.

I

Concerning the form of the text it should first be noted that the A-version of *Piers the Plowman* actually consists of two poems. The first is the *Vision concerning Piers the Plowman* (called the *Visio*). At the end of passus 8 occurs a colophon which tells us that the *Visio* ends here, and that now there begins the *Life of Do-well, Do-better, and Do-best* (called the *Vita*). This statement in the colophon receives support from the fact that the following passus are headed

prologus, passus primus and *secundus* of *Do-wel,* etc., in the manuscripts.[3] This point is worth stressing, since editorial tradition, which
I shall follow in citing passus and line numbers, has established the
practice of referring to these units of the poem as passus 9, 10, and
11 of the A-text. This is simply a matter of convenience, and should
not be allowed to obscure the circumstance that we are here dealing
with the prologue and first and second passus of a separate poem.

One other very important point which needs to be made about
the form of the *Vita* is that it consists only of the prologue and
two passus, or passus 9, 10, and 11 according to the traditional num-
bering. A twelfth passus appears in one manuscript (R), and parts
of it are to be found in two others (U and I), but the textual evidence does not favor the hypothesis that this passus was ever an
organic part of the original A-text. Furthermore, a certain John
But, writing in the time of Richard II, tells us explicitly that he
"made this end" (12.106 ff.). Hence the weight of manuscript evidence and the testimony of John But combine to make it wholly
unlikely that the author of the A-text was responsible for any part
of the "John But" passus. I have tried elsewhere to state this case
as impartially as possible, and therefore will not pursue the matter
here.[4]

To the evidence afforded by textual criticism and the testimony of
John But, however, should be added the observation of impartial
readers of the A-text that the *Vita* ends with a clearly recognizable
climax in the closing lines of its second passus (11.301–3):

> Souteris and seweris, suche lewide jottis,
> Percen with a *pater noster* the paleis of hevene,
> Withoute penaunce, at here partyng, in-to the heighe blisse.

W. W. Skeat, in the EETS edition of the A-text (1867), calls attention to the finality of these lines:

> Each poem [the *Visio* and the *Vita*] is complete in itself, and the concluding
> passages of each are wrought with peculiar care with a view to giving them
> such completeness, by stating, at the end of each, the result which in each
> case the author wished to bring out strongly.[5]

And I think it is significant that the outstanding student of the A-text in recent years, Father Dunning, believes that the *Vita* comes to a definite close at the end of passus 11, and that the John But passus is in all probability not the work of the author of A:

> After considering the line of thought in the *Vita*, I find that the poem ends perfectly with Passus ii; and that Passus iii [i.e., passus 12] constitutes a sort of epilogue which, so far from continuing the poem, re-emphasizes the fact of its conclusion: it is really unnecessary. This would agree with Dr. Chambers' view that the third passus is an afterthought of the poet, added when the poem itself already existed in some MSS. But, for my part, I should not be surprised were this passus—or fragment of one—definitely proved spurious.[6]

It has been necessary to stress the point that the *Vita* ends at the close of the eleventh passus, for it is still a very common experience to read in *Piers Plowman* criticism, especially the criticism written by scholars whose main concern is not the A-text, that the A-version "breaks off sharply." Thus we find in the latest book on the B-text: "The A-text comes to an abrupt close here. There is a hasty conclusion, but in it the Dreamer's questions are not answered."[7] The persistence of this belief about the A-text may be in part attributable to the presence of passus 12 in the parallel text edition (1886), following hard upon the eleventh passus without a break, and to the suppression, in this same edition, of the concluding lines, where John But signs his name. Yet it is to be feared that persistent statements to the effect that A "breaks off sharply" may also be due in part to considerations lying wholly outside the text itself. In short, if the text is read primarily as autobiography, rather than as poetry, then the "sudden end" provides an admirable means of showing how the poet, unable to answer the perplexing questions raised at the end of the A-text, brings his poem to an abrupt close, only to take these questions up later in B, where he successfully answers them.[8]

This biographical method of reading the A-text gains considerable strength, also, if the critic already believes that our poet to some extent lacks the ability to organize his thoughts, or, on the other hand, is careless about or disdainful of detailed attention to esthetic considerations in his poem.[9] Now it may be argued that those critics who would dispense with the John But passus as spurious, and regard the *Vita* as a unified work of art, are motivated by a biased desire to avoid recognition of incoherencies, uncertainties, or halting conclusions in the poem. If this is the case, then let me hasten to count myself among those whose prejudice leads them to believe that our poet is, in every way, in complete command of his poem. But the following interpretation of the *Vita* will, I hope, serve to establish that this attitude is based, not on bias, but on truth.

II

The only study of the A-text of *Piers the Plowman* concerned exclusively with the *Vita de Do-wel, Do-bet, & Do-best* is that undertaken many years ago by Otto Mensendieck.[10] He states:

> The Visions of Dowell, etc., contain experiences and confessions of the author in autobiographical chronology, where the different periods appear disguised as allegorical figures and following each other from passus to passus in the same order as they had followed each other in the actual life of the author.[11]

He then goes on, in his analysis, to make some valuable observations on the way in which the *trivium, quadrivium,* etc., figure in the poem. But he is mainly concerned, as the above quotation shows, with demonstrating that the poet is here setting forth his autobiography. And, as is so often true, this preoccupation leads the critic to make some rather harsh statements about the poet's abilities: "But it is not she [Dame Study] who is illogical, it is a man this time, the author. He cannot speak and write systematically. . . . We thank him this time, if not always, for the unsystematic bent of his nature. For he thus proves to us that here again we have a piece of autobiography. . . ." (p. 409). Later on Mensendieck summarizes passus 11 and then asks, "How are we to account for such an incongruity between the beginning and the end of this vision? . . . And all this under the heading: What is Dowell?" He then concludes that the incongruities and contradictions can only be explained as experiences from the author's own life.[12] Now in a sense the incongruities and contradictions to which Mensendieck refers are in the text, but they are there for a purpose, and I do not believe that he has understood what that purpose is.

No student will ever get very far with the A-text, of course, unless he builds on the foundation laid by Father Dunning,[13] whose study deserves attention, not only because of its learning, but also because of its penetrating analysis of the text, unimpeded by extra-textual considerations. The following summary is merely an effort to reproduce the main points in Dunning's analysis of the *Vita:*

First of all, Father Dunning notes, the *Vita* is a "finished poem." Even the twelfth passus confirms this. It adds nothing to what has gone before, and may well prove to be spurious, whereas the eleventh passus comes to an emphatic conclusion. In form, the poem is a *débat,* and some of the participants, e.g., "Thought" and "Wit," function precisely in accordance with the appropriate medieval definitions. In passus 9 (which is the prologue) the friars give the Dreamer orthodox instruction on the avoidance of deadly sin, and the Dreamer, though he doesn't understand them, thanks them and goes to sleep. In his vision he sees Thought, whose definitions of Do-wel, Do-bet, and Do-best as objective states of perfection fail to satisfy the Dreamer. However, in passus 10, Wit's discourse on Inwit and his definitions of the triad seem intended as the most acceptable to the Dreamer, the definitions evidently reflecting the subjective states, that is, the Purgative, Illuminative, and Unitive states or ways of perfection (well-doing). Wit teaches that man, through fear of God, can overcome self-will; that this is a matter independent of station, and that man should therefore not "covet to climb"; and, finally, that married folk should keep God's law. In passus 11, Study's rebuke to the Dreamer (11.86–91) accords well with what Wit said earlier about the subjective states, but it is in complete opposition to Thought's definition of the triad as repre-

senting objective states of perfection (9.69–100). Clergie's definition, in passus 11, is reminiscent of Thought's, and is equally unac-
ceptable to the Dreamer. In response to the Dreamer's question and
objection Scripture concludes the *débat* by stressing the law of love.
The Dreamer then sums up (11.250–303). After considering such
problems as predestination and the righteous heathen, he dismisses
them as unwarranted efforts to "wit the ways of God Almighty,"
and concludes by repudiating the value of learning. Salvation comes
soonest to unlettered poor people and plowmen. This ending is
carefully prepared (cf. 11.53–57), and accords perfectly with the
ending of the *Visio;* indeed, the two poems, though distinct, are
very closely linked.[14]

It is well to have this summary before us, I think, not only in
order to be reminded of the procession of ideas and definitions
presented in the *Vita,* but also because Father Dunning's analysis,
however inadequately summarized, sharpens and underscores some
of the questions that must be raised and, if possible, answered in
any further exploration of the form and meaning of the poem.
Here I call attention only to his statement concerning the close
relationship between the *Visio* and the *Vita,* for it is to this question
that we must now turn.

III

If anything is certain, it is that the *Vita de Do-wel, Do-bet, & Do-
best* has its origin in the pardon scene of the *Visio* (passus 8). We
must first of all, therefore, consider in some detail the significance
of this episode. The purpose of the clash between Piers and the
priest, and the tearing of the pardon, have challenged the ingenuity
of critics for many years. When the dust has settled, however, I
believe we shall find that it is R. W. Frank, Jr., who has taught us the
meaning of the pardon scene.[15] In the following remarks, therefore, I am greatly indebted to his interpretation.

It will be recalled that the *Visio* contains two very striking allegorical actions. The first centers on Lady Meed, who dramatizes the corrupting effect of cupidity in modern society. Then, in response to Conscience's appeal to the folk to repent and seek St. Truth, there follow the confessions of the deadly sins, which mark the transition leading to the appearance of Piers, the plowman, the central figure in the second part of the *Visio,* who agrees to lead the now penitent folk to St. Truth.

Piers, of course, stands in sharp contrast to Lady Meed. She reveals the way to damnation; Piers shows the way to salvation. The poet makes this particularly clear in passus 6, where Piers describes the way to Truth (God), described allegorically in terms of the Great Commandment and the decalogue (6.48–123). It is important to realize that this passage states fully the poet's view of the life of good works in the broadest sense, for it includes not only the commandments, but also stresses penance (6.85–87), grace (92), the danger of relying on good works as a means of "earning" salvation (95–103), the seven virtues (105–14), and mercy (115–23). I do not believe that the poet intends for us to have any reservations here whatsoever; this is the Way to salvation, and Piers, the humble plowman, is the guide. In the seventh passus occurs the plowing of the half-acre, that is, the actual life which the penitent folk must live on this earth. What happens is what we might expect. Some members of society do their assigned tasks as they should, but others help by singing in the tavern. In time of plenty, workers are lazy; when famine strikes, many a "beggar" is miraculously cured of his infirmities, and the wasters bestir themselves once more. At the end of passus 7, the pilgrimage to Truth seems as far away as ever, and workmen are sternly warned to win while they may, for another famine is coming soon.

With this warning of an approaching famine the seventh passus comes to the end, and passus 8 begins as follows (8.1–8):

> Treuthe herde telle here-of, and to Peris sente
> To take his tem, and tilien the erthe;
> And purchacede hym a pardoun *a pena et a culpa,*

> For hym and for hise heires, evere more aftir.
> And bad hym holde hym at hom, and eren his laighes;
> And al that holpen hym to eren or to sowen,
> Or any maner myster that mighte Peris helpen,
> Part in that pardoun the pope hath ygrauntid.

We learn from these lines, first, that Truth sent word to Piers not to set forth on the pilgrimage but to remain at home and plow his land, that is, live the life of good works on this earth in the manner already prescribed. The poet adopts this means of terminating, on the narrative level, a pilgrimage motif which has well served his purpose in passus 6 and 7.[16] Simultaneously, however, and more important, he is setting the stage for his final and most emphatic statement concerning the way to salvation, the statement given in the pardon itself (8.94). This pardon contains nothing new; it marks no transition in the character of Piers or in the poet's thinking; it serves, however, as the climax for the entire *Visio,* and is therefore of the utmost importance. Its phraseology is stark: Do well and you will be rewarded, do evil and you will be punished. But if this is true, then why call it a "pardon" at all? "I can no pardon find," says the priest to Piers, and he is correct; it is *not* a pardon. Yet the poet appears to be deliberately misleading us, for not only does he clearly state that Truth procured Piers a pardon, but to this he attaches the phrase *a pena et a culpa,* the exaggerated language familiarly associated with conventional pardons, and then he even goes so far as to specify that a share in this pardon has been granted to those who help Piers *by the pope.*[17]

But these things can be considered misleading only if we fail to perceive the poet's irony. This whole passage is building toward a sharp contrast between the way to salvation proclaimed by corrupt representatives of Holy Church in the poet's day and the true way to salvation represented by Piers the plowman. All the talk about pardons, therefore, is designed as a lure for the gullible (cf. A prol. 69 ff.) and as a means of providing a greater wrench when the pardon is shown to be "no pardon." As a matter of fact, the alert

reader has all the clues he needs in order to anticipate the denoue-
ment. The document sent by Truth is truly a pardon *a pena et a
culpa:* if you do well, there will be no punishment *and no guilt.*
The irony is unmistakable. Further, the lines describing those groups
affected by the pardon (8.9–88) are clearly designed to generate a
growing sense of incongruity. Surely no conventional pardon ever
contained such passionate language in defense of good laborers,
old folk, and women with child, nor such biting satire on the shortcomings of merchants, lawyers, and false beggars!

When the poet finally reveals this "pardon," the reader is leaning
eagerly forward with the Dreamer to see the document (8.93–94):

> In two lynes it lay, and nought a lettre more,
> And was writen right thus, in witnesse of Treuthe:
>   *Et qui bona egerunt, ibunt in vitam eternam;
>   Qui vero mala, in ignem eternum.*

By placing these two famous lines from the Athanasian Creed in the
"pardon" context which we have just examined, the poet fuses
powerfully the thematic extremes of the *Visio:* not only has Lady
Meed entered the pope's palace (2.18), but she has also found her
way to the very heart of Holy Church, the sacrament of penance.
Theoretically, of course, a man could not benefit by indulgences if
he were not truly repentant; but our poet has made it quite clear
in the prologue (65 ff.) that he is not interested in theory. When
the priest next exclaims that he can find no pardon, it becomes apparent that he is not in on the poet's grim joke, but rather belongs
with the gullible reader who expects to see the "real thing." More
to the point, he is clearly one of those priests who divide the silver
with false pardoners (prol. 78). He is, in short, to be viewed as a
quite worldly individual, and he functions here for the poet as a
villain.

Piers's response to the priest is to tear the pardon in anger ("for
pure tene"). His anger is clearly directed at the priest, and corresponds exactly to the "tene" of the poet in the prologue, where the
gullible folk ("lewide men") are addressed as follows (prol. 73–74):

> Thus ye yeven youre gold glotonis to helpe,
> And levith it loselis that leccherie haunten!

The actual tearing of the paper "pardon" symbolizes, as Frank has convincingly demonstrated, Piers's rejection of conventional pardons, bulls with seals, and, at the same time, his acceptance of Truth's message. Truth's message, after all, constitutes explicit divine authentication of the way of life which Piers represents.

But why does Piers then say (8.100 ff.) that he will cease his sowing and work not so hard, nor be so busy about his livelihood? Hasn't Truth just told him to stay at home and plow and sow his land (8.5–6)? To be sure. But the words "I shal cesse of my sowyng" function dramatically, to reveal the act of will by which Piers is able to free himself of overconcern for the things of this life, and the words immediately following confirm this: "and swynke not so harde, Ne aboute my liflode so besy be namore."

Yet one might still ask why Piers chooses this crucial time for expressing a resolve not to be too solicitous about his bodily welfare. To answer this question we should first remind ourselves that Piers's anger, directed at the priest, is a subordinate factor at this highly dramatic moment. It is of overriding importance that Piers has just received a message from Truth. And it should be observed that Piers is at no time in this passage (8.99–113) addressing the priest, or anyone else physically present in the narrative. He does, however, clearly address Truth Himself, in the words which he takes from the Psalter (the twenty-third psalm, or twenty-second in the Vulgate), *quoniam tu mecum es,* "for Thou art with me," constituting, as Frank points out, a traditional affirmation of faith. He then goes on to repent of his overconcern for his daily bread, and dedicates himself to prayers and penance.

The two elements in Piers's speech, *quoniam tu mecum es* (faith) and *ne soliciti sitis* (repentance), must be understood first in their relation to Piers himself. In a sense, they echo the two main components of traditional religious experience. *I have heard of thee by the hearing of the ear, but now mine eye seeth thee,* says Job; *where-*

fore I abhor myself, and repent in dust and ashes. Piers "sees" Truth; therefore he "repents." In this way the poet has added a profound dimension of religious experience to the scene. But I do not believe that this was his primary concern.[18] The main emphasis of the poet can be seen when we realize that Piers's words (8.100–13) are designed to provide an ideal example of true repentance. This demonstration of genuine contrition of heart is in no way a preparation for some new theme to be developed later in the poem;[19] rather it is a simple fulfillment of Piers's own injunction regarding penance (6.85–7), and it functions here as a direct refutation of conventional pardons.[20] Now pardons are granted only when preceded by true penance—so goes the theory. But Piers's tearing of the paper and his simultaneous enactment of genuine contrition dramatize this question: If a man is truly repentant, and performs his penance, but does not have the subsequent benefit of an indulgence, what then? Has he not fulfilled the law of Holy Church? And does this not show that a pardon is indeed "no pardon"? Theoretically, of course, the answer is that a pardon still "avails." And although I do not believe that the theology involved here (the doctrine of the treasury) was beyond the poet's comprehension,[21] I do believe that the pardon scene reveals it to have been beyond his patience. It should be understood, of course, that his impatience springs, not from any inborn dislike of intellectual refinements, but rather from the glaring discrepancy between theory and practice. Every reader of the *Visio* has certainly noted the poet's angry awareness of this discrepancy. *Faith* and *fait, preach* and *prove* run through the poem as a powerful theme.

Yet since the poet views the issue of pardons in the light of the discrepancy between theory and practice, we should not be surprised to find that in his eyes their intellectual justification seems relatively flimsy, if not indeed at one with the dark and fallacious persuasiveness of Lady Meed herself. But here the poet stops short (if indeed he ever got this far in conscious reflection), for he has reached holy ground. And if anything is clear in the poem, it is that the author believes loyally in the teaching of Holy Church. He is no heretic, nor is he, as earlier critics have thought, a forerunner of the Reformation. Still, though he can stop short intellectually, he cannot banish his anger, and he therefore lets loose the full force of his indignation against the idea that learning, as such, is of any value whatsoever. This can be seen in his characterization of the priest (8.114-15):

> "What!" quath the prest to Perkyn, "Peter! as me thinketh,
> Thou art lettrid a litel; who lernide the on boke?"

The delineation of the priest's character here is admirable. He could not remain unmoved by Piers's eloquent paraphrase of the passage from the Sermon on the Mount; he also senses, however, that spiritual issues are vibrant in the air around him, yet he (the learned man, the priest!) is failing to grasp their import, while Piers, the ignorant plowman, has evidently absorbed them fully. His praise of Piers's "learning" is therefore patently ironic. This is confirmed by the mild rebuke contained in Piers's reply (8.116-17):

> "Abstinence the abbesse myn a. b. c. me taughte,
> And Consience com aftir, and kennide me betere."

These are the first words spoken by Piers directly to the priest, and they function in a very important way as a bridge between the elevated tone of Piers's repentance in response to Truth's message and the open quarrel that breaks out in the following lines. But they also serve to stimulate a growing sense of inadequacy in the priest, to which the latter responds, however, not with a corresponding contrition of his own, but rather with the most withering sarcasm (8.118-19):

> "Were thou a prest, Piers," quath he, "thou mightest preche
> whan the likide:
> *Quoniam literaturam non cognovi*—that mighte be thi teme."

This is a riposte born of sheer desperation. Piers then replies scornfully in the priest's own terms (8.120-21), and the Dreamer awakes.

Thus it is clear that the open argument between Piers and the priest revolves around the value of learning, and that Piers, the un-learned man, is presented in a favorable light, while the learned priest is made to seem very small indeed. The Dreamer then sums up (8.127–81) by concluding that doing well, in accordance with Truth's message, is superior to indulgences such as the priest had in mind. But even here, in his conclusion, the poet manages one more thrust at learning. After discussing the reliability of dreams, the Dreamer says (8.146 ff.) that many times at midnight when men should be sleeping he thought

> On Peris the ploughman, whiche a pardoun he hadde,
> And how the prest inpugnid it, *al be pure resoun*.

The double meaning of the italicized phrase should be obvious. It is both a reaffirmation of Truth's message and an ironic comment on the value of learning: (1) the priest *quite rightly* impugned Piers's pardon, for it is not a "pardon"; and (2) on the other hand, al-though Truth's message is a leaf of the Athanasian Creed and is valid for all mankind, the priest impugned it *with impeccable reasoning*.[22]

The preceding analysis of the pardon scene has been designed to prepare the way for an answer to the question: How does the *Vita* grow out of the *Visio*? Perhaps I can atone for the length of the analysis by stating flatly and without qualification my answer to this question. The premeditated purpose of the poet in the *Vita de Do-wel, Do-bet, & Do-best* is to *prove* that Learning is *not* the way to salvation.

IV

There are two important reasons for considering the nature and function of allegory in the *Vita* before attempting to interpret it. One is that there is little general agreement on the role of literary criticism in interpreting allegory, or even on what constitutes a proper definition of allegory, whether as an artistic device, or as a literary form. The other reason is that there has been a notable lack of agreement on the application of allegorical interpretation to *Piers the Plowman*.[23] There is obviously not room to review these problems here. I will simply have to state my conviction that the allegory in the A-text is to be read literally, that is, that it says what it means and requires no probing for "levels of meaning" in the exegetical tradition.

There is, however, a distinction to be made between the allegorical methods employed in the *Visio* and in the *Vita*, which is valid, I think, so long as we keep in mind that few allegorical works ever adhere to a rigid system or "pure" allegorical form.[24] The personifications in the *Visio* frequently engage in a clear-cut allegorical action. For example: Meed seeks to obtain mercy for Wrong (who had attacked Peace), aided by the counsel of Wisdom and Wit, but Conscience refuses (passus 4). On the other hand, no such action takes place in the *Vita*. There we find speeches by Thought, Wit, Study, etc., whose names are to be understood literally: What Thought says is what the Dreamer can learn by thinking, etc. Thus in a very general way we might contrast the use of allegory in the two poems by saying that the *Visio* exhibits an allegorical action, while the *Vita* presents an allegorical meditation. The one is external and shows us the Way (to save our souls); the other is internal and considers a Problem (the value of learning).

The internal nature of the *Vita* allegory is of course evident in the personifications Thought and Wit. These are functions of the intellect. But not all of the speakers fit this rigid category. For Study is not a faculty, but something that the mind engages in, an activity, while Clergie is "learning"—that which the mind acquires —and Scripture is "writing," the means by which one acquires knowledge or learning. Nevertheless all of these personifications function harmoniously in what is clearly an internal *débat* taking place in the mind of the Dreamer. This is worth stressing, for we must not slip into the error of supposing that Study and Scripture, for example, are represented by the poet as entities outside the Dreamer's reach who would tell him what he ought to know if he could only understand them. Nothing of the sort is suggested anywhere in the text.

This brings us to the Dreamer himself, the most important single figure in the *Vita,* whose mind encompasses the debate. And it is important to note that although, as Mensendieck perceived,[25] the poet uses an educational motif, his Dreamer is not being educated. He never changes. Father Dunning's observations here are very important: [26]

> . . . I cannot regard the development of the poem as marking a definite progression towards the knowledge of *Dowel,* in the sense that each definition of Dowel, Dobet and Dobest rules out and is superior to the one preceding it: the development of the poem can be considered progressive only in so far as each new speaker provides further material for the dreamer's consideration, and for comparison with what he has already heard. It is the judgment of the dreamer, concluding the debate, that must finally decide what conclusions we are to carry away with us from the poem.

It is of course true that the Dreamer asks questions and protests his ignorance, but his questions are often loaded and his ignorance is Swiftian. Once we perceive these facts about the literary character of the Dreamer, it is then legitimate to point out that his views are, indeed, to be very closely associated with those of the author. But this is not "autobiography." Far from it. The Dreamer of the *Vita* sets out on a Quest which the poet has decreed shall end in failure.[27]

V

The *Vita de Do-wel, Do-bet, & Do-best,* as attested by the A-text manuscripts, is a complete and independent poem, with a beginning, a middle, and an end. Yet it is intimately bound up with the *Visio,* and grows out of the clash between Piers and the priest, the respective representatives of the unschooled and the learned. It is, further, cast in the form of an internal debate, the result of the

Dreamer's (and the poet's) meditations, "manye tymes at mydnight, whan men shulde slepe" (8.147). And the poet's unwavering purpose is to communicate the idea that learning is not the way to salvation. With these points in mind we are ready for a direct examination of the poem itself.

Prologue

> Thus yrobid in rosset I romide aboute,
> Al a somer sesoun, for to seke Do-wel.   (9.1–2)

Since I have said that the poet sets out to prove that learning is not the way to salvation, it is worth stressing that the *Vita* is obviously not formulated in exactly those terms. The poem is no mere diatribe against learning. Rather, as the opening lines indicate, it is cast in the form of a Quest, a search for Do-wel, to find "where Do-wel is," that is, where or among what groups in contemporary society one will find the good life which represents the way to salvation.

The Dreamer therefore wanders, as he tells us, until he meets two friars. This encounter is of considerable importance, for it sets the tone for the entire vision that follows.[28] The friars are introduced because of their great reputation for learning, and it is important to observe that the poet's delineation of them is clearly satirical. The learned are destined not to fare well in the *Vita*. Of course the conversation between the Dreamer and the friars is polite,[29] but that is just the point—it is *too* polite; and the first line describing these friars is meant to determine our attitude toward them (9.9):

> *Maistris* of the *menours*, men of gret wit.

Surely no one can miss this trenchant play on words: "Maistris" and "menours," as the poet would say, "mowe not dwelle togidere." [30]

The Dreamer opens the conversation by asking the friars where Do-wel is, and, when they tell him that Do-wel dwells with them, he then assumes the stance of a scholastic debater, and opposes them with *contra* and *ergo*. But it is an ironic pose: even the righteous (you friars) sin seven times a day, he says; hence Do-wel can't *always* be with you. Note that the Dreamer's argument is deliberately obtuse in its theology. It contains the same cutting oversimplification as did Truth's "pardon" in the *Visio,* and the response of the friar reveals that he, like the priest before him, is not in on the joke. For the Dreamer is getting a kind of bitter enjoyment out of the friar's use of a learned "forebisene" to deflect attention from the actual moral condition of the friars themselves. Thus the friar functions as a "straight man," and his sermon contains orthodox teaching. But the effect of his elaborate simile of the boat is clearly that of a homiletic *tour de force,* for while it admirably reveals his ability to *preche,* it is falling on the ears of a man (the Dreamer) who is looking for someone with the ability to *preve it him selve.* In this matter the friar fails to qualify, and his learning therefore has a hollow ring, however orthodox the ideas presented in his example.

"I have no *kynde knowyng,*" says the Dreamer politely, "to conseyve thi wordis" (9.48). The poet uses *kynde knowyng* here very deliberately. He means, literally, "natural understanding." [31] But it is not enough to recognize the literal meaning. In one sense, of course, the Dreamer means simply that he is not able to understand the friar. But it is the tone of his statement that is important, and to detect this we must be aware of the satiric context. In effect the Dreamer implies that he does not find Do-wel among the friars, for Do-wel cannot be recognized intellectually through words; rather it is a way of life, and will therefore be "naturally" known through its deeds, without need of learned window dressing. The emphasis is on an instinctive, almost "physical" apprehension, the kind of unlettered "knowing," in fact, which can penetrate intellectual disguises. [32]

The Dreamer bids farewell to the friars, and then, after wandering alone by a wood, he falls asleep under a tree to the sound of singing birds. In his dream he sees Thought, who gives him the first of a series of definitions of Do-wel, Do-bet, and Do-best. Now since Thought is the first to mention this important triad, we should pause here for a moment to consider, first, why the poet introduces it, and second, what specifically he means to convey through the use of it. The answer to these questions should be immediately apparent when we recall the purpose and form of the *Vita*. Its purpose, as has been pointed out, is to demonstrate that learning is not the way to salvation, but its form is that of a Quest (where is Do-wel?), and the Dreamer is therefore going to conduct a search through various groups and levels of society in an effort to find Do-wel. His encounter with the friars prepares us for this. The triad of Do-wel, Do-bet, and Do-best thus serves admirably to define the three levels of society that the poet wishes primarily to consider: the commons (Do-wel), the clergy, whether secular or regular (Do-bet), and the episcopate, or high ecclesiastical office in general (Do-best). It is important to realize that throughout the *Vita* this basic meaning of the triad never changes. Furthermore—and this is the beauty of the poet's invention—the triad enables the poet to avoid any appearance of animosity toward the main object of his satire (Do-bet), while at the same time he is able to affirm the lofty ideal to which the clergy (and all ranks) should aspire. It is a remarkable invention, and became justly famous in the poet's own day.[33]

Once it is understood that Do-wel stands for the commons, Do-bet for the clergy, and Do-best for the episcopate, then the form and emphasis of the actual definitions given in the *Vita* become immediately significant. Because of the poet's abiding interest in poor people, such as plowmen and pastors of beasts, i.e., the commons (Do-wel), we can expect him to devote considerable space to their condition and to exhortations for their betterment. Similarly, it should not be surprising to find (as we shall) that in this "loaded" Quest for the good life, the clergy, both secular and regular (Do-bet), are the main target of the poet's satire. On the other hand, little is said about the life of bishops (Do-best). This at first might be thought to imply that the poet is quite satisfied with existing conditions at that level of society, though a look at the prologue of the *Visio* (lines 75–76) suggests that this is unlikely. More to the point, however, I think the poet's own lack of experience in the world of high religious office (attested by the manner and content of both the *Visio* and the *Vita*) has led him to limit himself to statements concerning the theoretical function of Do-best in relation both to Do-wel and Do-bet, and to secular authority. The episcopal life as a whole lies beyond the horizon of his experience. Hence he has attempted no ersatz depiction or evaluation of that life. In this, as in so many other ways, our poet reveals the strict discipline of his art.

Thought defines Do-wel, Do-bet, and Do-best as "thre faire vertues" (9.70 ff.). Do-wel follows those who work for a living, and are meek, true, honest, and lead a sober, respectable life. Clearly this refers to the commons. Do-bet represents the life of those who, besides conforming to Do-wel, are humble and mild of speech (9.77–80):

> He is as lough as a lomb, lovelich of speche,
> Whiles he hath ought of his owene he helpith there nede is,
> The bagges and the bygirdles he hath broken hem alle,
> That the erl Averous hadde, or his eires.

With this compare Chaucer's description of the priest in the *Canterbury Tales,* General Prologue, 487–89, 515–23:

> But rather wolde he yeven, out of doute,
> Unto his povre parisshens aboute
> Of his offryng and eek of his substaunce.
>
> .   .   .   .
>
> And though he hooly were and vertuous,
> He was to synful men nat despitous,
> Ne of his speche daungerous ne digne,
> But in his techyng discreet and benygne.
> To drawen folk to hevene by fairnesse,
> By good ensample, this was his bisynesse.
> But it were any persone obstinat,
> What so he were, of heigh or lough estat,
> Hym wolde he snybben sharply for the nonys.

These two descriptions of an ideal man of religion are remarkably similar. Our poet does not often resemble Chaucer in this way, because he is rarely content to describe the ideal without reference to those who fail to measure up to it. In the lines quoted, however (9.77–80), he shows marked restraint, especially considering the fact that he is here contrasting the lowness and the lovely speech of his ideal with the characteristics of the arrogant and sarcastic priest in the *Visio*.

But four lines of objective description are about all that the poet can permit himself. Thought goes on to say of Do-bet (9.81–85):

> And with Mammones money he hath mad hym frendis,
> And is ronne to religioun, and hath rendrit the bible,
> And prechith the peple Seint Poulis wordis:
> > *Libenter sufferte, &c.*
> 'Ye wise, suffrith the unwise with yow for to libbe.'
> And with glad wil doth hem good, for so God hym self highte.

The scene has changed! Mention of the earl Averous marks a shift from the ideal to the real, from the pure to the corrupt, and the passage just quoted differs as sharply from the initial definition of Do-bet as Chaucer's friar differs from his parson. Our poet is, indeed, now talking about the friars.[34] Of course there is still a pretense of objectivity, but the reference to Luke 16:9 and the quotation from 2 Corinthians 11:19 reveal that something has happened to the tenor of Thought's remarks. He is now describing—"defining" is hardly the word—the typical worldly individual who, responding to the call of the gospel, *Make to yourselves friends of the mammon of unrighteousness* (properly "rendered"), has taken up religion and now preaches on the text: *For ye suffer fools gladly, seeing ye yourselves are wise.* And the last line (85) fairly radiates the very condescension which St. Paul is ironically condemning in the scriptural passage quoted![35] A sharper contrast between the ideal and the reality, as set forth in this "definition" of Do-bet, can scarcely be imagined. It should not be supposed, however, that the Dreamer has found a friend, "Thought," who now joins him in satirizing ecclesiastical corruption. Rather we are attuned to the "thoughts" of the Dreamer himself, meditating on the nature of the good life as it is to be found in the world around him, in theory and in practice, and musing on the value of learning as a way to salvation.

Thought's definition of Do-best (9.86–96) fits into the pattern of the triad very well, and is a fairly straightforward account of the relationship of church and state.[36] Do-best, we are told, bears a bishop's crosier, which is then described allegorically so as to reveal the bishop's authority and responsibility. At one end of this staff is the hook, for holding men in good life; at the other is the spike, for poking down such wicked men as may be planning to injure or annoy the commons (Do-wel). Then follows the description, in terms of the triad, of the church-state relationship. Do-wel and Do-bet have crowned one king to have authority over them, that is, a king whose jurisdiction embraces both the commons and the clergy (90–91). This arrangement enables the king to aid in the enforcement of episcopal authority, while at the same time the bishop can, if he so desires, intercede with the king on behalf of individuals from among either the commons or the clergy (92–96). Finally, Thought sums up (97–100) by saying that the king reigns by the consent and with the advice of the commons, clergy, and bishops. This would appear to be the extent of the poet's knowledge of or interest in such matters. For the Dreamer, though he has no doubt taken cognizance of the definitions of Thought, is anxious to know more, not about the status or relationships of Do-wel, Do-bet, and Do-best, but rather about how they "don on this erthe" (9.104), that is, where they are literally to be found (the Quest). In the next passus Wit provides some fresh definitions of considerable significance, but even these, important as they are, cannot, as we shall see, give the Dreamer that "kynde knowyng" which he so earnestly desires.

Passus 1

In his definition of the triad, Wit makes exactly the same equation that we found in Thought: Do-wel represents the commons, Do-bet the clergy, and Do-best the episcopate. But there is a difference in approach, for the poet clearly intends us to see that Wit (which he elsewhere equates, albeit pejoratively, with Wisdom) probes deeper than Thought. The latter has simply defined the three concepts in terms of their place and function in society; Wit is now going to define them with particular attention devoted to their internal or spiritual qualities.

Of fundamental importance in Wit's definition is the fact that Do-wel (the commons) is the real center of attention. Do-bet and Do-best (clergy and episcopate) are derived therefrom and they have no function or *raison d'être* apart from Do-wel. In the figure of the castle (10.1–75), "man with his soule" (39), is Everyman; this is obvious enough. But Wit tells us that since the soul (*Anima*) was in danger from the wiles of the devil (*Princeps huius mundi*), God (Kynde) "hath don hire to Sire Do-wel" (10.11). Thus the soul is in the keeping of Do-wel, that is, mankind as a whole is represented by the commons. Wit then goes on to show how the devil's wiles are thwarted through the relationship of the rest of the triad to Do-wel (10.12–15):

> Do-bet is hire [*Anima's*] damysele, Sire Do-welis doughter,
> And servith this lady lelly bothe late and rathe.
> Thus Do-wel and Do-bet and Do-best the thridde
> Beth maistris of this maner this maide to kepe.

Do-bet is very aptly described here as the servant of *Anima,* for the clergy is charged with the cure of souls. Likewise Do-best, by implication, is the *servus servorum.*[37] In the terms of the Castle figure, of course, members of the triad are "maistris" of the manor. But it should be obvious that the poet is here emphasizing humility, the ideal spiritual condition, in sharp contrast, for example, to the "maistris of the menours" in the prologue (9.8).

Having thus revealed how the structure of society, ideally conceived, serves to protect the soul, Wit next examines "man with his soule" in order to show how God has placed within mankind the instruments necessary for living the good life, that is, an ability to comprehend what is good (Inwit, aided by the five senses), and a will to act ("chief sovereyn over hym self," 72) in response to his recognition of the good. There are, of course, as Wit explains, exceptions to this (10.56–70). Sots who sit drinking in the ale house pour ale into their heads until Inwit is drowned. Such men, deprived of their protector, "the cunstable of the castel," are easy prey to the devil's wiles. Children and "fools," however, are the responsibility of parents, guardians, and Holy Church. This whole passage is an admirable illustration of the poet's ability to set forth the mechanics of the soul with clarity and force.[38]

God has placed man in a society organized for his spiritual security. He has likewise granted men the ability, if they will use it, to live the good life. Having established these facts, Wit now goes on to define Do-wel, Do-bet, and Do-best in such a way as to emphasize a certain spiritual quality for each. For Do-wel, this is fear of the Lord; for Do-bet, it is patience ("suffraunce"); for Do-best, humility. These definitions are not intended, of course, to serve as an exhaustive analysis of the virtues attributable to the triad. Rather they are chosen because these particular virtues stand in direct opposition to contemporary abuses which Wit is going to denounce. This can be seen to apply clearly to Do-wel and Do-bet. Do-best receives little detailed attention, for the reasons I have already given. Nevertheless, the ideal for the episcopate is beautifully expressed, as we shall see, in the figure of the rose.

After explaining Do-wel as fear of God, Wit starts to define Do-bet by first pointing out that the latter includes the former. Do-bet is "to ben ywar for betyng of the yarde," i.e., fear of God's chastisement, as witnessed in the Psalter (quoting Ps. 23:4). But then,

instead of proceeding directly to his definition of Do-bet ("suffraunce"), Wit pauses to give the Dreamer some advice, which, although it is related to the forthcoming definition, seems extremely
personal. Here it is (10.87–99):

> Ac yif clene consience acorde that thi self dost wel,
> Wilne thou nevere in this world for to do betere;
> For, *Intencio indicat hominem, &c.*
> Be counseil of consience, accordyng with holy chirche,
> Loke thou wisse thi wyt, and thi werkis aftir;
> For yif thou comist ayen consience thou combrist thi selven;
> And so witnessith Godis word and holy writ bothe:
> > *Qui agit contra conscientiam, &c.*
> Ac yif thou werchist be Godis word, I warne the for the beste,
> What so men worden of the, wraththe the nevere.
> Catoun counseillith so—tak kep of his teching:
> > *Cum recte vivas, ne cures verba malorum.*
> But suffre and sit stille, and sek thou no ferthere,
> And be glad of the grace that God hath i-sent the;
> For yif thou comsist to clymbe, and coveitest herre,
> Thou mightest lese thi loughnesse for a litel pride.

In order to convey my understanding of the tone of this passage, I
offer the following paraphrase of it:

> Before I define Do-bet, says Wit in effect, let me warn you that if in good
> conscience you do well, then do not desire to do better in this world, for
> "the purpose reveals the man." See to it that you direct your wit, and your
> works as well, in accordance with the dictates of conscience and Holy
> Church; for if you go against conscience you injure yourself, as both God's
> word and the Fathers attest. But if you act in accordance with God's word—
> I tell you this for your own good—then never become angry no matter what
> men say about you. Heed Cato's advice: "As long as you live uprightly, pay
> no attention to scandal." Rather be patient and sit still, seek to go no further,
> and be thankful for the grace God has sent you; for if you begin to climb,
> and covet a higher degree, pride of position may destroy your humility.

If there is anything relating to the private life of the author in the
Vita, surely it is to be found in these lines.[39] Of course the passage is
not "autobiography" such as critics like Mensendieck would have

[27]

us see running throughout the *Vita,* but the advice here seems so personal and so circumstantial that one is tempted to read between the lines.

On the other hand, Wit's statement is an excellent introduction to his definition of Do-bet. Disregarding the possibility of personal allusion, we may interpret what he says as this: Beware lest you set out to ascend the scale of perfection, and end up climbing the ladder of success. The *intencio* is all. This leads Wit into a denunciation of "climbers" (10.100–8). To avoid this, he says, one must have "suffraunce" (10.109–16). This is the virtue which is now most urgently in need of cultivation among the clergy. *He that humbleth himself shall be exalted.*

Wit's definition of Do-best, though it is brief, is very important because it gives us, in a single well-conceived figure, the relationship of all three members of the triad (10.117–26):

> And thus of dred and his dede Do-best arisith,
> Which is the flour and the fruyt fostrid of bothe.
> Right as a rose, that red is and swet,
> Out of a raggit rote and a rough brere
> Springeth and spredith, that spiceris desirith,
> Or as whete out of weed waxith of the erthe,
> So Do-best out of Do-bet and Do-wel gynneth springe
> Among men of this molde that mek ben and kynde;
> For love of here loughnesse oure Lord yiveth hem grace
> Such werkis to werche that he is with paied.

The figure of the rose now reinforces that of the castle (which the poet introduced mainly to delineate the machinery of the soul), and serves admirably to reveal the essential unity of the triad, and hence also the ideal, unified society that the poet here envisions. The figure also gives apt expression to the poet's attitude toward each group: Do-best, the episcopate, is capable of developing the highest expression of spirituality (the rose); Do-bet, the clergy, is necessary to "foster" Do-best, though it is by no means as attractive

[28]

(the brier!); while Do-wel, the commons, if not decorative, is nevertheless the very source of life to which the others owe their existence (the root). A more appropriate and effective simile could scarcely be imagined. Particularly enjoyable, in view of what we have observed about the poet's attitude so far, is the equation of the clergy with the brier. As is so often the case, the poet here inserts, in one of his most idealistic passages, the hidden barb of his satire. But it is especially important to note what this definition does and does not say about the episcopate. On the one hand, there is not the slightest hint (here or anywhere else in the poem) that learning is a prerequisite for Do-best; on the other hand, what Do-best *must* have is humility.

Thus the poet has clearly set forth, by the use of the castle and the rose, Wit's explanation of man's responsibility for his own moral welfare, and the spiritual qualifications of the commons, clergy, and episcopate. He has also stressed the fact that Do-wel, the commons, is the very foundation of society, the root from which spring all higher forms of spiritual expression. Precisely for this reason, therefore, the poet now turns, in the remainder of this passus, first, to a consideration of the nature of marriage, the institution which makes it possible for Do-bet and Do-best to "spring" from Do-wel, and, second, to a satiric description of what happens to this institution when Do-wel lacks its most important spiritual attribute, the fear of God.

God is pleased first and foremost, says Wit, with wedded folk who respect the laws of marriage, "for thorugh wedlak the world stant, who so wile it knowen" (10.129). From marriage come those representing all levels of society, from the highest to the lowest, *including* maidens and martyrs, monks and anchorites. This observation resembles, of course, the point made by the Wife of Bath (*Canterbury Tales,* WB Prologue, 71–72):

> And certes, if ther were no seed ysowe,
> Virginitee, thanne wherof sholde it growe?

except that whereas the Wife introduces this point in an amusingly specious way, Wit in all seriousness wishes to stress the fact that if the institution of marriage should crumble, society itself will disintegrate. Unlike Chaucer, whose moral concern is rarely visible in any form stronger than the most refined irony, our poet expresses his indignation directly and often in considerable detail. We have a good example of this in the present instance, for from 10.135 virtually to the end of the passus, Wit sketches the history of marriage and its debasement from the beginning, in Genesis (10.135–75), and then reviews some of the abuses of the "children of Cain" in the present generation (10.176–90). But the central thesis of this passage is perfectly clear: abuse of marriage began as a violation of God's law, and those who perpetuate these abuses today are guilty of the same violation, showing that they lack the fear of God, which Wit has stressed as the most important spiritual requisite of Do-wel. Wit then concludes this discussion of marriage by citing the laws and motives which should govern wedded folk (10.191–202), and warning of the evils that can result from the multiplication of illegitimate offspring (10.203–9). This final section of passus 10 contains some of the poet's liveliest verse, especially his description of the "cheste" and "choppis" of quarreling couples (10.176–90).

The final three lines of the passus provide a concise summary of the whole (10.210–12):

> Thanne is Do-wel to dreden, and Do-bet to suffre,
> And so comith Do-best aboute, and bringeth doun mody;
> And that is wykkide wil, that many werk shendith.

The commons, says Wit, must fear God; the clergy must have sufferance; from these come the bishops, who must have humility, for they are charged with the responsibility of abasing the proud— those who, by ignoring or perverting the knowledge of the good which they possess, break God's law, either through selfish desire to better themselves or through commercialized matrimony or adultery.

Passus 2

The final passus of the *Vita* begins with an explosion. Suddenly, and without warning, the Dreamer is confronted by Study, Wit's wife, who fairly shouts at her husband, Don't cast pearls before swine! It is both startling and amusing to find Dame Study, by far the most colorful figure in the *Vita,* appearing so dramatically on the scene and scolding her husband in the manner which Wit had just finished condemning in the preceding passus.[40] Yet the poet's purpose here at the beginning of passus 11 goes beyond the mere desire to amuse. Dame Study is the most important instrument in his evaluation of learning, which, as we have seen, is the central purpose of the poem. Her appearance also marks the point at which the allegorical structure of the *Vita* undergoes a radical change, designed to prepare the way for the poem's conclusion.

The change in the allegorical structure of the poem at this point might better be called a modification, for I am not suggesting that passus 11 contains anything that could be termed allegorical "action," on the model of the *Visio.* If it did, perhaps we might expect to see some such character as Humility attack Pride-of-Perfect-Learning, and drive him to a retreat called Know-Thyself. Nothing like this occurs in the poem. Rather what does develop here is a kind of dramatic interplay between the Dreamer and the personifications. Whereas up to now Thought and Wit have responded directly and, for the most part, soberly to the Dreamer's questions, from this point on we must be prepared for anything.

Dame Study's denunciation of the Dreamer (Pearls before swine) is based on her assumption that he is one of those "faitours" who enjoy tinkering with theological concepts as a kind of game. This is an amusing turn of events. The good dame proceeds to condemn the Dreamer for being guilty of the very abuses which the Dreamer himself has been satirizing, overtly in his encounter with the friars, and implicitly in the definitions of Thought and Wit emerging from his own internal *débat.* In other words, he agrees absolutely with everything she says (11.5–91): Wisdom is corrupted by cupidity and serves the devil—why do the wicked prosper? Minstrels can tell you that artistic integrity is worse than useless—"harlotrie" is all the rage. But if conversation at feasts does get around to religion, then clerks, and laymen too—you don't need a degree—dream up questions about the Trinity, how two slew the third, while the poor and hungry cry at the gate with none to take them in. O Lord (with great eloquence) blessed be Thou, and all shall be as Thou wilt, whatever we tell! Thus does Dame Study denounce the abuses of learning. Ability to discuss doctrinal problems has become a mark of social distinction, of belonging to the elite. It is a brilliant passage. The clergy, especially friars, take a merciless beating. But note: dramatically speaking, Dame Study's entire speech is a scathing denunciation of the Dreamer, and yet (who can doubt it?) the Dreamer is silently cheering her on. The skill with which the poet manages this joke on himself (as the Dreamer) and uses it to such satiric advantage reminds us of Chaucer's amusing self-portraits in his dream-visions and in the *Canterbury Tales*.

Amid all of her outpourings of satiric abuse, however, Dame Study manages two positive points which the poet wishes to stress. One of these is to be seen in her sharp contrast between the learned and the unlearned (11.53–57):

> God is muche in the gorge of this grete maistris,
> Ac among mene men hise mercy and his werkis.
> And so seith the Sauter—seke it in *Memento*:
> *Ecce audivimus eam in Effrata, invenimus eam in campis silve.*
> Clerkis and kete men carpen of God faste,
> And han hym muchel in here mouth, ac mene men in herte.

This is the first explicit statement (though the theme is implicit throughout) of what is to be the conclusion of the entire poem, fully stated at the end. The other point is brought out when Dame Study, at the end of her opening discourse, turns savagely on the Dreamer, and says (11.86–91):

And now comith a conyon, and wolde cacche of my wittes
What is Do-wel fro Do-bet—now def mote he worthe!
Sithen he wilneth to wyte which thei ben alle:
But he lyve in the leste degre that longith to Do-wel,
I dar be his bolde borugh Do-bet wile he nevere,
Theigh Do-best drawe on hym day aftir other.

Here the poet has a last fling with the joke on himself. Nevertheless he is, at the same time, quite serious: Before you can "know"
what the good life is, you have to "live" it. Perhaps these learned
men can define the good life; but they still do not know it. This is
precisely the point that the poet makes elsewhere in his use of the
words "kynde knowyng."

In the course of the poem so far the Dreamer has opposed the
friars, disputed with Thought, and failed to respond to Wit (though
of course he was given no opportunity in the latter case); he will
later question the definition of Clergie and say *contra* to Scripture.
To Dame Study, however, he gets down on his knees. Why? For
one thing, as we have seen, she has said exactly what he wants to
hear; he admires her. Further, this action is a dramatic necessity:
she has assumed him to be one of the learned carpers, and he wishes
to correct this erroneous impression. He does so, very easily, with a
demonstration of humility. Since Study has said that he can't possibly know Do-bet and Do-best without first knowing at least the
essentials of Do-wel, he gets down on his knees and asks her to
tell him what Do-wel is; never mind the other two. Study is
properly impressed, and commends him for his "meknesse" and
"mylde speche" (11.103).

Dame Study does not, however, proceed to define Do-wel; this
she delegates to Clergie, and in the course of so doing provides the
Dreamer with one of those allegorical maps which our poet particularly enjoys (11.113–22), and which, incidentally, in this case,
has some very valuable and pointed advice on how to come to
learning. On the other hand, she goes on to speak at length

(11.123–62) of Clergie himself (i.e., learning), and his wife Scripture (writing, books). She describes the typical medieval curriculum, and makes observations on the futility and deceptiveness of certain of the sciences. At the same time, she points out what is valuable. Learning is the basis, for example, of crafts such as carpentry and masonry. Most important, however, are her remarks on theology. Theology, she says, has vexed me ten score times; the more I study it, the mistier it seems. And if it were not for its emphasis on love, it would be a useless thing (11.139–42):

> It is no science for sothe for to sotile there inne,
> Ne were the love that lith there in, a wel lewid thing it were.
> Ac for it lat best be love I love it the betere;
> For there that love is lord lakkith nevere grace.

What theologian would dispute that statement? It is important, I think, to avoid the patronizing assumption that our poet is simply confessing his inability to cope with the intricacies of theological study. What theologian worthy of the name has not, after prolonged effort, found that the greatest religious truths elude adequate intellectual formulation? And yet—paradoxically—if *caritas* is not the foundation of theology, what is? While the "maistris" continue to talk interminably about the Trinity, and the friars preach smoothly about Charity the Champion, the poet here distinguishes the very essence of theology.

Thus it is evident that Dame Study performs a number of valuable services for the poet. She breaks in, colorfully and dramatically, to interrupt the sequence of definitions by Thought and Wit, and makes the delightful mistake of assuming the Dreamer to be a quibbling carper; she denounces the abuses of learning with passionate eloquence; she affirms the piety of poor men as against the pride of the learned; and she then reveals, finally, the extent to which learning is of genuine value. All this the poet accomplishes, not by stating it flatly in the person of the Dreamer (as he might have), but by putting it in the mouth of his most intriguing and obstreperous personification.

From the time that the Dreamer takes leave of Dame Study and comes to Clergie (learning), the poem moves rapidly toward its conclusion. Clergie, of course, first gives us a definition of the triad.[41] His definition, however, though it is in essential agreement with the definitions of Thought and Wit, does not in any way go beyond them. Yet the poet has a very good reason, as we shall see, for putting it in the poem at precisely this point.

Like Thought and Wit before him, Clergie identifies Do-wel with the commons, Do-bet with the clergy, and Do-best with bishops. His description is closer to Thought's than it is to Wit's, however, for he deals almost solely with externals. Do-wel, for example, represents the laboring class, pure and simple; there is not even the emphasis on ethical conduct which we find in Thought's definition. Do-bet does charitable deeds, clothing and feeding beggars and prisoners, and dwelling together in unity. Do-best is a bishop's peer, and both does and teaches; hence he has power to preach and chastise. These statements are perfectly straightforward. If there is any irony here it is in the applicability to Do-bet of the verse quoted from Psalm 133: *Behold, how good and how pleasant it is for brethren to dwell together in unity!* This is, of course, commendably optimistic, if taken at face value; but we may well doubt that the poet's serenity here is anything more than a momentary pose, especially at a time when storms are raging around the friars, and "the moste meschief on molde is mountyng up faste" (prol. 64).

The reader's skepticism is borne out by what follows the definition of Do-best. For Clergie now returns to Do-bet, and observes (11.196–200):

> Do-bet doth ful wel, and dewid he is also,
> And hath possessions and pluralites for pore menis sake.
> For mendynauntz at meschief tho men were dewid;
> And that is rightful religioun—none renneris aboute,
> Ne no leperis over lond ladies to shryve.

Once again we see that the poet, having given his ideal definition, suddenly confronts us with the corresponding reality. Clerks, he says, are endowed and given the right to own property, in order that they might discharge their responsibilities efficiently.[42] And this is as it should be. The alternative is the anarchy of the friars (11.199–200). On the other hand, the possessions and pluralities of the regulars do not guarantee spirituality. Clergie quotes the old saying (here attributed to Gregory the Great) about a monk ("religioun") out of his cloister resembling a fish out of water (11.201–7), and then concludes with a denunciation of Do-bet which exactly matches Chaucer's portrait of a Monk, except that our poet is by no means as sympathetic in his portrayal of the regulars (11.208–15):

> Ac now is religioun a ridere, and a romere be stretis,
> A ledere of love-daies and a lond biggere,
> Poperith on a palfrey fro toune to toune,
> A bidowe or a baselard he berith be his side;
> Godis flessh and his fet and hise fyve woundis
> Arn more in his mynde than the memorie of his foundours.
> This is the lif of *this lordis* that lyven shulde with Do-bet,
> And wel-a-wey wers, and I wolde al telle.

It is important to note that Clergie calls the religious *this lordis,* for this is the trigger that sets off the "dispute" with which the vision is brought to an end. Clergie's purpose in using these words is of course to emphasize what his description clearly shows, namely, that the religious are now imitating the dress, manners, and life of the secular aristocracy, a tendency which is equally clear in the portrait of Chaucer's Monk. Now if there is anything that is certain, it is that the Dreamer concurs wholeheartedly in this judgment. But his foredoomed quest for the good life among learned men, the clerks, is at an end, and he is ready to hand down his decision. He therefore breaks in on Clergie's discourse with this withering objection (11.216–20):

> I wende that kinghed and knighthed and caiseris with erlis
> Wern Do-wel and Do-bet and Do-best of alle;
> For I have seighe it my self, and siththen red it aftir,

How Crist counseillith the comune, and kenneth hem this tale:
> *Super cathedram Moisi sederunt principes.*

For-thi I wende that tho wyes wern Do-best of alle.

Surely, says the Dreamer, if we may judge by the life of *this lordis* (the religious, in Clergie's words), we must conclude that the secular aristocracy should be our model for the good life. He then compounds the irony by deliberately misquoting Matt. 23:2—In the chair of Moses sit, not "the scribes and the Pharisees," but *princes!* The poet's hand is well nigh quicker than the reader's eye: he places the religious on a throne of dubious distinction,[43] and simultaneously gives them the aristocratic title which their secular manners and dress would seem to demand. But our admiration of this master stroke should not cause us to lose sight of the function of this passage as an instrument in the termination of the vision: the Dreamer is here "finding up" a question in the manner of the quibbling friars mentioned by Dame Study (11.58), which leads to his closing "dispute" with Scripture.

The exchange between the Dreamer and Scripture, however, is not really a dispute, for they are actually in perfect agreement. What gives it the appearance of a dispute is the Dreamer's ironic pose. "I nile not scorne," quoth Scripture (11.221), that is, *you* may be as ironic as you please, but *I* will not "scorne." She then proceeds to answer his objection in all seriousness. Neither social rank nor wealth help one to heaven (11.225–27):

> Poul provith it unpossible, riche men in hevene,
> Ac pore men in pacience and penaunce togidere
> Haven eritage in hevene, ac riche men non.

The very refusal of Scripture to "scorne" intensifies the satire, for in the act of correcting the Dreamer she is now attacking the clergy on the most embarrassing grounds possible. The unlucky object of the poet's ire is indeed squirming on a pin! But the Dreamer, warming to his role, comes gallantly to the defense (11.228–29):

[37]

"Contra," quath I, "be Crist! that can I with-seye,
And proven it be the pistil that Petir is nempnid:
Qui crediderit et baptizatus fuerit, salvus erit."

Once again Scripture, refusing to "scorne," patiently explains that this is *in extremis,* relating to the conversion of the heathen, but that Christian men have a responsibility to love God and their neighbor, lead the life of good works, and live together as brothers (11.230–43). Furthermore, she says—and here, in the fading moments of the vision, the poem's horizon suddenly expands—furthermore, says Scripture, it is the Christian's responsibility to help the heathen: God never ordered us to harm them or slay them!

What does this mean? Are we to suppose that the poet ends his vision with a truism from Scripture? By no means. The poet's dramatic contrast between *love thy neighbor* and *slay the heathen* is simply his final extension of a theme that echoes throughout both the *Visio* and the *Vita: preach and prove.* And, unlike the typical "one hundred per cent" Christian of his day, he feels no tingling of the blood at a call to arms against the heathen. Our poet falls far short of the apparent equanimity of Chaucer, whose worthy knight had

foughten for oure feith at Tramyssene
In lystes thries, and ay slayn his foo.[44]

To this rather widespread view of the heathen, Scripture opposes the commandment, *Thou shalt not kill.* And the complacent reader, who has long since dissociated himself from the hypocrisy of those ridiculous "learned" clerks denounced in the poem, is suddenly propelled into self-examination. At this opportune moment, Scripture wields her two-edged sword. First, *Vengeance is mine, saith the Lord, and I will repay,* from which it follows, second (11.248–49),

"I shal punisshen in purcatory, or in the put of helle,
Eche man for his misdede, but mercy it make."

On this strident note the dream in the *Vita de Do-wel, Do-bet, & Do-best* comes to an end.[45] We have learned that the commons must

[38]

be honest and faithful, and fear the Lord; that the clergy must be charitable and patient in maintaining the spiritual welfare of the commons; and that bishops must be humble in order to carry out their function of chastising the sinner and rebuking the proud. Thus the poem, as its title suggests, has a positive theme from beginning to end. On the other hand, the critical views of the author are equally clear. The commons must not, by forgetting the fear of the Lord, corrupt the institution of marriage and thus destroy society's foundation. But above all, the poet's sharpest criticism is directed against Do-bet. The clergy, making friends with Mammon's money, preach condescendingly to the people; they are the brier of the rose of society; and they talk of the Trinity at banquets while poor men hunger and thirst. Further, it is clear from this that the poet's primary intent is to expose the futility of their learning. This is what gives the sharp edge to virtually every line of the satire. Clerks are educated, but they do not "know." They can discuss theology, but they do not know charity. This point is emphasized again and again.

Although the poet has been careful to point out, by the introduction of Dame Study, the ways in which learning itself can be useful, it is nevertheless clear that he has now presented his case against learning. But lest there be the slightest shadow of doubt in any reader's mind, he now restates this conclusion in the most direct and forceful language at his command.[46]

In order to understand fully the meaning of the poet's conclusion, it is absolutely essential to recognize the rhetorical form of lines 11.250–84. This passage is a *reductio ad absurdum*. The poet's irony is, I think, quite plain. Yet I am never the nearer, says the Dreamer, for all my walking, to know what is Do-wel "witterly in herte."[47] Does learning help us toward heaven? I'll give you some "learned" examples; judge for yourself. It doesn't make any difference whether I do well or evil in this world; I'm predestined either for salvation or damnation (if you don't believe me, look at John 3:13!). Good men of past ages, like Solomon and Aristotle, gain nothing by their wisdom and virtue; for all Holy Church says they are in hell; so why should I follow their example to my eternal damnation? What about the thief on the cross? Aren't we told that he was, after all, a *thief?* And yet merely because he had faith and confessed himself to Christ, he obtained salvation sooner than the holiest of men. Take Mary Magdalene—who could do worse? Or David, who destroyed Uriah? Or Paul, who killed Christian men? Yet there is none so certainly in heaven as these very ones, *who lived such wicked lives when they were in the world!*

It is one of the wonders of literary history that critics have actually supposed this passage to be the poet's own sober confession of serious theological doubt or uncertainty. For even if everything that he has said up to this point in his poem is thrown out (in the mad search for autobiography), the rhetorical form of the passage is unmistakable. The ascending irony, the increasing absurdity of the examples, the obtuse theology, the scripture quoted out of context, all combine to stimulate in the reader who is watching this parade a growing sense of incongruity.[48] It is important to note, in this connection, that the absurdity of the passage *grows:* a mere parade of straw men will not do. Predestination and the fate of the righteous heathen were among the questions most hotly debated in the schools. They were (and are) outstanding examples of theological paradox. Perhaps these facts will help us avoid the condescending idea that the poet is here reducing theology to the absurd because he can't understand it, whereas he should know, after all, that predestination does not affect morality and that the righteous heathen is saved. The truth is that our poet *does* know these things, but through "kynde knowyng," not theology.

Having completed his *reductio ad absurdum,* the poet drops the mask, and, now completely serious, he presents his explicit condemnation of learning (11.285 ff.). And yet, says the Dreamer, I'm forgetting the teaching of my five wits ("kynde knowyng" again!), namely, that Christ never did commend learning. See his words to some of his disciples in Mark 13:9, 11. He said (here the Dreamer "translates," 289-92):

> "Whanne ye ben aposid of princes or of prestis of the lawe,
> For to answere hem have ye no doute;
> For I shal graunte yow grace, of God that ye serven,
> The help of the holy gost to answere hem alle."

The translation is of course quite free, as is common enough in the poem. But the variations are highly significant. First observe the form of the Latin text itself: *Dum steteritis ante presides nolite cogitare,* etc. The poet has omitted *reges* from the Vulgate phrase *ante reges et presides.* Second, in the translation, *Dum steteritis* is given as "Whanne ye *ben aposid,*" while *ante presides* is rendered "of princes or of *prestis of the lawe.*" Thus the poet's modification of the scriptural passage clearly reveals the application of it which he intends: Take no thought what you shall speak when you *are opposed by priests.*[49] Suddenly we are thrust back to that scene in the *Visio* (8.122) where

> The prest and Perkyn aposide either other.

And I have not the slightest hesitation in affirming that the poet, in the *Vita,* has indeed "answered them all."

Finally, says the Dreamer, I am, after all, only pointing out what "Austyn the olde" said long ago: *Ecce ipsi ydioti rapiunt celum, ubi nos sapientes in infernum mergemur.* His paraphrase of this is both a refutation of the priest and a vindication of Piers (11.297-300):

> "Arn none rathere yravisshid fro the righte beleve
> Thanne are thise grete clerkis, that conne many bokis;
> Ne none sonnere ysavid, ne saddere of consience,
> Thanne pore peple as ploughmen, and pastours of bestis."

Learning can undermine faith; the unlettered plowmen and shepherds achieve salvation. These lines are forceful in themselves; but their impact is derived primarily from the fact that they express beautifully the conclusion toward which the poet has been moving throughout the *Vita*. And for this same reason nothing—not even the fulminations of learned biographers—can obscure the brilliance of his closing lines (11.301–3):

> Souteris and seweris, such lewide jottis,[50]
> Percen with a *pater noster* the paleis of hevene,
> Withoute penance, at here partyng, in-to the heighe blisse.

Two

PRINCIPLES OF ORDER
IN THE B-CONTINUATION

———⋰•◆•⋱———

The so-called B-continuation (B, passus 11–20) of *Piers the Plowman* is a complete poem in its own right, with a beginning, a middle, and an end. But it is so intimately connected with the A-version, both in its genesis and in its actual structure, that we must keep the A-text constantly in mind as we consider the form and meaning of B. The literary relations of the two texts are indeed very complex and need first of all to be viewed as a whole. Before attempting any detailed analysis of the B-continuation, therefore, I wish in the following pages to sketch briefly its literary tradition, the motivation of the poet in writing it, and the methods that the poet uses to accomplish his purposes and to meet the problems he must face in the intricate task of continuing the A-version in accordance with the plan that he has adopted.

Literary Tradition

The B-continuation is based on the Bible. The poet does not, however, merely "use" scriptural tradition in order to present a doctrinal thesis. Rather the poem begins with the book of Genesis and ends with the book of Revelation. The opening scene in passus 11 is envisioned as the world ("middle-earth") of the Creation, and the closing scene in passus 19–20 is conceived in terms of the Apocalypse, with the coming of Antichrist and the threat of doom hanging in the air. Between these two extremes is to be found the familiar procession of the patriarchs, prophets, and of course the life, passion, and resurrection of Christ, followed by the depiction of the apostolic age. The poem is one more testimony to the tremendous popularity and influence of Holy Scripture in the Middle Ages. It also reveals that our poet had an impressive grasp, not only of scriptural tradition, but also of the Bible itself as a whole.

Yet having said that the poem is based on the Bible, I must add what is perhaps obvious, namely, that the Bible in the Middle Ages was not studied in a vacuum. Rather it was viewed, first of all, in the light of commentaries extending through the centuries from St. Augustine (and even earlier) down to the poet's own day. In the fourteenth century one of the most popular of reference works was the *Glossa Ordinaria,* which summarized the important interpretations of Scripture from Genesis to Revelation, chapter by chapter, verse by verse. Our poet was almost certainly familiar with this work and no doubt with other commentaries as well. More important, however, is the fact that he was familiar with and uses in his poem the multilevel allegorical interpretation of Scripture which represents one of the great achievements of the exegetical tradition in the Middle Ages.[1] This is *not* to say that the B-continuation uses the fourfold allegorical system on the analogy of biblical exegesis as a fundamental element of its poetic structure; this is not the case. What I am saying is that the specifically biblical materials in the poem are, at times, susceptible of interpretation on the various levels in accordance with the commonly accepted allegorical method of reading the Bible. The importance of this distinction will, I hope, be made clear when we come to a direct analysis of the poem.

Important as it is to be aware of medieval exegesis, it is probably even more important in a reading of the poem to be acquainted with scriptural influence in literary tradition. By this I mean the

Bible as it is employed in the drama, poetry, and prose of the period in which our poet is practicing his art. One of the most important influences on the B-continuation in this literary tradition is of course the medieval drama. In particular I refer to the cycle plays, where the story of the Bible was set forth dramatically in a series of episodes, each complete in itself, but linked together in such a way as to present in graphic form an entire cosmology, in short, the medieval "world picture." These plays began with the Creation (often preceded by the fall of Lucifer) and then presented successively the Fall, Cain and Abel, the Flood, and so forth, scenes from the patriarchs, prophets, the life, passion and resurrection of Christ, and so on through to the end of the world, or Doomsday. Four major cycles are extant in English, and one in Cornish. Although the surviving manuscripts are late, there is good evidence that they were performed in England quite early in the fourteenth century. It has been observed in the past that *Piers the Plowman* shows the influence of the medieval drama, but this fact has not been used, as I think it should, in arriving at an understanding of the B-continuation as a whole.

Subsequent analysis will confirm, I believe, that our poet knew and used the medieval drama as a part of his literary tradition. But in view of his obvious sophistication and learning it will be well, also, to pay some attention to other literature in the biblical tradition. One of the most popular poems in the fourteenth and fifteenth centuries in England was the *Cursor Mundi*.[2] This "omnibus" work, composed in the late thirteenth or early fourteenth century, is more than three times as long as the entire B-text of *Piers the Plowman*. It begins with Genesis and ends with Revelation, but includes much legendary material, commentary, and homiletics. The author tells us that he has written his poem in English for the common people. It is quite likely that the *Cursor Mundi* provided materials for some of the dramatists responsible for the cycle plays in England. Its manner of presenting the biblical materials accords well with that governing the cycle plays themselves. Often what appears in the *Cursor Mundi* as doctrinal exposition of the scriptural narrative is reflected, in condensed form, in the cyclical drama as a speech assigned to the "doctor" or "expositor," who wishes to make certain that the spectator grasps what is often the allegorical meaning of a particular scene. The same holds true for the poem's legendary material, some of which is reflected in the cycles. The striking picture of the traditional debate of the Four Daughters of God, though it does not survive in any of the extant cycles, was no doubt one of the major contributions of the *Cursor Mundi* to medieval drama. The famous treatment of the Four Daughters motif in the B-continuation (passus 18), though it is used in an independent way by our poet, is nevertheless in the tradition of *Cursor Mundi* and the drama.

One other work of the omnibus type should be mentioned as a part of the biblical tradition which we are considering. Ranulf Higden's *Polychronicon,*[3] a Latin prose history, was phenomenally popular in England in the fourteenth and fifteenth centuries. The fourteenth century *Stanzaic Life of Christ* was partly based on it, and it was twice translated into English during this period, once in the fourteenth century by John Trevisa, and again, anonymously, in the next. Although it begins with an extended word-map of the world, and although its emphasis is historical rather than didactic, nevertheless the *Polychronicon* has the same basic pattern that we find in the *Cursor Mundi*. Both divide history into the seven ages of the world, and both progress from Genesis to Revelation, though of course the *Polychronicon* stresses the historical, extending up to the middle of the fourteenth century. Continuations were added by various hands during the second half of the century, and eventually Caxton brought it up to date and printed it in 1482, using the translation of John Trevisa. Like the *Cursor Mundi,* it is not improbable that Higden's *Polychronicon* was a source book for the medieval dramatists. According to one tradition, Ranulf Higden himself composed the Chester cycle in 1328.[4]

The medieval drama, the *Cursor Mundi,* and Higden's *Poly-*

chronicon do not, of course, constitute anything approaching a complete list of the sources of the B-continuation of *Piers the Plowman.* But they do, I think, adequately represent the literary tradition, the context for viewing the poet's use of the Bible. Once we realize this, as I hope to show, the poem suddenly comes to life.

There is, however, one further stream of tradition, second only to the Bible in its importance for understanding the B-text. Medieval romance, which flourished on the Continent in the twelfth and thirteenth centuries, reached a new pinnacle of popularity in England in the latter half of the fourteenth century, at the very time that *Piers the Plowman* was being composed. It would indeed be strange if our poet were unaware of this. I think his poem reveals that he was quite familiar with the romance tradition, and exploits it very effectively in his poetry. The precise nature of the "romance tradition" which the poet used is not easy to define, since it is not at the center of his poem in the sense that the Bible is. Nevertheless it will be useful to review briefly the main developments in romance which preceded the composition of *Piers,* as an aid to understanding the romance elements to be found in the text. Arthurian romance provides us with a convenient unified example.

The earliest Arthurian romances in the twelfth century appear to have arisen from the desire to adapt materials from popular lore and myth for the entertainment of sophisticated audiences. Leaving aside King Arthur himself, we find that the type of hero in these early romances is best represented by Gawain, the protagonist whose strength and might of arms gain the victory. In the later English versions, of course, especially in the alliterative *Sir Gawain and the Green Knight,* Gawain's sheer prowess is modified and enhanced by a courtly setting of considerable sophistication and moral depth. On the Continent, however, the indomitable representative of the chivalric ideal, both on the battlefield and in the bower, was Lancelot, the hero of *Le Chevalier de la Charrette,* by Chrétien de Troyes. The great prestige of Lancelot, however, proved vulnerable.

In the early thirteenth century, when the Vulgate cycle of French prose romances was being composed, the chivalric ideal on which Lancelot's popularity had been based was subjected to severe scrutiny, and as a result there arose a new hero, Galahad, who became the central figure in the Grail quest, which now began to dominate the Arthurian scene. In fairness to the literary creator of Lancelot, it should be said that Chrétien's *Conte del Graal,* the last and in my opinion the greatest of his romances, was the poem most responsible for the new religious emphasis in the Vulgate cycle.[5] Although Galahad eventually became the "Christ in armor" of the religious tradition, it was Chrétien's masterly treatment of Perceval in the *Conte del Graal* that first called the secular ideal of Arthurian romance in question. Perceval is cast in the role of "God's Fool," who rises to the heights of worldly reputation, only to discover that the chivalric ideal is dust and ashes. The impressive scene at the hermitage on Good Friday in the *Conte del Graal* provided the requiem of the Arthurian world. The Cistercian author of the prose *Quest del Saint Graal,* who substituted Galahad for Perceval as the Grail hero, was not equipped to use or develop Chrétien's subtle characterization of Perceval. Nevertheless Perceval in his role as God's Fool continued to be popular in the thirteenth and, in England especially, in the fourteenth century. An English poem, *Sir Perceval of Gales,* based ultimately on Chrétien's poem, was composed in England about 1350. The pre-eminence of Galahad was by no means so obvious in the time of *Piers the Plowman* as it is to modern readers of Tennyson.

Generally speaking, the "romance tradition" of the B-poet, though it undoubtedly embraced a variety of texts from Geoffrey of Monmouth's *Historia Regum Britanniae* (1137) down to the latest native versions of the older French texts, had as its perspective the religious emphasis that began with Chrétien's *Conte del Graal,* and spread thence through the Vulgate cycle to virtually every area of medieval romance. In short, our poet appreciated romance and used it, but he saw it as a means of conveying truth to a popular audience, and as a way of expressing in human terms God's plan for the salvation of mankind. He belongs, therefore, to what might be called the "exegetical" romance tradition.

Romance is particularly obvious in the pervasive Christ-knight theme of the B-continuation. That this theme had become widespread in literature before *Piers the Plowman* is certainly true, and for this reason it is possible that the poet derived the concept from earlier treatments of the theme rather than directly from the romances. In fact the Christ-knight is a prominent feature of the cycle plays themselves. But the impressive development and skilled elaboration of the motif throughout the poem suggest that it is no mere imitation of earlier examples, but rather a revitalization of the original idea, an achievement based on the poet's own intimate knowledge of a wide selection of romance literature, both chivalric and religious.

The poet's reading of course goes beyond what has been thus far presented. He was unquestionably familiar, for example, with the *Legenda Aurea,* and with numerous compendiums on the order of *The Book of Vices and Virtues,* but works of this type, though extremely valuable for seeing some of the poet's ideas in relation to the thought of his age, shed very little if any light on the literary form of the poem. Once we see that the B-continuation is a unified work, with a Creation to Doomsday cosmology and with thematic developments from medieval romance, we have all the facts necessary for a proper apprehension of the basic literary structure of the work as a whole. One word of caution, however, is in order. Although the poem is in the biblical and romance traditions, and although its structure stands in a significant relation to them, the poet is not bound in any respect whatsoever by these facts. Like Chaucer, though in his own way, our poet has created something new out of the old. The task of the critic, therefore, is not to force the poet to do what he "should" do by virtue of his belonging to a particular literary tradition, but rather to understand what he has in fact done with that tradition. But before we can do even this, we must try, first, to define what motivated the poet in composing his continuation and, second, to ascertain the method which he devised for the execution of his complex design.

Motivation

From what has just been said about the literary tradition of the B-continuation it should be apparent that the poet's purpose is to compose a cosmological poem which begins with the Creation and ends with Doomsday. But because the poem is a continuation (or a *suite* in romance terms) we must qualify such a flat statement of the poet's aim. If his poem is to be attached to the A-version, then it automatically assumes the form of a dream-vision. Furthermore, to the degree that his continuation is in harmony with the A-text's satire on contemporary conditions, it will not extend literally to Doomsday, but rather will come to an end in the poet's own time, in the tradition of Higden's *Polychronicon*. In attempting to write a cosmological poem in the form of a dream-vision, and then to attach it to an already existing poem, the author would seem to have set himself an impossible task. Yet he succeeds magnificently. Whereas in A the field of folk (the world) is viewed *statically* against eternity (heaven and hell), in B the field of folk is presented to the reader *dynamically,* that is, it appears in passus 19–20 at the end of a mighty stream of divinely ordained historical events. The way in which this is achieved, despite the apparent difficulties involved, will be dealt with below.

But of course the desire to write a poem does not exist in a vacuum. What motivated the poet to undertake this formidable task? Any answer to such a question is bound to involve oversimplification. Yet I think that the B-continuation reveals at least two features which throw light on the poet's motivation. First, note that a large part of B passus 11–15 is devoted to teaching the Dreamer the value of learning. When we recall the unequivocal condemnation of learning as a way to salvation in A, then it is easy to see that the B-poet wishes to modify, if not indeed completely negate, the anti-intellectual and anticlerical views expressed in the A-version. On the other hand, the poet also elaborates and expands much of the earlier satire on contemporary conditions. This he obviously endorses. Above all, however, I believe the poet has an unwavering hostility toward the friars. And although his hostility by no means dominates him, it is certainly an important motivating factor in the composition of the B-continuation.

Method

The literary complexity of the B-continuation requires that we look briefly at the poet's method of organizing his materials before we undertake an analysis of the text itself. First let us consider the biblical chronology of the poem. The Creation occupies no less than five passus, that is, B 11–15. Then we have the Fall (16.1–166), Patriarchs and Prophets (16.167–17.350), the Passion and Resurrection (18), Ascension (19.1–193), Pentecost (19.194–256), the Apostolic Age (19.257–330), Signs of Judgment (19.331–478), and the Coming of Antichrist (20). This narrative progression from Genesis to Revelation is the central feature of the poem's structure. It must be emphasized, however, that the treatment of this biblical narrative is determined by the poet's use of commentaries, the cycle plays, and other literary treatments of Scripture such as the *Cursor Mundi* and the *Polychronicon*. Furthermore, to the familiar story of the Bible is added the trappings of medieval romance. Abraham, for example, is a herald who proclaims the coming of a Knight (Christ) who will joust at a tournament in Jerusalem. Finally, of course, in the last two passus (19–20), we return to the field full of folk, where the plowing of the half acre, the tournament motif of romance, and the ominous atmosphere of Apocalypse are combined by the poet to provide an impressive conclusion.

The structure of the B-continuation as outlined above presents us with a very common pattern, one with which most readers, even in the twentieth century, are certainly familiar. Yet it is by no means obvious in a first reading of the poem. Why is this? One reason is that to perceive this structure the reader must first regard the B-continuation in its *literary* relation to the A-version, something which few readers of *Piers the Plowman* have been willing to do. The B-version has been regarded as the "received" text, and we read this from beginning to end, the prologue and all twenty passus of it. Thus by the time we reach passus 11, we are not prepared to begin all over again with the Creation, as the poem requires.

There is yet another difficulty in reading the B-continuation. I have said that passus 11–15 are concerned with the Creation, and so they are. But this is a vast oversimplification. The poet deals directly with the Creation in but one relatively brief passage in passus 11 (311–94). The remainder of passus 11 and all of passus 12–15 are a part of the poet's complex method of welding his continuation to the original poem. And in reading this section we must be prepared to follow the poet as he takes us back over the ground covered in the A-text and offers his comments upon it, here criticizing some of the views expressed in A, and there expanding and developing hints contained in A's satire on contemporary conditions. In terms of the B-poet's method, therefore, passus 11–15 might well be entitled "The A-text Revisited."

The details of the author's method in revisiting the A-text in passus 11–15 will be taken up in my analysis of that section. There is, however, one feature of his method of joining his poem to A which requires mention here because it seriously affects the reading of the entire B-continuation. I refer to his characterization of the Dreamer. As we have seen, the Dreamer in the A-text, although he professes ignorance and asks many questions, is nevertheless a tool of the poet's satire, in that his questions are often loaded and his ignorance Swiftian. The Dreamer in the continuation, though he reveals occasional affinities with the satirical questioner in A, is a completely different person. The B-poet very skillfully casts him in the role of the Fool, on the model of Perceval (and other similar protagonists) in the romance tradition. In Chrétien's *Conte del Graal* the adventures of the hero, Perceval, are presented as one long series of incredible blunders. He misunderstands or fails to grasp everything that is told him. His initial errors, of course, are those of the crude Welshman, and are treated comically by the poet. But as the narrative progresses, his ignorance gradually becomes more serious, reaching a climax in his failure at the grail castle. And even after the grail episode his foolishness continues, down to the very end of the poem, the scene at the hermitage on Good Friday. The hermit has to teach him the simplest lessons of the faith. In a scene containing profound truth and cosmic humor, Perceval, the now famous Arthurian hero, learns to recite the *Pater Noster*. He is God's Fool to the bitter end.

The Swiftian Dreamer of the A-text becomes God's Fool in the B-continuation. The poet's idea may have originally been suggested by that amusing development in the A-version, passus 11, in which Dame Study mistakenly berates the Dreamer. But his use of it in the B-continuation is an independent and strikingly different development. At the very beginning of the poem, in passus 11, the allegorical figures who in the A-text had cooperated beautifully with the Dreamer and his satirical aims suddenly surround him in hostile fashion, and begin to rebuke and teach him. He is forced to blush for shame. He admits he may have been wrong. This is something that never happens in the A-text.

The immediate strategic advantage afforded by this revision of the Dreamer's character should be obvious. It is a primary instrument in the poet's modification of the points of view expressed in the A-text. His personifications can now legitimately address the Dreamer in words to this effect: You were wrong about this; or, You are right in stressing the law of love, but what you say needs qualifying in this manner; and so forth. The Fool-Dreamer is in fact used primarily in this way throughout passus 11–15. At the end of passus 15 the Dreamer's character has been established, the continuation is solidly linked to the A-text, and hence the poet can in passus 16 once more resume the biblical narrative with the Fall of Man.

The poet's use of the God's Fool motif, however, is not limited to passus 11–15. Like Perceval in the *Conte del Graal,* the Dreamer in the B-continuation is being educated, and this fact the poet keeps constantly in mind, to the very end of the poem. If we rightly understand the function of God's Fool in romance, of course, we will not expect to find this expressed in the form of a conventional *Bildungsroman.* As Chrétien remarks of Perceval, "It is a very heavy thing to teach a fool." [6] This applies perfectly to our poet's Fool. He is willing to be corrected, and eager to learn, but he takes everything literally, and it is exceedingly difficult to make him grasp even the simplest of ideas. He has to be told over and over again. This device is used in the B-continuation to build toward a climax. The spring is wound tighter and tighter, as it were, until it finally uncoils with tremendous force at the end, thus providing both the climax and resolution of the poem, insofar as it relates to the Dreamer himself. The passage in passus 20 where this occurs will be discussed later. Here I will only say that it corresponds perfectly in function to the scene at the hermitage in Chrétien's *Conte del Graal.*

The "Estoire de Piers"

A proper understanding of the literary function of Piers in the B-continuation is of the utmost importance. No interpretation can safely afford to slight the figure that gives the poem its title. Yet Piers's actual role seems relatively unimportant. He does not put in an appearance until passus 16, and, except for his function as the plowman in passus 19, he seems to be merely alluded to by the poet, rather than actually depicted in the allegorical action. Surely this is a strange way for the author to treat his hero. As a matter of fact, students of *Piers the Plowman* have been unable to agree on the role of Piers in the B-continuation, and the latest authority, R. W. Frank, Jr., rejects most of the efforts that have been made in this direction as worthless. Frank's comments on earlier efforts to define the role of Piers are interesting:

> These explanations assume that Piers was the poet's own creation. But what if Piers was not a completely original figure? The poem itself does not explain him clearly. It treats Piers as though he needs no explaining. Perhaps he existed in some context outside the poem that made him more easily intelligible to fourteenth-century readers than he is today. And why did Piers give the poem its title? He appears infrequently in the action and, except for the second vision, rarely plays a leading role. But if the figure of Piers were, in some form, popular and important in his own right, there would be more reason for him to give the poem its name.[7]

Frank then goes on to suggest that the popularity of Piers can be explained by Konrad Burdach's theory of a tradition, already existing in the fourteenth century, concerning the good plowman who is an embodiment of the mysterious, semidivine essence to be found in human nature. Now I agree with Frank that the B-continuation treats Piers as if he needs no explaining. I further agree that Piers is not an original figure in the B-continuation. But we do not have to resort to an elusive mystical tradition in order to explain these things. Piers's popularity and his independent existence are sufficiently attested in the A-text of *Piers the Plowman*.

There still remains, however, the necessity of understanding the strange way in which Piers actually does function in the poem. To explain this I suggest that the B-continuation is, in a sense, an *Estoire de Piers*. The analogy involved here refers to the literary development of the grail quest in Arthurian romance. The grail romance of Chrétien de Troyes was extremely popular from the time that it first began to circulate. Imitations and continuations were begun almost immediately after Chrétien's death, and these became the focal point in the development of the vulgate cycle of prose romances in the early thirteenth century. The most popular work was the *Queste del Saint Graal*. In addition to elaborations and exegetical rewritings of the quest itself, however, there also arose histories of the grail of which the best-known example is undoubtedly the *Estoire del Graal* of the Vulgate cycle. These Estoires (each in its own way) were designed to capitalize on the popularity of the grail story and to use it to present religious teachings to a secular audience. In point of time the *Estoire* was written after the original grail story had become popular, but in the terms of its own chronology the *Estoire* is a backward projection, a history of the grail before it appears on the scene in the author's own day. Hence the typical romance of this kind may perhaps begin with the incarnation, passion, and resurrection of Christ, and then proceed to give the history of the Church seen in the allegorical history of the grail custodians beginning with Joseph of Arimathea. Yet the later grail romances often ranged as far back in history as the book of Genesis itself. The episode of Solomon's ship in the *Queste del Saint Graal*, with its elaborate, highly baroque allegory of the white, green, and red spindles from the Tree of Life, takes us all the way back to the Garden of Eden.[8]

From this brief description of the literary development of the *Estoire* in medieval romance, we can see that these prose writers were using the grail to shed light on the biblical history of God's plan for man's salvation from the Creation, especially from the incarnation, and continuing down to the author's own day. Taking a popular symbol, they employed it for edifying purposes in the *Estoire* form. This, of course, is precisely analogous to what our poet is doing with Piers in the B-text. He is writing a continuation which is actually a backward projection in the terms of his biblical chronology, and he is using Piers to shed light on his history of God's plan for the salvation of mankind. Since Piers was already a popular figure (thanks to the popularity of the A-text), and since the humble plowman was so intimate and familiar a part of life in England in the fourteenth century, this employment by the poet of a kind of "you are there" device serves admirably to present an old, familiar story in a new and exciting form. Its tremendous popularity, which was evidently not limited to theologians, is sufficient evidence of this fact. It is in this sense, then, that the B-continuation is an *Estoire de Piers.*

A proper understanding of Piers's role is of great value in reading the B-continuation. It helps us understand how he can dominate the poem, as he does, without having to put in an appearance at every turn. It also helps us interpret the allegory. For once we realize that Piers stands above the allegory of the poem as a whole, rather than in it, then we will never make the mistake of trying to "read him into" the allegorical action without the poet's permission. This is particularly evident in the allegory of the Fall at the beginning of passus 16. Piers shows the Dreamer the tree, he chases the devil with the Trinitarian props supporting the tree, but—strange as it may seem for me to say so—he is not involved in the allegorical action. The supposition that he is involved in the allegory has led to some fantastically complex and generally unsatisfactory interpretations of this scene. I will defer my own analysis of the allegory of the Fall until later. Here it will suffice to say that Piers can initiate an allegorical action and comment on it, but the poet will not allow him, unless we are clearly shown otherwise (as in passus 19), to become a part of the action itself.

What has been observed so far, of course, is concerned strictly with the position of Piers in the structure of the B-continuation; it says nothing about the meaning of Piers himself. Fortunately, however, there is no difficulty here. In the B-continuation Piers stands for *exactly* the same values as are exhibited in the A-text. He is the representative of the good life, the humble follower of St. Truth, that is, of God. This is his symbolic value throughout the B-continuation, from beginning to end. But this will be clear to the reader only if he understands the difference that exists between the literary function of Piers in the A and B versions. In the A-text Piers is *in* the poem, that is, he appears in the field full of folk and participates in the allegorical action. He stands, as we have seen, in direct contrast to Lady Meed. In the B-continuation, however, as I have just tried to make clear, he for the most part stands outside of the allegory. Any attempt, therefore, to fit Piers into the action on the analogy of the A-text will be doomed from the start. Yet Piers in the B-continuation *is* the familiar plowman of the A-text, used, however, as the central figure of the poet's *Estoire*. The way in which this bears on our understanding of the poem will, I trust, be made clear in the following analysis.

Three

CREATION: THE A-TEXT REVISITED

The portion of the B-continuation dealing with the Creation, which I have called "The A-Text Revisited," occupies passus 11–15, and constitutes a well-defined unit of the poem. Furthermore, within this unit are four clearly marked sections. The first section (passus 11) establishes the Dreamer as the Fool, shows him God's creation, and in the process begins the work of revising his opinions as represented in the A-text. The second section (passus 12) is devoted entirely to Imaginatif's refutation of the Dreamer's former views. In the third section (passus 13–14), however, we find the first dramatization of ideas that the poet wishes to introduce. The worldly Doctor is presented at the dinner table in order that he may be contrasted with Haukyn the active man. But, as we shall see, both of these scenes are derived from the A-text and are intended to provide further modifications of the views there expressed. The last section (passus 15) returns us to the scene of the Creation, where the Dreamer is addressed by *Anima* (the Soul), whose long discourse on Charity includes the final response of the poet to the A-text and simultaneously prepares us for the biblical drama that is to follow. It is worth noting, finally, that each of these four sections begins with an elaboration of the Dreamer-as-Fool motif. With this over-all view of passus 11–15 in mind, we may now turn to an analysis of the first section.

Passus 11

It will be recalled that the A-text ended with the Dreamer's ringing denunciation of the learned, and his exaltation of ignorant plowmen and shepherds. In response to this, at the beginning of B passus 11, Scripture scornfully tells the Dreamer: "Know thyself." With these words the Dreamer falls asleep and dreams that Fortune leads him into the land of Longing and makes him look upon a mirror called Middle-Earth. Fortune's damsels, Lust-of-the-Flesh and Lust-of-the-Eyes, accompanied by Pride-of-Perfect-Living, urge the Dreamer to despise learning. Fortune and her crew entice the Dreamer with fair promises to abandon himself to worldly delights, while Old Age and Holiness warn him against trusting in Fortune. But this good advice is brushed aside by Recklessness and Childishness, who encourage him to "let himself go." This the Dreamer proceeds to do, and he tells us that Lust-of-the-Eyes followed him for more than forty winters, during which time he gave no thought to Do-wel or Do-bet (11.1–50).

Acting on the advice of Lust-of-the-Eyes, the Dreamer, while he is Fortune's friend, makes arrangement, presumably for a certain sum, to let the friars hear his confession and sing masses for his benefit. But when he becomes old, and Fortune abandons him, the friars break their agreement with him, merely because he expressed a desire to be buried at his own parish church. The Dreamer suspects that the friars are interested only in his money, and he asks them why they are so inordinately concerned with the rites of burial, when baptism, which is essential for salvation, is surely more important. At this point a character named Loyalty (here representing "fair play") appears, and he and the Dreamer discuss the propriety of exposing the falseness of the friars. Loyalty concludes that although one should not cast the first stone, there can certainly be no objection to a denunciation of something that is already notorious; but one must, of course, be certain that his motives are pure (11.51–102).

Next Scripture preaches on the text, *Many are called, but few are chosen* (Matt. 22:14), and the Dreamer ponders the question of his own election. He concludes that the Christian who believes and is baptized, though he may at times deny his faith, can nevertheless be saved at last with the aid of reason and conscience. Scripture confirms this, pointing out that God's mercies are over all his works (Ps. 145:9). But at this point Trajan, the Roman Emperor and famous example of the righteous heathen, breaks in scornfully on the theological exchange between the Dreamer and Scripture. "As for books," he cries, "I say bah!" and he goes on to state that he was saved, not by prayers or masses, but by love and because of his "pure truth." He then begins a long speech, in which he functions primarily as a spokesman for the author, in praise of love, Christian brotherhood, and patient poverty, and concludes his discourse with a critique on the abuses of covetous and ignorant priests (11.103–310).

Next Kind (Nature) takes the Dreamer to a mountain called Middle-Earth; from this point he can see God's Creation: the waters, the sun, dry land, animals, and finally man, male and female. The Dreamer observes how reasonably all the animals behave, in contrast to the unreasonableness of mankind. When he questions Reason about this, Reason rebukes him for his lack of sufferance, and implies that he is questioning the goodness of God's Creation (11.311–94).

Reason's rebuke makes the Dreamer blush for shame, and he awakens, concluding that Do-wel means to see much and to endure more. To this a new personification (identified in the next passus as Imaginatif) responds that Reason would have taught him much if he had had patience. Like Adam, the Dreamer wants to have the wisdom of God, and is therefore not fit company for Clergie or Reason. The Dreamer acknowledges this criticism and asks this new teacher his name (11.395–431).

From the above summary it can be seen that passus 11 has several very important functions. First, of course, the poet establishes the

Dreamer in his new role as the Fool. This leads very smoothly to the second scene, in which the friars are satirized and the Dreamer discusses with Loyalty the propriety of writing a poem that will expose their evil ways. As we shall see, the friars are destined to emerge at the end of the B-continuation as a group of terrifying villains, the cohorts of Antichrist. It is my belief that our poet has already envisioned at this point the main outlines of his entire poem, and that he presents, in this discussion between the Dreamer and Loyalty, a justification for the attack on the friars which his poem is to contain. The passage reveals some humorous touches, but it has, nevertheless, a fundamentally serious purpose.

The next scene (11.103–310) presents a discussion involving Scripture, the Dreamer, and Trajan. This is our first example of a theme to which the greater part of passus 11–15 is devoted: the A-text revisited. And it is difficult if not impossible to follow the thought of this part of B passus 11 unless we have well in mind the eleventh passus of the A-text, especially Dame Study's denunciation of the pride and hypocrisy of the learned (A 11.13–85), and the ironic dispute of the Dreamer which interrupts Clergie's definition of the triad, together with his closing observations on the futility of learning (A 11.216–303). Once we perceive this relationship between the A and B texts, the meaning of B 11.103–310 becomes perfectly clear. And since no one has hitherto attempted a detailed analysis of this complex passage, we may let the following explication of it serve to illustrate the importance of reading the B-continuation with the A-text constantly in mind.

The Dreamer in A, reflecting on his vision at the end of the *Vita,* had observed (11.250–54):

> Yet am I nevere the ner, for nought I have walkid,
> To wyte what is Do-wel witterly in herte;
> For how so I werche in this world, wrong other ellis,
> I was markid withoute mercy and myn name entrid
> In the legende of lif, longe er I were.

As we have seen, the A-poet is not actually troubled by this; he introduces it in his *reductio ad absurdum* as an example of the futility of learning. But of course predestination was one of the problems being seriously debated in the schools; it was no straw man. And so in the B-text Scripture reopens this question by preaching a sermon on the text, *Many are called, but few are chosen* (Matt. 22:14), a text which was, of course, a focal point in the argument. Upon hearing the familiar parable of the marriage feast, the Dreamer's heart trembles, and he disputes within himself on whether he is one of the chosen. With very little effort (B 11.114–31) he concludes that he can be saved. Scripture then confirms this, and the problem of predestination is settled.

Suddenly Trajan bursts into the scene. His immediate purpose is to correct the Dreamer's allegation concerning the fate of the righteous heathen in the A-text (A 11.256–70). This he does very quickly (B 11.135–53). But then he goes on with a long speech in which he is clearly speaking for the poet himself (B 11.165–310). In this passage the author undertakes a diplomatic modification of many of the ideas expressed in the eleventh passus of the A-text. I offer below a paraphrase of this passage, stripped of its diplomacy in order to make the poet's meaning perfectly clear, and at the same time to indicate its relationship to the relevant portions of A passus 11. Statements which reveal the author's modification of ideas expressed in the A-text are italicized. The statements in parentheses supply transitions of thought which I believe are implied rather than openly stated. In my paraphrase the author of B is addressing the A-poet.[1]

> You are certainly correct in pointing out [A 11.127–62] that learning is useless without love, and that *very often* [B 11.167–69] the learned are corrupted by cupidity [A 11.13–23] and pride [A 11.58–71]. And I agree that it is our duty to love our fellow man, both enemy and friend, and give to the poor [A 11.237–44]. Those learned clerks whom you describe as carping about the Trinity at feasts while the poor cry at the gate [A 11.38–50] have

failed to conform to the law of love. We should help the poor. It is also true, as you say [A 11.51–54], that God's mercy and his works are to be found among poor men. Christ himself appeared on earth as a poor man, and he tells us in the Gospel [Luke 14:12] to invite the poor and helpless to dinner rather than our friends. *On the other hand, we are all brothers, rich and poor alike* [B 11.191–202]. *Therefore let us love one another, and freely give, both of our possessions and of our knowledge; and let us not blame anyone, though he may know more Latin,*[2] *nor foully rebuke him, for none is without fault* [B 11.203–9].

Now I am sure we can agree that faith is above learning, as both the Gospels and saints' lives attest, so that in this sense you have done good service, and I join you in urging all Christians not to rely *too heavily* [B 11.219] on learning. It is far better for us to love, *and to know ourselves* [B 11.223].

But to return to the subject of the poor. I said that Christ appeared in the likeness of a poor man. This is true. *But his followers recognized him, not by his poor clothing, nor by his learning, but by his deeds* [B 11.226–31]. Do you see what this means? *Christ's poverty was not an end in itself; it was an example of humility which we should all follow, whatever our rank or condition in society* [B 11.232–34]. Now Scripture certainly does give many examples in praise of poverty; no one will deny this. *But all the wise men I have ever read on the subject praise poverty over riches only if it is patient* [B 11.247–49]. True, the poor have a hard life; but the reward of eternal life makes it worth it, and it has its practical advantages too. (But don't misunderstand me: I do not claim that poverty as such has any inherent value. It is the will of the individual that is important.) *Surely you will agree, as Luke bears witness* [Luke 18:22–23], *that perfect poverty is voluntary, for it clearly reveals one's faith in God's promise to provide for the needs of the body* [B 11.261–73].

(Perhaps you are thinking that I am all in favor of poverty for the common people, but that I make an exception in the case of priests. This is not true.) Priests should have exactly the same faith in God's promise to provide that I have just mentioned as characteristic of perfect poverty. There is no need for them to take money for singing masses [e.g., A 3.228–30]. If they are worthy, the bishop should provide for them. Furthermore—while I am on the subject—there is absolutely no excuse for ignorant priests, who, endowed with nothing but a shaved head, expect to get a cure automatically, making no effort to acquire learning or holiness of life. Why the bishop ordains such "priests" I will never understand. They stumble in the Gospel, they skip passages at mass, and I am convinced that for this the bishop will have to answer to God. *Priests, after all, are God's knights* [B 11.304]. Nay, I will add that both the bishop and the chaplain stand condemned.—But these reflections on ignorant priests have caused me to digress: my main point is that poverty is preferable to riches *if it is patient* [B 11.309–10].

This is indeed a remarkable passage, and it does a lot to prepare us for the modification of ideas expressed in the A-text which we can expect to find in the B-continuation. A glance at the italicized lines will show that the poet has softened A's condemnation of the rich; distinguished between poverty as an economic condition and patient poverty as a spiritual condition (adding the case of the rich man in the Gospel as a potential example of perfect poverty); affirmed the value of learning, with appropriate qualifications; warned the Dreamer once again to know himself; and, finally, condemned covetous and ignorant priests. The entire speech—if it is a speech—has a highly personal tone. I cannot read it without feeling very close to the author himself. The B-continuation is of course not autobiographical: we have already had occasion to take note of the literary convention which governs the characterization of the Dreamer. But this passage is not spoken by the Dreamer,[3] nor does it seem to relate to him in any significant way. He certainly fails to respond to it, as he does to the other rebukes directed at him.

Is this one of those personal reflections (similar to A 10.87–99) that a poet occasionally permits himself? If so, I must say that it does not seem to me to fit the conventional account of the poet's life and position. W. W. Skeat says of the author:[4] "It thus appears that he had received the tonsure, but probably had only taken minor orders, and, being a married man, was hardly in a position to rise in the church. He has many allusions to his poverty." But unless I grossly misread this passage, it reveals that the poet is a man who has been intimately associated with wealthy men (and knows that they are not all bad), and is, in fact, a ranking member of the secular clergy. His criticisms of priests, be it noted, are directed not so much at the miserable examples of ignorance that he cites, but rather at the bishop who will make such men "goddes kniȝts."[5] He then adds this significant statement (B 11.306–8):

> Ac neuer neyther is blamelees, the bisshop ne the chapleyne,
> For her eyther is endited, and that of *"ignorancia*
> *Non excusat episcopos nec* idiotes prestes."

Is the poet a chaplain? If so, the lines quoted might be boldly paraphrased: "But I am just as much to blame as the bishop; both of us stand indicted."

We now come to the passage (B 11.311–94) that most clearly sets the stage for the biblical drama that is to come in the B-continuation. Kynde (Nature) takes the Dreamer to a mountain called Middle-Earth, whence he can see the created universe (B 11.318–21). Kynde's purpose, of course, is to let the Dreamer learn to love God by observing nature, *For the invisible things of him from the creation of the world are clearly seen, being understood by the things that are made, even his eternal power and Godhead* (Rom. 1:20). The Dreamer then looks and sees the world of the Creation as it is written in the first two chapters of Genesis. The details of his description fit remarkably well into the literary tradition of the Bible as represented by the cycle plays, *Cursor Mundi* and Higden's *Polychronicon*.

Note first of all the Dreamer's description of the animals. He is struck by the fact that they seem to behave very reasonably (B 11.332–53):

> There ne was cow ne cowkynde that conceyued hadde,
> That wolde belwe after boles, ne bore after sowe;
> Bothe horse and houndes and alle other bestes
> Medled nouȝte wyth here makes that with fole were.   335
> Briddes I bihelde that in buskes made nestes;
> Hadde neuere wye witte to worche the leest.
> I hadde wonder at whom and where the pye lerned
> To legge the stykkes in whiche she leyeth and bredeth;
> There nys wriȝte as I wene shulde worche hir neste to paye;   340
> If any masoun made a molde ther-to, moche wonder it were.

And ȝet me merueilled more how many other briddes
Hudden and hileden her egges ful derne
In mareys and mores, for men sholde hem nouȝt fynde,
And hudden here egges whan thei there-fro wente,   345
For fere of other foules and for wylde bestis.
And some troden her makes and on trees bredden,
And brouȝten forth her bryddes so, al aboue the grounde;
And some bryddes at the bille thorwgh brethynge conceyued;
And some kauked, I toke kepe, how pekokes bredden.   350
Moche merueilled me what maister thei hadde,
And who tauȝte hem on trees to tymbre so heighe,
There noither buirn ne beste may her briddes rechen.

Of course this is based on the account of the creation of the animals
in Genesis, but it is a highly distinctive and unusual list. For the
animals traditionally associated with the Creation are the lion
and the lamb, wolf and sheep, etc., stressing the ideal nature of the
world before the Fall, the state of things corresponding to the time
predicted in the prophets, when *the wolf also shall dwell with the
lamb, and the leopard shall lie down with the kid* . . . (Isaiah 11:6).
We find this, for example, in the *Cursor Mundi*.[6] The B-poet's
source for the passage quoted, however, strange as it may seem,
appears to have been the depiction of the Creation in the first drama
of the Cornish *Ordinalia,* the *Origo Mundi*.[7] In this play God creates
the animals, and Adam gives them their names (Gen. 2:19–20). I
quote from Norris' translation (123–34):

ADAM

I name cow, and bull,
And horse, which is a beast without equal
   For helping mankind;   125
Goat, deer, stag,
Sheep, in few words,
   Let it receive its right name.
Now I name goose and hen,
Which I consider birds without equal   130
   For food of man on the earth;
Duck, peacock, pigeon, partridge,

Swan, kite, crows, and the eagle
Further by me shall be named.

The first thing that strikes the eye, of course, is the presence in both passages of cow, bull, and horse, in that order (our poet adds "cowkynde," "bore after sowe," and "houndes" for purposes of alliteration). But the correspondences do not stop there. The words "and alle other bestes" are perhaps intended to supplant Adam's naming of the goat, deer, stag, and sheep; then follows a rather full description of the magpie and her nest (B 11.336–41), possibly reflecting the poet's own observation, since it is the only bird he names here that does not also appear in the cycle play. Our poet next describes, without mentioning names, the nesting habits of the Cornish goose, hen,[8] duck, and swan (B 11.342–46), the breeding of the pigeon [9] (347–48), partridge [10] (349), and peacock (350), and, finally, the nesting habits of the kite, crow, and eagle (351–53).

Thus it can be seen that the poet has either mentioned or described the habits of virtually every one of the creatures named by Adam in the passage quoted, and, except for the swan (included by the author in his description of the water fowls) and the peacock (mentioned by name in both texts), all of these creatures appear *in precisely the same order*. Further, it does not seem likely that the Cornish text is derived from our poem.[11] To suppose that the dramatist delved into the B-text of *Piers,* found this passage, applied it to Adam, and then converted the descriptions of nesting habits, and so on, into the appropriate names of the birds, would be extremely dubious, to say the least. Perhaps it might be argued that there is a common source for both passages, or that our poet borrowed from some intermediate text. In the absence of any direct evidence of this, however, I conclude that the author is here indebted to the *Origo Mundi,* and that he had, therefore, in all probability, some knowledge of the Cornish language.

We next return to a description of the Creation, still based on Genesis, but with traditional elaborations (B 11.354–59):

And sythen I loked vpon the see, and so forth vpon the sterres,
Many selcouthes I seygh ben nought to seye nouthe.
I seigh floures in the fritthe, and her faire coloures,
And how amonge the grene grasse grewe so many hewes,
And somme soure and some swete, selcouthe me thouȝte;
Of her kynde and her coloure to carpe it were to longe.

This is the well-known *hortus deliciarum,* as we find it, for example, in the description of paradise in the *Cursor Mundi* (1012-14,
1027-8):

> Þe gresse es euer ilik grene,
> Wit alkin blis þat þar es elles;
> Flours þar es wit suete smelles;
>
> .   .   .   .   .   .
>
> It es a yard cald o delites
> Wit all maner o suet spices.

The same garden is evident in the Towneley *Creation:* [12]

> *Adam.* Eve, felow, abide me thore,
> ffor I will go to viset more,
> To se what trees that here been;
> here ar well moo then we have seen,
> Gresys, and othere small floures,
> That smell full swete, of seyr coloures.

There can be little doubt, I think, that the Dreamer is gazing
upon God's Creation as it is described in Genesis, and as it is
elaborated in biblical tradition and the medieval drama. But we
have not yet taken cognizance of the fact that the poet is using his
traditional materials in a very special way. When he describes
Adam and Eve, for example, he envisions simultaneously the
ominous consequences of their Fall (B 11.322-25):

> Man and his make, I myȝte bothe byholde;
> Pouerte and plente, bothe pees and werre,
> Blisse and bale, bothe I seigh at ones,
> And how men token mede, and mercy refused.

[69]

And then he has the Dreamer comment on the perversity of man, as compared to the reasonableness of beasts (B 11.360–66):

> Ac that moste moeued me, and my mode chaunged,
> That Resoun rewarded and reuled alle bestes,
> Saue man and his make; many tyme and ofte
> No resoun hem folwed; and thanne I rebuked
> Resoun, and riȝte til hym-seluen I seyde,
> "I haue wonder of the," quod I, "that witty art holden,
> Why thow ne suwest man and his make, that no mysfait hem
>   folwe?"

This is of course the basic idea expressed by Isaiah (1:3): *The ox knoweth his owner, and the ass his master's crib: but Israel doth not know, my people doth not consider.* But this passage was usually interpreted allegorically in scriptural tradition (note the ox and the ass in most medieval representations of the nativity) and not generally applied to the creation. Perhaps, then, this application is the poet's own. On the other hand, it is quite possible that he derived the suggestion for the Dreamer's complaint from the discussion of man's state, before and after the Fall, in Higden's account of the Creation in his *Polychronicon*.[13] I quote from the translation of John Trevisa:

> But he [man] is feblere þan eny oþer beest; he can non helpe, he may nouȝt doo of hym self, bot wepe wiþ alle his myȝt. No beest haþ lyf more brutel and unsiker. Noon haþ siknesse more grevous, noon more likynge to doo oþer wise þan he shulde. Noon is more cruel. Also oþer bestes loveþ eueriche oþer of the same kynde, and woneþ to gidres, and beeþ not cruel but to bestes of oþer kynde þat beeþ contrarye to hem. But man torneþ þat manere doynge vp so down, and is contrarye to hym self and cruel to oþer men; and he may not reche for to greue oþere, þan he bycomeþ angry and cruel to hym self.

Clearly this idea governs the poet's exploitation of the Creation scene. The pure description from Genesis and the details taken from the *hortus deliciarum* tradition combine to set the stage, but the animals, which in the Cornish *Origo Mundi* are a mere catalogue, serve in our poem as an exemplum showing the reasonableness of these creatures in contrast to the irrationality of man, a motif in the *de contemptu mundi* tradition. Hence the poet's description of their mating and nesting habits. But this is not all. What is the purpose of this passage in relation to the eleventh passus as a whole? Does the poet in fact wish to stress here the reasonableness of animals? I think not. The whole creation scene has a dramatic function in relation to the Dreamer. As we have already seen, Kynde is giving the Dreamer an opportunity to learn to love God by observing Creation, "the things that are made." But instead of finding God, he sees only the irrationality of man. His first lesson is over, and he has failed it miserably. The poet's transformation of his sources is truly remarkable. With great skill and originality he has given the conventional representation of the Creation a satiric twist, and, what is most impressive, used the *de contemptu mundi* theme as an exhibition of the Dreamer's spiritual blindness. The Fool has *worshipped and served the creature more than the Creator* (Rom. 1:25).

To the Dreamer's questioning of Reason the latter responds by saying, in effect, this is none of your business; improve it, if you can. What you lack is sufferance (cf. A 10.115). And do you dare question God's Creation? Scripture tells us that *God saw everything that he had made, and, behold, it was very good* (Gen. 1:31). At this the Dreamer blushes with shame, and awakens.[14] He now thinks he knows what Do-wel is, and, when questioned by Imaginatif (who is to be his guide in the next passus), he says that Do-wel is "to see much and endure more" (11.402). There is more than a tinge of bitterness in this statement. The Dreamer still feels the sting of his shame. And his new tutor proceeds to rebuke him, telling him that just as his impertinent interruption of Clergie (A 11.216–20) prevented his learning what Clergie could teach him, so now his rude questioning of Reason has lost him another chance to learn. He is not worthy of Clergie's company. However, there is still hope, for shame is a healthy sign. To this the Dreamer responds, in the closing lines of the passus (11.425–31):

"ȝe seggen soth," quod I, "ich haue yseyne it ofte,
There smit no thinge so smerte, ne smelleth so soure,
As Shame, there he sheweth him, for euery man hym shonyeth!
Why ȝe wisse me thus," quod I, "was for I rebuked Resoun."
  "Certes," quod he, "that is soth," and shope hym for to walken;
And I aros vp riȝt with that, and folwed hym after,
And preyed hym of his curteisye to telle me his name.

Fortune's Fool has at last turned, and is now taking his first step on the long road that will lead him to God.

Passus 12

In the twelfth passus the poet takes us on a quick journey through the entire *Vita* of the A-text, pausing here and there to modify or correct what he considers a misleading or erroneous statement. Imaginatif is our guide. He corresponds to Thought in the ninth passus of A, and represents very nearly the same thing as Thought. If there is a difference, it is that Imaginatif signifies a more intense "reflection" or "meditation," which is a salutary consequence of the Dreamer's shame, described at the end of the preceding passus.

The opening passage (12.1–29) is a rather amusing reiteration of the Fool motif, which simultaneously prepares us for the ensuing discussion. Imaginatif tells the Dreamer that he has followed him for forty-five winters (compare Thought's words, A 9.66), and urges him to amend himself before it is too late. But you meddle with making (composing poetry), he says, when you should be reciting the Psalter (12.17–19):

                              for there ar bokes ynowe
        To telle men what Dowel is, Dobet, and Dobest bothe,
        And prechoures to preue what it is, of many a peyre freres.

The allusion to the friars is a sharp thrust, but delivered without malice. The reference to the Dreamer's "meddling with making" reveals the poet's bantering tone. I do not see how anyone can take this passage seriously. The author has Imaginatif accuse the Fool of doing exactly what he himself is doing at that very moment. The Dreamer responds with a good-humored defense, but the two of them, poet and Dreamer, are obviously enjoying this brief moment of rapport at the expense of the Philistines. The Dreamer next remarks that if someone would tell him about Do-wel, etc., he would spend all of his time (except for eating and sleeping) at prayer in the church. This gentle observation provides the opening for Imaginatif. The remainder of the passus is at his disposal, and his theme, of course, is "the A-text revisited."

Imaginatif begins by defining Do-wel in accordance with St. Paul's famous triad: faith, hope, and charity. This helps prepare us for his later emphasis on grace. But he has no desire to spin out a new definition of his own as a replacement for the definitions in A. He is more interested in correcting the views already expressed there. Hence he plunges immediately into a revision of Wit's definition of Do-wel, etc. (A 10.76 ff.). It will be recalled that Wit in A defined the triad (commons, clergy, and episcopate) in terms of particular spiritual requisites of each: fear of God, sufferance, and humility. He then went on to emphasize the importance of marriage as the foundation of society (A 10.127–29):

> Formest and ferst to folk that ben weddit,
> And lyuen as here lawe wile, it liketh God almighty;
> For thorugh wedlak the world stant, who so wile it knowen.

This is eloquent praise of the married state. And it is followed by several more lines in praise of wedded folk somewhat at the expense of both the secular and regular clergy. Now it is evident that the B-poet is not entirely satisfied with this emphasis on marriage. I can see him wincing especially at the statement that God is pleased *first and foremost* with wedded folk (cf. 1 Cor. 7:25–40). Imaginatif therefore provides the following correction (B 12.33–40):

> For he doth wel, with-oute doute, that doth as lewte techeth;
> That is, if thow be man maried, thi make thow louye,
> And lyue forth as lawe wole while ȝe lyuen bothe.
> Riȝt so, if thow be religious, renne thow neuere ferther

[73]

> To Rome ne to Rochemadore but as thi reule techeth,
> And holde the vnder obedyence that heigh wey is to heuene.
> And if thow be mayden to marye, and miȝte wel contynue,
> Seke thow neuere seynt forther for no soule helthe.

Clearly, this presents the more conventional triad of spiritual states: marriage, continence, and virginity, following St. Paul. Marriage no longer holds the center of the stage. To this, Imaginatif adds a warning against climbers, suggested by the criticism of regulars in the A-text (A 10.102 ff.), which serves to demonstrate his objectivity. He is no special pleader. Just as Wit (in A), who is mainly interested in wedded folk, launched into a denunciation of abuses of marriage, so Imaginatif, who seems more interested in the clergy, warns against runners and climbers. He has nothing to add in the way of a critique on marriage.

The next unit in Imaginatif's discussion (B 12.41–65) is a transitional passage, designed to prepare the way for the Dreamer's acceptance of his evaluation of clergie (learning) and kynde wit (natural understanding). It is a rhetorically skillful and persuasive argument, but despite this it is virtually impossible to follow unless the reader keeps relevant portions of the A-text constantly in mind. It opens with the *de casibus* theme: Why did Lucifer lose heaven, or Solomon his wisdom, or Samson his strength? This is clear enough in itself, but what is its connection with the preceding definition of the spiritual states? The answer lies in Imaginatif's allusion to the denunciation of climbers in the A-text, where we read (A 10.96–99):

> But suffre and sit stille, and sek thou no ferthere,
> And be glad of the grace that God hath i-sent the;
> For yif thou comsist to clymbe, and coveitest herre,
> Thou mightest lese thi loughnesse for a litel pride.

The transition, then, is begun with a shift from the pride of those not satisfied with a particular state to the pride of Lucifer, thus introducing the *de casibus* theme. But to what end? The answer to this is evident when we observe that, although the examples given are in part merely conventional illustrations of fall from high degree, they nevertheless include a significant number of men renowned either for their wealth (Job, Alexander), or their wisdom (Solomon, Aristotle, Hippocrates, Virgil). Imaginatif calls attention to this fact by saying, admittedly with some exaggeration: "Catel and kynde witte was combraunce to hem alle" (B 12.46). He then goes on, as the *de casibus* convention demands (cf. Chaucer's Monk's Tale), to bring his list up to date—albeit with an anti-feminist turn—by citing the instances of Felice and Rosamund. But then he immediately returns to the main point, warning of the dangers that threaten those who abuse either wealth or wisdom.[15] Imaginatif concludes this transitional passage by affirming that the tendency to abuse wisdom and wealth can be checked by grace (B 12.62–65):

> Ac grace ne groweth nouȝte but amonges lowe;
> Pacience and pouerte the place is there it groweth,
> And in lele-lyuynge men and in lyf-holy,
> And thorugh the gyfte of the holygoste, as the gospel telleth,
> *Spiritus vbi vult spirat, etc.*

These lines constitute a judicious statement, not only of the poet's earlier conclusion about patient poverty as a spiritual state (B 11.247–73), but also of its application to the present passage. True humility and patience (whether literally among the poor, or among the poor in spirit), with the help of the Holy Ghost (contrast A 11.289–92), can amend the faults of improperly used wealth and wisdom. This is our poet's soft answer to the angry tone of the A-version of *Piers the Plowman.*

But there is one further function of these transitional remarks which I have not yet mentioned. Whereas in the above summary I refer to "wisdom," the poet actually uses the words "kynde witte." His reason for this choice of words will be evident in our analysis of the next unit of Imaginatif's discussion. Suffice it to say here that his association of "kynde witte" with riches is a skillful strategic move, for the Dreamer, who of course represents the point of view expressed in A, will be attentive to any denunciation of riches (cf. A 8.162 ff., 11.13 ff., 11.221–27). The B-poet here is not particularly interested in denouncing the rich; but he does so at this point in order to get the Dreamer on his side. And his coupling of riches with "kynde witte" is the first step in his diplomatic downgrading of a faculty which in the A-text (e.g., A 11.250–303) was exalted at the expense of learning.

The way in which Imaginatif revises the Dreamer's attitude toward kynde witte and clergie is an admirable illustration of the poet's skill and diplomacy in argument. Clergie, says Imaginatif, comes from what we know; kynde witte comes from what we see. But grace, which is a gift of God *through the Holy Ghost* (B 12.65), is above both clergie and kynde witte. In reference to the Holy Ghost he uses John 3:8, 11, but his argument reveals that what he has in mind primarily is the passage in Isaiah, chapter 11, verses 2–5, perhaps the most famous text on the Holy Ghost in the Old Testament: *and he shall not judge after the sight of his eyes, neither reprove after the hearing of his ears: but with righteousness shall he judge the poor, and reprove with equity for the meek of the earth* . . . (Isa. 11:3–4). Grace, which is the gift of God through the Holy Ghost, goes beyond the sight of eyes (kynde witte) and the hearing of ears (clergie), in order to judge with righteousness and reprove with equity. This power is perhaps best illustrated by Christ's knowledge of men's thoughts (Matt. 9:4, Luke 11:17), but it is a power which all men of true charity and humility may possess in some degree. With these facts in mind, Imaginatif's introduction to his discussion of clergie and kynde witte reveals itself to us as a model of clarity and persuasiveness (B 12.62–71):

> Ac grace ne groweth nouȝte but amonges lowe;
> Pacience and pouerte the place is there it groweth,
> And in lele-lyuynge men and in lyf-holy,
> And thorugh the gyfte of the holygoste, as the gospel telleth,
>> *Spiritus vbi vult spirat, etc.*
> Clergye and kynde witte comth of siȝte and techynge,

As the boke bereth witnesse to buirnes that can rede,
>   *Quod scimus, loquimur; quod vidimus, testamur.*
Of *quod scimus* cometh clergye, and connynge of heuene,
And of *quod vidimus* cometh kynde witte, of siȝte of dyuerse
>   peple.
Ac grace is a gyfte of god, and of gret loue spryngeth;
Knewe neuere clerke how it cometh forth, ne kynde witte the
>   weyes,
>   *Nescit aliquis vnde venit, aut quo vadit, etc.*

Once the Dreamer accepts this statement, he has automatically relinquished his old position (in the A-text), and is well on the way toward the acceptance of learning as a partner of kynde witte, if not indeed the latter's superior. Imaginatif now proceeds to his formal argument, but in effect the battle is already won.

Both clergie and kynde witte are to be commended, says Imaginatif, but especially clergie. With learning, Christ saved the woman taken in adultery (contrast A 11.285–86). Without learning, we would not have the sacraments. Clergie and kynde witte are cousins; both are guides for learned and unlearned alike. So do not dispute with clerks, for no "kynde-witted man" can be saved without their teaching. Furthermore, it is a sacrilege to despise the clergy and their science, whatever shortcomings they may have personally. Remember what happened to those who meddled with the ark of the covenant (1 Sam. 6:19, 13:8–14; 2 Sam. 6:6–7). On the other hand, kynde witte comes from the observation of nature, resulting in the apprehension of half-truths and deceits (compare A 11.160–61). Kynde witte, in fact, compared to the "clergye of Cryst," is *sapiencia huius mundi* (1 Cor. 3:19): *For the wisdom of this world is foolishness with God.*

Imaginatif then concludes this phase of his argument by adapting for his own use the closing lines of the A-*Vita* (A 11.301–3):

>   Souteris and seweris, suche lewide jottis,
>   Percen with a *pater noster* the paleis of hevene,
>   Withoute penaunce, at here partyng, in-to the heighe blisse.

Here is Imaginatif's version of these lines (B 12.141–43):

> For the heihe holigoste heuene shal to-cleue,
> And loue shal lepe out after in-to this lowe erthe,
> And clennesse shal cacchen it, and clerkes shullen it fynde.

He refers, of course, to the incarnation, and this lends particular force to his emphasis on the supremacy of charity, humility, and grace over both clergie and kynde witte. But his daring use of A's climactic lines is, in addition, an important instrument in his persuasion of the Dreamer. It will be recalled that the Dreamer in A, citing St. Augustine, had concluded (A 11.297–300):

> Arn none rathere yravisshid fro the righte beleve
> Thanne arn thise grete clerkis, that conne many bokis;
> Ne none sonnere ysavid, ne saddere of consience,
> Thanne pore peple as ploughmen, and pastours of bestis.

Imaginatif seizes upon the reference to "pastours of bestis," that is, shepherds, and replies: *both* shepherds *and* great clerks (the three wise men) came to worship Christ at Bethlehem! [16] The gospels, he goes on, do not speak here of rich men (cf. A 11.13 ff.), or learned hypocrites and ignorant lords (A 11.38 ff.), but of the greatest of learned men, the Magi. If any friar were found there (A 11.58 ff.), I'll give you five shillings! [17] Imaginatif then concludes (B 12.149–51, 154–55): [18]

> To pastours and to poetes appiered that aungel,
> And bad hem go to Bethlem goddis burth to honoure,
> And songe a songe of solas, *gloria in excelsis deo!*
> Clerkes knewe it wel and comen with here presentz,
> And deden her homage honourablely to hym that was almyȝty.

This is a brilliant and incisive response to the challenge provided by the ending of the A-*Vita*.

We have seen how everything that Imaginatif says has a direct bearing on some portion of the *Vita* poem of the A-text of *Piers the Plowman*. This is confirmed—if indeed confirmation were needed —by Imaginatif's own frank admission (B 12.156–59):

> Why I haue tolde the al this—I toke ful gode hede
> How thow contraryedest Clergye with crabbed wordes,

[78]

"How that lewed men liȝtloker than lettred were saued,
    Than clerkes or kynde-witted men, of Crystene peple." [19]

And what you say is true in part, Imaginatif admits, but let me explain—and he goes on to give the example of two men, one a swim-
mer and one not, who are thrown into the Thames. Which man
is in more danger? The nonswimmer, of course. Hence the learned
man, not the ignorant one, is sooner saved. This actually concludes
the formal argument. But Imaginatif adds some curiously intimate
remarks on the clergy's superior knowledge concerning the nature
of sin, the importance of contrition, and the reprehensibility of
priestly ignorance (B 12.175–86). We are inevitably reminded of
the earlier passage (B 11.274–308), evidently a part of Trajan's
speech, containing an eloquent denunciation of ignorant priests.
The present remarks, put in the mouth of Imaginatif, have the
same tone. And once more it is difficult to avoid the inference that
the author's own thoughts are rising to the surface of his poem,
and that they show him to be one whose viewpoint is that of the
priesthood.

After a brief reference to the value of the neck-verse—which is a
bone tossed with good-natured condescension to the Dreamer-Fool—
Imaginatif attacks the problem raised by the reference in A to the
apparent injustice of Dismas' salvation (A 11.271–78). As we have
seen, the A-poet was not really worried about this; it was simply
one of the *exempla* in his *reductio ad absurdum,* which reaches its
climax with the mention of such wicked men as David and Paul.
But Imaginatif does not want to leave any loose ends in his critique
of the *Vita,* so he proceeds to assure the Dreamer that the penitent
thief, though he was saved, does not have as exalted a position at
the heavenly feast as those who led holy lives (B 12.208–9):

> And forto seruen a seynt and such a thef togyderes,
> It were noyther resoun ne riȝt to rewarde hem bothe aliche.

It is possible that Imaginatif considered the calling in question of
Dismas' salvation something of a quibble, for he now tries to an-

ticipate further quibbling questions which he supposes the Dreamer might wish to "find up." Do you ask where Trajan is? He is undoubtedly placed the lowest in heaven. Do you ask why one thief on the cross was saved and not the other? Not all the learned men under Christ could answer that question. You are a fool. You argued with Reason, you wanted to know all the secrets of nature. Nature knows why the magpie builds in bushes, etc. Nature taught Adam and Eve to cover themselves with leaves. Some ignorant men even ask (is this the kind of thing you're interested in?) why Adam didn't first cover his mouth, which ate the apple, instead of the lower part of his body. Nature knows the answer, but not clerks! Throughout this passage (B 12.210–35) there is a kind of hesitation between seriousness and jocularity, as if Imaginatif were feeling his way, wondering if his observations were hitting or missing the mark. The Dreamer maintains a discreet silence.[20]

At this point Imaginatif has an inspiration. The Dreamer, he reasons (and here I am supplying the transition which is implicit at line B 12.236), is scornful of the rich and takes the part of the poor. Perhaps some learned examples which support his point of view, at least in part, will help to make him see the value of learning. And so Imaginatif launches into an exposition of the peacock, who signifies, in the bestiary tradition, the shortcomings of rich men, or rather of *proud* rich men, as the poet is careful to specify (B 12.240). He then gives the *significatio* of the lark, which stresses the superior qualities of humble men, and concludes (B 12.266–67):

> Arestotle the grete clerke, suche tales he telleth;
> Thus he lykneth in his logyk the leste foule oute.

But as soon as Imaginatif invokes Aristotle, he is faced with the vexing problem of the righteous heathen. Perhaps we may say (without straying too far from the text) that he sees a gleam in the Dreamer's eye. In any case, he immediately protests that he doesn't know whether Aristotle, Socrates, and Solomon are saved or not (cf. A 11.257–70), but that we certainly ought to pray God to give their souls rest.

The Dreamer is not satisfied with Imaginatif's ambiguous hope regarding the heathen, and he repeats (from A 11.263–67) his assertion that all clerks of Holy Church say that the unbaptized heathen are in Hell. Whereupon Imaginatif frowns (meaning, in effect, "Don't push me too far"), and proceeds to walk a theological tightrope, concluding that God may well reward the just man who obeyed the best law that he knew. Then Imaginatif vanishes, before the Fool has a chance to ask him any more questions.

Passus 13–14

The thirteenth and fourteenth passus must be considered together, for they constitute a well-defined unit in the "Creation" section of the B-continuation. This unit, however, is closely related to the preceding passus, in that it presents a dramatization of Imaginatif's discussion of clergie and kynde witte (B 12.41–191). The learned Doctor, whom we meet first, represents clergie; Haukyn, the wafer-seller, represents kynde witte. Both are subjected to searching criticism, just as Imaginatif criticized both clergie and kynde witte in the preceding passus. But this is an oversimplification. Other characters appear in the action, and, before considering the text in detail, we must first take due note of the ways in which these other figures serve to qualify the above generalization.

The Dreamer, obviously, is one of the participants in the allegorical action. His role here is a further elaboration of the Fool motif which governs his characterization throughout the poem. He is used by the poet with particular effectiveness in satirizing the Doctor. And although he does not function dramatically in the confession of Haukyn, the whole scene involving Haukyn is designed for his enlightenment. It is true, as we shall see, that he doesn't appear at first to learn much, and that he even draws the wrong conclusions from what he has been taught, but this is because he is a Fool.

Conscience, who is introduced here for the first time in the B-continuation, is a very important figure, both in the present action and also in the closing passus (19–20) of the poem. He has a multiple function throughout. He "monitors" the action. He directs the Dreamer's (and the reader's) attention to important features of the allegory. He is a guide on the pilgrimage through time which is an implicit feature of the poem's progression. When he joins forces with one of the personifications, the reader knows that this personification is to be respected. The role of Conscience, in short, is that of the individual's conscience, which selects and rejects the good and the evil in this world, the conscience which is our "guide." [21]

Clergie (learning) appears only in the banquet scene with the Doctor, but he has a very significant function here. I have said that the Doctor represents clergie, and one might well ask how this could be, since Clergie appears as a separate character. The answer is that the Doctor specifically embodies *corrupted* learning, not learning per se. The poet introduces Clergie in order to make this point, since, as we have observed (B 12.72 ff.), he holds learning in very high esteem. This fact is brought out clearly, as we shall see, at the close of the banquet scene.

By far the most important character in passus 13–14 is Patience. He teaches the Dreamer and Haukyn, exposes the Doctor, and commands the respect of Conscience. If the Doctor and Haukyn embody clergie and kynde witte, then Patience is the embodiment of that humility, patience, and charity which Imaginatif has declared (B 12.62–65) to be the fruit of grace, the gift of God through the Holy Ghost, and which is superior to both clergie and kynde witte. Indeed, Patience is a virtue which the author has praised implicitly or explicitly from the beginning of the B-continuation, particularly in the long speech assigned to Trajan (B 11.165–310). Furthermore, as we shall see, this virtue is the center of attention throughout passus 14, which ends with a highly charged and impassioned eulogy of patient poverty. Thus, although Patience actually appears as a character only in passus 13–14, he is an extremely important functionary in the poet's articulation of the major theme of passus 11–15: the A-text revisited.

Why is Patience so important? It is not enough to say that patient poverty and the doctrine of *ne solliciti sitis* were commonplace teachings of the poet's day. For this merely sets the stage, so to speak, and cannot explain their use in the poem; and, as R. W. Frank, Jr., has pointed out, the particular emphasis they receive in the B-continuation is the poet's own creation.[22] Nor do I think it sufficient to say that the poet's emphasis on patience is a call to reform *in vacuo,* as it were. For the important thing to note is that his emphasis on patience is *always* intimately associated with his revision of ideas put forth in the A-version of *Piers the Plowman.* In view of this, therefore, I offer the following suggestion. If the B-poet did not actually regard the A-text as dangerous in itself, he may yet have feared that its angry denunciation of learning and riches might incite others to a dangerous course of action. If this is the case, then in fairness to our poet we should add that his worst fears were realized in the Peasants' Revolt of 1381.[23]

Having observed the relation of passus 13–14 to the larger context of the "Creation," and having seen the function of the characters who participate in the action, we are now in a position to examine the allegory in detail. There is, however, one other question to be considered. What inspired the colorful banquet scene, and the confession of Haukyn? As we have come to expect, the answer is to be found in the A-text.[24] The banquet scene dramatizes Dame Study's brilliant description of corrupt clerks and secular lords (A 11.24–71), who gnaw God in their gorge when their guts are full (A 11.44).[25] Its satire, however, concentrates specifically on the evils of the friars. The confession of Haukyn, of course, as has been frequently observed, is based on the confessions of the personified Deadly Sins in the fifth passus of A. The details of both scenes support these generalizations. More important, however, we must realize that the B-poet is not merely elaborating ideas from the earlier text. Both scenes in the B-continuation contain explicit directives, designed, first, to make us *revise* our opinions concerning corruption among the learned, and, second, to *dispel* any illusion we may have had (from reading the A-text) about the superior spirituality of the commons.

At the beginning of passus 13 the Dreamer tells us that when Imaginatif vanished he awoke and wandered many years as a beggar, "witles nerehande" (well-nigh senseless). He then briefly summarizes everything that has happened to him from the beginning of the poem, that is, passus 11–12. The complexity of the poet's theme, of course, clearly warrants such a review; but it is interesting to note that summaries of this kind are to be expected in the literary tradition in which the poet is writing. They often occur, for example, at the beginning of individual cycle plays in the medieval drama. An even closer model for the summary here, perhaps, is this typical example from the *Cursor Mundi* (9375 ff.).

> Now lordingis haue ȝe herd
> Of the bigynnyng of þis werd,
> How he þat neuer had bigynnyng
> Made heuen, erþe & al þing.
> Also to alle þinge he ȝaue
> Her kyndely shap for to haue.
> Sonne & mone þat is so briȝt
> Had seuen so michel more liȝt;
> Alle þinges þat þo dud grow
> Were myȝtiere þen þei are now.
> A greet harm bifel vs þore,
> Þat alle shulde deȝe, lasse & more,
> Þat of Adam & Eue coom.
> But ȝitt was hit riȝtwis doom,
> As ȝe shul se bi riȝtful skil. . . .

Our poet writes in this same tradition, but of course the review is of his own poem (B 13.5–20):

First, how Fortune me failled at my moste nede,
And how that Elde manaced me, myȝt we euere meten;
And how that freris folwed folke that was riche,
And folke that was pore at litel prys thei sette,
And no corps in her kirkeȝerde ne in her kyrke was buryed,
But quikke he biquethe hem auȝte, or shulde helpe quyte her dettes.
And how this coueitise ouercome clerkes and prestes,
And how that lewed men ben ladde, but owre lorde hem helpe,
Thorugh vnkonnynge curatoures to incurable peynes.
And how that Ymagynatyf in dremeles me tolde,
Of Kynde and of his connynge, and how curteise he is to bestes,
And how louynge he is to bestes on londe and on water;
Leueth he no lyf, lasse ne more;
The creatures that crepen, of Kynde ben engendred.
And sitthen how Ymagynatif seyde *vix iustus saluabitur,*
And whan he had seyde so, how sodeynelich he passed.

Here we are reminded of the poet's treatment of the Dreamer as Fortune's Fool; satire on the friars; criticism of corrupt priests, but at the same time recognition of the importance of the priesthood for the salvation of the commons; and, finally, Imaginatif's teaching of the essential goodness of God's creation, together with his critique on the A-text (represented by the case of the righteous heathen). This is indeed a judicious summary of the poem up to this point.

Once more the Dreamer falls asleep, and this time Conscience appears and invites him to go dine with Clergie. Evidently the teachings of Imaginatif have had some effect, for the Dreamer is now eager to meet Clergie, and so they come to a court (cf. A 11.119 ff.) where they meet a "maistre," that is, the Doctor, who is portrayed unmistakably in this scene as a friar of the worst sort. Everyone washes and goes to dinner. At this point Patience first appears on the scene (B 13.29–30):

> Ac Pacience in the paleis stode in pilgrymes clothes,
> And preyde mete for charite for a pore heremyte.

This is a fine touch, inspired by Dame Study's description in the A-text (A 11:45–46):[26]

[85]

> Ac the carful may crighen and carpe at the yate,
> Bothe for hungir and for threst and for chele quake.

But it is particularly interesting to note that Conscience allows this poor pilgrim a place, be it ever so humble, in the dining hall. Patience is needed, of course, in the forthcoming satire on the Doctor; but the poet also wishes to revise the A-text's savage picture of uncharitable wealthy lords and their harsh treatment of the poor man (A 11.47–48):

> Is non to nymen hym in his noye to amende,
> But honesshen hym as an hound, and hoten hym go thennes.

The allegory of the dinner itself is transparent enough. The learned Doctor has the place of honor, and eats rich stews and soups. The others eat spiritual food, the Scriptures, and the bread and drink of repentance (Psalm 42:3; cf. A 8.106). One is reminded of the famous scene at the grail castle in Chrétien's *Conte del Graal,* where Perceval is served rich food at dinner with his host, while at the same time, though he does not know it, he is being urged to partake of the spiritual food in the grail.[27]

There is one striking feature of the dinner scene, however, that demands our attention. The Dreamer, watching the Doctor, is indignant at the rate he drinks his wine, and quotes Isaiah (5:22): *Woe unto them that are mighty to drink wine, and men of strength to mingle strong drink!* Not four days ago, says the Dreamer, this fellow preached on penance at St. Paul's (though he skipped an important verse: *Periculum est in falsis fratribus*), and now, look at him! These friars preach that penance is profitable to the soul (B 13.75 ff.),

> "Ac this goddes gloton," quod I, "with his gret chekes,
> Hath no pyte on vs pore; he performeth yuel;
> That he precheth he preueth nouȝt"—to Pacience I tolde,
> And wisshed witterly with wille ful egre,
> That disshes and dobleres bifor this ilke doctour,
> Were molten led in his maw and Mahoun amyddes!

> "I shal Iangle to this Iurdan with his Iust wombe,
> To telle me what penaunce is, of which he preched rather."

At this point Patience winks at the Dreamer to be still, but then goes on himself to describe satirically the probable after-effects of the Doctor's gluttony. This is truly an amusing development. Our poet allows the Fool to be the spokesman for his own criticism of the friars. We can be sure that he has not allowed Patience to quiet the Dreamer until the latter has fully expressed the author's contempt for the Doctor. But this is yet the best game of all: the ostensible purpose of this scene is to teach the Dreamer patience! The whole passage is a brilliant tour de force.[28]

The Doctor then proceeds, at Conscience's request, to define Dowel, Do-bet, and Do-best. Once more the indignant Dreamer interrupts, only to be silenced by Conscience and Patience. Conscience here acts as a kind of referee, maintaining order and a surface politeness, but it is obvious that the Dreamer, Conscience, and Patience are all instruments in the exposure of the Doctor. The Doctor's definitions of Do-wel, etc., are of course perfectly acceptable,[29] for they are meant to be in contrast with his behavior at the banquet.

Clergie is next asked by Conscience to give *his* definition of Dowel. This is Clergie's first call to active participation in the allegory, and we might expect the author to take this opportunity to distinguish between true learning and the corruption of learned individuals. But he does not. Yet what Clergie says is important. I quote his reply in full (B 13.119–29):

> "I haue seuene sones," he seyde, "seruen in a castel,
> There the lorde of Lyf wonyeth, to leren hym what is Dowel;
> Til I se tho seuene and my-self acorden,
> I am vnhardy," quod he, "to any wyȝt to preue it.
> For one Pieres the Ploughman hath inpugned vs alle,
> And sette alle sciences at a soppe, saue loue one,
> And no tixte ne taketh to meyntene his cause,
> But *dilige deum* and *domine, quis habitabit, &c.*

And seith that Dowel and Dobet aren two infinites,
Whiche infinites, with a feith, fynden oute Dobest,
Which shal saue mannes soule; thus seith Piers the Ploughman.

Critics of *Piers the Plowman* have apparently found these lines difficult to understand; few have even attempted to explain what they mean.[30] We must therefore pause to consider them, for they contain our poem's first reference to Piers the plowman. I do not believe that anyone can speak authoritatively on the role of Piers in the B-continuation unless he understands these lines.

Clergie's reply consists of three separate statements. The first is a simple disclaimer. I cannot tell you what Do-wel is, he protests, until I consult with my seven sons (the seven arts). Translating the allegory, this of course says merely: Let me think it over. But why should Clergie say this? One reason for this strange reply is dramatic. Clergie is embarrassed by the conduct of the Doctor, his real life representative in this scene. His embarrassment will be further emphasized, as we shall see, at the end of the banquet. Another reason, however, and more important, is the poet's desire to show that in fact learning has its limits. This paves the way for Patience's definition, which immediately follows Clergie's speech. Patience has the gift of grace, humility, patience, and charity (B 12.62–71), and is above both clergie and kynde witte.

In his second statement Clergie alleges that Piers the plowman has declared all sciences to be worthless, save love alone, and takes as his texts only *dilige deum* and *domine, quis habitabit, &c.* (Matt. 22:37–39; Ps. 15). Now it is important to realize that Piers has actually said no such thing.[31] All of these points, however, *are* made in the A-text of *Piers the Plowman*,[32] and so at first glance Clergie would seem to be guilty of that error concerning our poem which the late Professor Skeat warned against:[33]

Hence careless readers at once jumped to the conclusion that Piers Plowman was the name of the *author*, not of the *subject*. . . . There seems to be quite an attraction in this curious error; for it is still constantly made even by those who must to some extent have read the book; thus Mr. Bardsley,

in his book on English Surnames, ed. 1873, p. 406, actually has the words—
'Piers, in his Vision, says,' &c.

Yet it is by no means necessary to assume this about Clergie's remarks. The pre-existing popularity of Piers, based, as we have already seen (chapter 2), on the popularity of the A-text, is sufficient explanation for the assignment of any idea expressed in A to Piers himself. But why should the poet himself do this? This question naturally arises, since up till now our author has consistently assigned all ideas expressed in the A-text to the Dreamer, not Piers. The answer is simple. The views set forth in A that the poet wishes to criticize he assigns to the Dreamer; those that he wishes to accept and even emphasize (though in his own way) he assigns to Piers, whether they were actually spoken by Piers in the A-text or not. This is an integral part of his method of adapting Piers for use in the B-continuation.[34] One could argue, I suppose, that if the poet is going to exploit the popularity of Piers in a continuation of the A-text, he obviously cannot afford to criticize Piers himself. But I do not believe that our author has the slightest desire to criticize the plowman. Rather, he sees him as the same good plowman that we find in the A-text—the ideal representative of the humble poor. He *portrays* Piers, however, in the B-continuation specifically, as an embodiment of that spiritual state which we have already been told is superior to learning and kynde witte: humility, patience, and love, the fruit of grace, the gift of God through the Holy Ghost. Piers in the B-text is patient poverty personified. But the poet judiciously avoids assigning Piers that role in any specific allegorical action. Instead, Piers's emphasis on love, his possession of grace, these things are subtly hinted at in passages like the present one. On the other hand, Patience is Piers's "stand-in" in the allegorical action. And I must express my unqualified admiration of the poet's skill in avoiding the slightest suggestion that he is manipulating the plowman in order to gain an argumentative advantage.

Now for the last part of Clergie's speech. Piers, according to Clergie, says that Do-wel and Do-bet are two infinites, which infinites, with a faith, lead to Do-best, which shall save man's soul. Viewed dramatically, this is a "learned" summary of the A-*Vita,* the deliberate obscurity of which represents Clergie's ironical admission that matters of faith are beyond him. And we have already seen that one of the purposes of this scene is to show that learning does have its limitations. But this mysterious statement also has a larger function in the structure of the B-continuation. Note that it is cast in the form of a prophecy, and belongs to the literary tradition of prophecy in medieval romance, as represented by the ecstatic and often highly obscure utterances of such men as Merlin and Thomas the Rymer. The poet uses this device more than once; nor should this be surprising if we keep in mind the many evidences of the influence of romance in the poem. But why should Piers be reported as prophesying here, and what does the prophecy mean, if anything?

In order to understand why the poet here assigns Piers a prophecy, we must remind ourselves that we are engaged in reading the "Creation" section of the B-continuation, that the whole poem is based on biblical history from Genesis to Revelation as qualified and enhanced by the poet's intimate knowledge of the medieval drama. Now the cycle plays frequently insert such prophecies very early in their dramatization of events taken from the book of Genesis. In the Norwich *Creation,* for example, the Holy Ghost speaks to Adam and tells him of the coming Redemption.[35] In the Chester *Creation,* Adam tells of a vision he had when God caused a deep sleep to fall upon him, in which he saw a parade of future historical events, including the Incarnation and Last Judgment.[36] The words attributed to Piers by Clergie constitute such a prophecy. What this prophecy foretells is precisely what is going to take place in the poem, that is, the dramatization of the Fall, the Redemption, and the Apostolic Age, which is the author's central theme in the B-continuation. In spite of all its deliberate mystification, Piers's prophecy helps us understand why the poet chose the titles "Do-wel," "Do-bet," and "Do-best" for the major divisions of his poem.[37] They are designed to express the gathering momentum of the divine plan, God at work in human history, as expressed in his Old Law (Do-wel), New Law (Do-bet), and the establishment of the Faith through Holy Church in the Apostolic Age (Do-best), "which shal save mannes soule" at the Last Judgment, the consummation of history. We cannot pursue the implications of Piers's prophecy any further at present, for to do so would be to anticipate the outcome of the entire B-continuation. Let it suffice to point out once more that Clergie's speech, which contains the poet's first reference to Piers, is extremely important, and cannot be safely ignored in an analysis of the B-continuation.

In response to Clergie's words, Conscience appropriately disqualifies himself as an interpreter of prophecy (B 13.130–32):

> "I can nouȝt her-on," quod Conscience, "ac I knowe wel Pieres;
> He wil nouȝt aȝein holy writ speken, I dar wel vndertake;
> Thanne passe we ouer til Piers come and preue this in dede."

But these lines reveal that Conscience, so to speak, does in fact understand the prophecy. That which Piers later "proves in deed" is the whole biblical drama of the poem, over which he "presides" in the manner suggested in my discussion of the *Estoire de Piers* (chapter 2, above).

Conscience then calls upon Patience to define the triad, and at the same time indicates to the reader that he is about to hear the gospel truth (B 13.133–34). Patience proceeds to define Do-wel as *disce* (learn), *doce* (teach) and *dilige inimicos* (love thine enemy), and speaks eloquently in praise of love. He then apparently brandishes a scroll, which he says contains Do-wel, and describes its contents in another of those deliberately obscure utterances, framed in the tradition of romance prophecy (B 13.152–56):

> I bere there-inne aboute fast ybounde Dowel,
> In a signe of the Saterday that sette firste the kalendare,
> And al the witte of the Wednesday of the nexte wyke after;
> The myddel of the mone is the miȝte of bothe.
> And here-with am I welcome, there I haue it with me.

It is certainly true, I think, as Skeat suggests,[38] that this passage alludes to the great events of Christianity. I hesitate to venture beyond this generalization. But as the following lines clearly indicate, Patience intends for us to understand that his mysterious packet or scroll contains charity, which is, of course, what he has just finished praising.[39] The important thing to observe, however, in this passage, is the action. "Undo it, late this doctour deme if Dowel be therinne," says Patience.[40] The Doctor then apparently examines the document, or whatever it is, and makes the following cynical observations (B 13.172–76):

> "It is but a *Dido*," quod this doctour, "a dysoures tale.
> Al the witt of this worlde and wiȝte mennes strengthe
> Can nouȝt confourmen a pees bytwene the pope and his enemys,
> Ne bitwene two Cristene kynges can no wiȝte pees make,
> Profitable to ayther peple."

Thus the Doctor is finally exposed as completely ignorant of *caritas,* the basis of all theology, a subject in which he is, in the eyes of the world, a "maistre." What was the poet's inspiration for this climactic drama in the banquet scene? Surely it was that memorable passage at the end of the *Visio* (A 8.89 ff.):

> "Piers," quath a prest tho, "thi pardon muste I rede;
> For I shal construe iche clause, and kenne it the on Englisshe."
> And Peris, at his preyour, the pardoun unfoldith,
> And I, behynde hem bothe, beheld al the bulle. . . .

There is, however, an important difference. In the A-text the villain was a priest; in the B-continuation, the villain is a friar. This accords well with the priestly point of view so frequently apparent in B.

The banquet is now at an end, and the company breaks up. There is, however, an epilogue, which is important in what it adds to our understanding of the function of Clergie. Conscience announces that he is going on pilgrimage with Patience (that is, Patience has won the victory). To this Clergie replies (B 13.183–87):

> "What?" quod Clergye to Conscience, "ar ȝe coueitouse nouthe
> After ȝeresȝyues or ȝiftes, or ȝernen to rede redeles?
> I shal brynge ȝow a bible, a boke of the olde lawe,
> And lere ȝow, if ȝow lyke, the leest poynte to knowe,
> That Pacience the pilgryme perfitly knewe neuere."

These words clearly reveal Clergie's embarrassment, to which I have already referred, over the behavior of the Doctor. To cover up, he jokingly offers to teach Conscience how to turn an education into cash. His offer to teach him the Old Law, though possibly an allusion to the "glosing" of the friars, is essentially a plea for mercy. Judge me not, he says in effect, by the behavior of this Doctor! But Conscience stays with Patience, demonstrating his affiliation by a polite farewell to the friar. He then whispers to Clergie (B 13.200–1):

> Me were leuer, by owre lorde, and I lyue shulde,
> Haue pacience perfitlich than half thy pakke of bokes!

Clergie, however, no longer jocular, says very seriously that Conscience will see the time when he will wish for learning. With this Conscience agrees. We three, he says (Patience, Conscience, and Clergie), working together, could reform the world. Meanwhile, says Clergie (B 13.212–14):

> I shal dwelle as I do, my deuore to shewen,
> And conformen fauntekynes and other folke ylered,
> Tyl Pacience haue preued the, and parfite the maked.

Thus the poet re-establishes, after all, the dignity of true learning. Clergie has shown that he, too, is in reality a companion of Patience. But he must now leave the stage, for we are ready to turn our attention to Haukyn, *Activa-vita,* the embodiment of kynde witte and the representative of the commons in the B-continuation.

Conscience and Patience set forth on an allegorical journey reminiscent of that described by Dame Study in the A-text (A 11.113–22), until they meet a man who identifies himself as *Activa-vita,* a minstrel and waferseller. The poet seems to have established this dual role for Haukyn primarily in order to expand

[93]

his satirical function. For Haukyn, in response to Patience's questioning, first comments on his poverty, explaining that if he knew how to be a comedian, he could earn plenty of money entertaining lords. This reminds us by contrast of the banquet scene just concluded, where, despite the performance of the Doctor, a certain decorum was maintained by Conscience, who "carped us mery tales" (B 13.58). Both passages, however, are derived ultimately from Dame Study's denunciation of jesters (A 11.24–37). This passage seems to have had a particular fascination for the poet, for he alludes to it many times.

Haukyn next delivers an amusing discourse on his fortunes as a waferseller. In the course of these remarks we learn that Haukyn makes bread for people from all ranks of society, from beggars to the Pope. The most recompense he ever got from the Pope was a pardon, and he says he would much prefer that the Pope send him a cure for the pestilence. After all, he says, Christ prophesied that true believers would lay hands on the sick, and heal them (Mark 16:17–18), and the Pope has the power of Peter; so why doesn't he say: *Silver and gold have I none; but such as I have give I thee: In the name of Jesus Christ of Nazareth rise up and walk?* There is some suggestion of satire on indulgences here, but the tone of these remarks is bantering, and I think their main purpose is to present a rough and ready commoner, who will speak irresponsibly on any subject at the slightest provocation. In any case, Haukyn withdraws his criticism of the Pope, and remarks that if miracles fail it is because men are not worthy. What we need is another famine! Remember the big famine of 1370? Here the author clearly alludes to the episode involving Hunger in the seventh passus of A, and his purpose in so doing is, I think, to suggest that the sociological approach of the A-text to the problem of "wasters" is inadequate. This point is made very skillfully by letting Haukyn present the argument of the A-text in his own amusing and irresponsible way. It is important to note also that this is a criticism of the *Visio* which directly involves Piers (A 7.156 ff.), yet the author gets away with it. He does not, however, ignore Piers altogether; in fact he very delicately suggests (B 13.234–37) that Haukyn is Piers's man. If we lose sight of what the poet is doing here, it is because he has charmed us with his entertaining portrait of *Activa-vita*.

The picture of Haukyn which emerges from his opening discourse is of great importance in the poet's strategy. If we are inclined to be sympathetic, at the same time we tend not to regard him seriously as a thinker. Kynde witte can occasionally be incisive (as in Haukyn's remarks about pardons and a salve for the pestilence), but we must not expect it, after all, to be of much use in solving the problems of mankind. Viewed in relation to the conversation between Conscience and Clergie (B 13.202–10), the remarks of Haukyn sound like those of a child interrupting the conversation of adults.

Having established Haukyn as an amiable but fallible representative of the commons, the poet next proceeds, in the remainder of passus 13, to enumerate the sins which stain his clothes. *Activa-vita's* sin-spotted coat is, of course, an adaptation of the confession scene in the A-text, and requires no detailed analysis. It is enough to see how centering the seven deadly sins in a single individual serves to emphasize the sinfulness of the commons. There is, however, one irregularity in the catalogue of sins that is worthy of note. The poet's discussion of Sloth suggests that he did not consider this sin particularly prevalent among the poor. True, he applies it generally to those who, for example, neglect the penance enjoined by the priest. But he goes on specifically to warn of the dangers which Sloth holds for the wealthy, who support worldly entertainers or jesters and turn away the poor. Once again the poet joins Dame Study (A 11.24 ff.) in his indignation at the thought of these devil's disciples. Clerks, he says (B 13.432 ff.), should teach lords holy writ, which condemns this sort of thing.[41]

After all the sins have been enumerated and discussed, Conscience asks Haukyn why he has not cleaned his coat. And so we come to passus 14. This passus continues the poet's treatment of the sins motif, but, unlike the preceding catalogue, it does not depend on the A-text for its material. In fact, the poet here supplies what he evidently considered a serious deficiency in the confession scene of the A-text: the spiritual counsel which a penitent sinner requires.[42] Imaginatif has already prepared us for this development (B 12.107–10):

> And as a blynde man in bataille bereth wepne to fiȝte,
> And hath none happ with his axe his enemye to hitte,
> Namore kan a kynde-witted man, but clerkes hym teche,
> Come for al his kynde witte to Crystendome and be saued.

Hence when Haukyn complains that he cannot keep his sin-spotted coat clean, Conscience explains to him the cleansing power of contrition, confession, and satisfaction. But it is Patience who is the real spokesman in passus 14, and his spiritual counsel, although it echoes the teaching of the penitentials, is no routine exhortation to sinners. The words of Patience are the words of our author, who here addresses, in a tone of considerable urgency, the poor men of England in the fourteenth century.

Patience begins with the spiritual counsel of *ne solliciti sitis,*[43] the warning against overconcern for material things. Haukyn is skeptical about this, but Patience asks him to consider the lilies of the field, how they grow, and then offers him a portion of the Lord's prayer, *Thy will be done,* saying (B 14.49–58):

> "Haue, Haukyn!" quod Pacyence, "and ete this whan the hungreth,
> Or whan thow clomsest for colde, or clyngest for drye.
> Shal neuere gyues the greue, ne grete lordes wrath,
> Prisone ne peyne, for *pacientes vincunt.*
> Bi so that thow be sobre of syȝte and of tonge,
> In etynge and in handlynge and in alle thi fyue wittis,
> Darstow neuere care for corne ne lynnen cloth ne wollen,
> Ne for drynke, ne deth drede, but deye as god lyketh,
> Or thorw honger or thorw hete, at his wille be it;
> For if thou lyuest after his lore, the shorter lyf the better:
>   *Si quis amat Cristum, mundum non diligit istum.*

[96]

In this passage we see the poet's clearest and most direct definition of what he means by patient poverty. It is indeed an austere doctrine, although it cannot be accurately assessed apart from the context of the all-embracing medieval concept of *caritas,* the law of love (cf. B 14.97 ff.). We cannot stop to consider the implications of Patience's doctrine. I will only say that the twentieth-century reader, who perhaps has tired of hearing modern literary critics praise the "beauty" of the Sermon on the Mount, may feel refreshed to discover that our poet understands its meaning.

Having presented his stark definition of poverty, Patience goes on to assure Haukyn that God will provide, citing the example of Israel's forty years' wandering in the wilderness, the famine in the time of Elijah, and the seven sleepers of Ephesus, and warning him ominously about what prosperity did to the city of Sodom. He then concludes this section of his discourse by emphasizing the value of contrition, confession, and satisfaction as a means of eradicating deadly sin.

Suddenly Haukyn asks (B 14.97–98):

> "Where woneth Charite?" quod Haukyn, "I wiste neuere
>   in my lyue
> Man that with hym spake, as wyde as I haue passed!"

As we have already noticed, patient poverty is rooted in the all-embracing doctrine of *caritas* (cf. B 12.62–71), and this is undoubtedly why Haukyn is made to ask this question here. But his interruption also serves to lead into Patience's discussion of poverty *versus* wealth, a subject which occupies the remainder of the passus. We need not consider this section in detail, for its meaning is perfectly clear, once we understand the poet's purpose in writing it: it is here that he presents his most eloquent argument concerning the problem of poverty and wealth, and advocates the cultivation of humility, patience, and love, those spiritual virtues which should guide all men on the road to the New Jerusalem.

Let us briefly review Patience's argument. Some rich men, says Patience, live as if there were no heaven other than this earth, and they will suffer for it. But if you rich obey the law of love, and give to the poor, you will be saved. O Lord, have pity on those wealthy men who are cruel to the poor! (B 14.103–73, especially note 162–63; cf. A 11.45–52).

Patience goes on to say (B 14.174–200), in a passage reminiscent of the pardon scene in the *Visio* (A 8.1–126), that Christ's patent is for rich and poor alike. The difference in point of view of the A and B texts is particularly striking here. Truth's pardon in A devotes most attention to problems intimately associated with the commons; for example (A 8.67–68):

> Beggeris and bidderis ben not in the bulle,
> But yif the suggestioun be soth that shapith hem to begge.

On the other hand, Christ's patent in B seems to deal with the weaknesses of the wealthy (B 14.193–94):

> Of pompe and of pruyde the parchemyn decorreth,
> And principaliche of alle peple but thei be pore of herte.

Of course the A-text deals with the shortcomings of the rich (e.g., A 8.162), but what I am trying to suggest is that there is a difference in attitude. It is only in the B-text that the rich are specified in the patent and warned, like the beggars in A, not to abuse their position. And I think that this basic difference in point of view helps to explain, in part, Patience's elaborate comparison in the B-text between poverty and wealth, which we are now considering.

This difference in "attitude" which I find in reading the A and B texts together is of course one of those delicate matters about which it is difficult to be dogmatic. Yet it seems so striking to me that I venture to add another example. After discussing Christ's patent, Patience goes on to argue that the seven sins attacks the rich much more fiercely than they do the poor (B 14.201–72). The rich man, for example, is reverenced for his wealth, and this tempts him to pride, whereas the poor man, by virtue of his position, is better able to cultivate humility and wisdom. Therefore it is easier for the poor to attain salvation. Note particularly this passage (B 14.210–14):

> For the riche hath moche to rekene, and riȝe softe walketh;
> The heigh waye to-heuene-ward oft ricchesse letteth,
>> *Ita inpossibile diuiti, etc.,*
> There the pore preseth bifor the riche with a pakke at his rugge,
>> *Opera enim illorum sequuntur illos,*
> Batauntliche, as beggeres done, and baldeliche he craueth,
> For his pouerte and his pacience a perpetuel blisse:
>> *Beati pauperes, quoniam ipsorum est regnum celorum.*

The reader has to pinch himself to remember that in the context of this argument Patience is proving to Haukyn that the poor are in a better position than the rich. For unless I am badly misreading the text, this passage is a wry parody of the ending of the *A-Vita* (A 11.301–3), in which poor plowmen and shepherds are pushing rudely past rich men in order to claim their too easily won salvation. Skeat glosses the word *batauntliche* as "hastily," but surely its connotations in this passage might better be expressed by some such word as "raucously" or "clamorously." This is not a very flattering picture of the heroes of the A-version of *Piers the Plowman*. Furthermore, we cannot dismiss this passage as mere rhetoric, for it cannot serve in any way to dramatize the character of Patience in the poem. If the passage is rhetorical, then what we see before us is the rhetoric of the author himself. The lines quoted above might then be summarized: "You see how much I envy you poor men."

Patience concludes his discourse, significantly, by pointing out that voluntary poverty is the most praiseworthy condition of all. Haukyn then asks him to explain "pouerte with pacience." This paves the way for Patience's peroration, an eloquent and impassioned eulogy of patient poverty (B 14.273–319). In response to this Haukyn begins to weep, revealing his genuine contrition (B 14.329–32):

> "I were nouȝt worthy, wote god," quod Haukyn, "to were any
>> clothes,

Ne noyther sherte ne shone, saue for shame one,
To keure my caroigne," quod he, and cryde mercye faste,
And wepte and weyled, and there-with I awaked.

The vision is at an end. The corruption of learning has been exposed in the friar, and the limitations of kynde witte have been revealed in Haukyn, representative of the commons. The poet has devoted most of the space of these two passus to the latter figure, for it is in the analysis of *Activa-vita* that we find his most penetrating critique of the A-text. He wishes to show us that the highway to salvation is perhaps beset with more obstacles than are immediately apparent in the A-text. It may be true that learned men often stray from the Faith, says our author, but it is also true that Haukyn and his kind, to be saved, must do more than

Percen with a *pater noster* the paleis of hevene,
Withoute penaunce, at here partyng, in-to the heighe blisse.

Passus 15

This last passus of the "Creation" section is actually designated in the manuscripts as the Prologue to Do-bet. But it matters not whether we regard it as the epilogue of the "Creation" (Do-wel) or the prologue to the "Fall and Redemption" (Do-bet). For passus 15 in fact contains both a final presentation of "the A-text revisited," and a preparation for the coming of Christ, the main theme of passus 16–18. At the same time passus 15 is well-organized, and has a unity of its own. It begins with a reiteration of the Fool motif (B 15.1–10). The poet then introduces Soul, who defines his nature and corrects the Dreamer's attitude (B 15.11–144). But the main business of this passus is Soul's discussion of charity and its implications (B 15.145–601). This reaches a climax at the end which admirably prepares us for the dramatic entry into the poem of Piers the Plowman himself.

The Dreamer tells us that when he awoke from his dream concerning Haukyn, it was long before he achieved a natural under-standing of Do-wel (B 15.3–10):

> And so my witte wex and wanyed til I a fole were,
> And somme lakked my lyf, allowed it fewe,
> And leten me for a lorel, and loth to reuerencen
> Lordes or ladyes or any lyf elles,
> As persones in pellure with pendauntes of syluer;
> To seriauntz ne to suche seyde nouȝte ones,
> "God loke ȝow, lordes!" ne louted faire;
> That folke helden me a fole, and in that folye I raued. . . .

This is one of the poet's most amusing uses of the Fool motif. The Dreamer admits his complete intellectual defeat as a result of the dizzying onslaught of personifications in passus 11–14; his wit "waxes and wanes"; he is now putty in the hands of the author. Did Patience say that the poor are really far better off than the rich? All right, he will never again show rich men the customary deference. If they only knew what miserable creatures they are! Here we see a typical instance of the Fool's literalistic interpretation of what he has been taught. In this respect our Dreamer is exactly like Perceval in the romance tradition.

Reason has pity on the Dreamer and rocks him to sleep, thus be-ginning his next vision. He sees a ghostly figure, whom he con-jures in the name of Christ to identify himself. This creature, who speaks without benefit of tongue or teeth, identifies himself as the Soul, and proceeds to define his nature and enumerate his various names and functions (B 15.23–39). Soul's introductory remarks need not detain us; they are perfectly conventional. Yet we may legiti-mately ask why it is that the poet chooses Soul as the Dreamer's tutor at this point in the poem. To answer this question we need first to be reminded that the "scene" of the B-continuation, in spite of its intricately developed theme of the A-text revisited, is still the Creation, and, furthermore, the Creation as it is represented in the literary tradition of the Bible. In this tradition, as represented here by the *Cursor Mundi,* the soul is introduced at the close of the ac-

count of God's creation. After telling us that God rested on the
seventh day, the author of the *Cursor Mundi* goes on to describe the
creation of the angels and the fall of Lucifer, and then explains how
man's body is a microcosm reflecting the macrocosm of the creation.
He next provides us with a description of the soul (553–80):

> But resoun ȝitt herde ȝe nouȝt
> Wherof mannes soule is wrouȝt;
> Of goostly liȝt men say hit es,
> Þat god haþ made to his likenes,
> As prent of seel in wax þrest
> Þerynne he haþ his likenes fest;
> He haþ hit wrouȝte as frend & fere,
> No þing to him is so dere;
> His godhede is in trinite.
> Þe soule haþ propur þinges þre,
> Menynge & þat of þinges to se,
> Þat is & was and euer shal be.
> Vndirstondynge haþ hit riȝt,
> Of þingis seyn & out of siȝt.
> Wisdome also hit haþ in wille,
> Þe good to do & leue þe ille.
> Alle þe myȝtes þat may be
> Wonen in þe holy trynite.
> Alle vertues haþ a soule I-wis,
> Þat out of synne clensed is,
> And as god þat is in oon & þre,
> Wiþ no manere creature may be
> Vndirgroped ny ouergone.
> But he ouertakeþ euerychone
> So þe soule wiþouten wene,
> To alle þinge hit is vn-sene,
> Þouȝe hit of alle þingis haue siȝt,
> To se a soule no man haþ myȝt.

As far as literary tradition is concerned, therefore, we see in this
passage that a description of the soul and its functions is associated
with the Creation. But of course our poet is no slave to tradition;
he uses it. And, since passus 15 contains the Dreamer's final in-

structions (before the drama begins), it is appropriate that he employ every faculty at his command, so to speak, in absorbing the poet's last and most important message: the doctrine of charity.

The Dreamer, however, is in a joking mood, if indeed his head is not still spinning from the wealth of instruction he has received. You have as many names as a bishop! he says to Soul. Soul is evidently puzzled by this remark at first. All he can say is, "That is soth." We can almost hear the wheels turning as the typical schoolmaster searches for an opening. Suddenly Soul thinks he sees it (B 15.44–46):

> "That is soth," seyde he. [*pause*] "Now I se thi wille!
> Thow woldest knowe and kunne the cause of alle her names,
> And of myne, if thow myȝtest, me thinketh by thi speche!"

One is reminded here of that delightful pedagogue, the eagle in Chaucer's *Hous of Fame* (991–98):

> With that this egle gan to crye,
> "Lat be," quod he, "thy fantasye!
> Wilt thou lere of sterres aught?"
> "Nay, certeynly," quod y, "ryght naught."
> "And why?" "For y am now to old."
> "Elles I wolde the have told,"
> Quod he, "the sterres names, lo,
> And al the hevenes sygnes therto. . . ."

Unlike Geoffrey, however, our Dreamer professes a great interest, not only in the names of bishops and of the soul, but in everything under the sun (B 15.47–49):

> "Ȝe, syre," I seyde, "by so no man were greued,
> Alle the sciences vnder sonne and alle the sotyle craftes
> I wolde I knewe and couth kyndely in myne herte!"

To which Soul replies (B 15.50–51):

> "Thanne artow inparfit," quod he, "and one of Prydes knyȝtes;
> For such a luste and lykynge Lucifer fel fram heuene:
> > *Ponam pedem meum in aquilone, et similis ero altissimo.*"

No one except Christ, he says, can know everything. Too much honey cloys; a desire for knowledge drew Adam and Eve out of Paradise. And he concludes (B 15.66–67):

> For in the lykyng lith a pryde and a lycames coueitise,
> Aȝein Crystes conseille and alle clerkes techyng,
>> That is, *non plus sapere quam oportet sapere.*

The wheel has come full circle! The Dreamer is now being told the very same thing which he heard with such delight from Dame Study in the A-text (A 11.72–73):

> Ac Austyn the olde for alle suche prechide
> And for suche tale telleris suche a teme shewide:
>> *Non plus sapere quam oportet.*

This is indeed a striking development in the B-poet's characterization of the Dreamer, and we should pause for a moment to consider how it serves his purposes. First of all, obviously, the Dreamer's extreme desire to embrace all knowledge matches his disdain for the rich. It is now part of his role as the Fool to accept literalistically and with abandon all advice offered him. Patience convinced him that he was superior to the wealthy; hence he will have nothing to do with them. His conversation with Soul indicates that Imaginatif (B 12.72–191) has persuaded him that learning is to be respected. So the Dreamer says that he will not merely respect learning, he will worship it. We see here a truly skillful use of the literary tradition of the Fool.

But the poet is not merely having a little fun at the expense of his Dreamer, for this reversal of the Dreamer's character has a very important function in passus 15. The poet has now completed his modification of the views expressed in the A-text, and is ready to present his final message on the law of love. And it is important to realize that in this presentation much of what he says is in very close agreement with the views expressed in the A-version of *Piers the Plowman.* He can afford to do this now without being misunderstood, because he has made his disagreements with the ideas in A abundantly clear. But he is aided immensely, from a dramatic point of view, by maneuvering his Dreamer into the position of actually *needing* the kind of exhortation which he plans to deliver. It is hard to imagine any more effective strategy than this.

There is one other preliminary point that needs to be made, and that is the difference in tone between passus 14 and 15. Although there are exceptions in both cases, it is safe to say that, in general, Patience addressed his remarks in passus 14 to the poor, especially those whose impatience, as we know, eventually erupted in the Peasants' Revolt. On the other hand, in the present passus, the poet is going to talk to those members of the secular aristocracy and those of the wealthy clergy whose pride of position and complacency in the face of corruption have led to the present explosive state of affairs. This is a completely different audience, and the poet accordingly alters his tone. And it is for this very reason that so much of passus 15 accords perfectly with the views expressed in the A-text, which the poet now revisits, not in order to refute it, but rather to take from it the ammunition which he needs.

Although the A-text becomes the poet's arsenal in much of passus 15, it is important to realize that he never makes use of it with such abandon as to contradict his established views. He is very severe with the priesthood, for example, but never to the point of questioning its importance in the scheme of salvation, as is the case in the A-text. Students of the B-text have observed that there is considerable criticism of friars, priests, the regulars, and even bishops in passus 15, but they do not seem to have noticed that the poet's criticism of the priesthood is handled in a very special way. A good illustration of this can be found in Soul's criticism of friars and priests in the passage immediately following his "correction" of the Dreamer (B 15.68–144).

Soul begins by attacking the friars. These friars that preach to ignorant men, he says, tell of the Trinity, etc., in such a way as to cause the people to question their faith (B 15.68–70; cf. A 11.62, 71). They are motivated, not by charity, but by a desire to make a display of learning. Further, they reveal their cupidity in their excessive respect for the wealthy. But then Soul pauses and turns his attention to the priesthood with these words (B 15.87–89):

> Of this matere I myȝte make a longe bible,
> Ac of curatoures of crystene peple as clerkes bereth witnesse,
> *I shal tellen it for treuth sake, take hede who so lyketh!*

One might question the reliability of a single line, such as the one italicized above, as an indication of the poet's particular concern for the priesthood. But similar statements occur throughout the passus, and they all suggest that the poet is writing with a strong consciousness of an audience of potentially hostile colleagues. Here are some examples:

> Doctoures of decres and of diuinite maistres,
> That shulde konne and knowe alkynnes clergye,
> And answere to argumentz and also to a *quodlibet,*
> (*I dar nouȝt seggen it for shame*) if suche weren apposed,
> Thei shulde faillen in her philosofye and in phisyk bothe.
> (B 15.373–77)

> *Ac for drede of the deth I dar nouȝt telle treuthe,*
> How Englissh clerkes a coluer feden that Coueityse hatte,
> And ben manered after Makometh, that no man vseth treuth.
> (406–8)

> Ac who beth that excuseth hem? That aren persounes and prestes,
> That heuedes of holycherche ben, that han her wille here,
> With-oute trauaille, the tithe del that trewemen biswynkyn.
> *Thei wil be wroth for I write thus,* ac to witnesse I take
> Bothe Mathew and Marke. . . .
> (478–82)

> Wyte ȝe nouȝt, wyse men, how tho men honoured
> More tresore than treuthe? *I dar nouȝt telle the sothe.*
> (510–11)

But if we return to the original passage under consideration (B 15.87–144), we find even more specific evidence of the poet's special way of criticizing priests. At first glance one might suppose that he is flatly anticlerical, for his language is certainly uncompromising (B 15.101–8):

> For-thi, wolde ȝe lettred leue the leccherye of clothynge,
> And be kynde, as bifel for clerkes, and curteise of Crystes goodes,
> Trewe of ȝowre tonge and of ȝowre taille bothe,
> And hatien to here harlotrye and nouȝt to vnderfonge
> Tythes of vntrewe thinge, ytilied or chaffared,
> Lothe were lewed men but thei ȝowre lore folwed,
> And amenden hem that mysdon more for ȝowre ensamples,
> Than forto prechen and preue it nouȝt, ypocrysie it semeth.

These remarks are reminiscent of the anticlerical view of A, and, as a matter of fact, most of them are clearly derived therefrom. Compare, for example, the passage just quoted with the following lines from the A-text:

> Manye chapellenis arn chast, ac charite is aweye;
> Arn none hardere than heo whanne heo ben avauncid,
> Unkynde to here kyn and to alle cristene,
> Chewen here charite and chiden aftir more;
> Such chastite withoute charite worth cheynid in helle.
> Ye curatours that kepe yow clene of your bodies,
> Ye ben acumbrid with coveitise, ye conne not out crepe,
> So harde hath avarice haspide yow togideris!
> That is no treuthe of trinite, but treccherie of helle,
> And a lerning to lewide men the lattere to dele.
> (A 1.164–73)

> Til clerkis and knightes be curteis of here mouthes,
> And haten to here harlotrie or mouthe it;
> Til prestis here prechyng preve it hem selve,
> And do it in dede to drawe us to goode.
> (A 4.105–8)

In some instances the B-poet paraphrases the idea; in others he uses the very wording of the A-text. But whereas the A-passage is a ringing denunciation of chaste but "chewing" chaplains, the B-text here is cast in the form of an appeal: If you learned clerics would only amend yourselves, the unlearned would follow your example.

The best evidence of the contrast between the A and B texts in their attitude toward the priesthood is in their poetic imagery. Recall, for example, the very effective use of the rose in the A-text (A 10.119–24), where the root is the commons (Do-wel), the brier is, amusingly enough, the clergy (Do-bet), and the rose is the episcopate (Do-best). The poet then goes on to praise married folk, ideal representatives of the commons (A 10.130):

> Thei be the riccheste of reaumes, and the *rote* of Do-wel.

We have already seen that our author in the B-text is not satisfied with this emphasis on marriage to the detriment of widowhood and virginity (B 12.33–40). On the other hand, observe how neatly his own image (the tree) serves to stress the importance of the clergy (B 15.94–100):

> And se it by ensample in somer-tyme on trowes,
> There somme bowes ben leued and somme bereth none;
> There is a myschief in the more of suche manere bowes.
> Riȝt so persones and prestes and prechoures of holy cherche,
> That aren *rote* of the riȝte faith to reule the peple;
> Ac there the rote is roten, reson wote the sothe,
> Shal neure floure ne frute ne faire leef be grene.

Thus the "brier" of A is neatly transformed into the "root" of B. Also, in an exhibition of true charity, the B-poet, by his use of the "tree" image, represents the people, not as a brier, but as flower, fruit, and fair leaf, whose flourishing, however, is *dependent* on the integrity of the secular clergy.

The B-poet then goes on to denounce the cupidity of worldly priests (B 15.101–44), frequently employing ammunition from the A-text. But he has made it perfectly clear, in so doing, that his criticisms are based on a firm belief in the indispensability of the priesthood, whose role in the salvation of poor plowman and shepherds is as important as the *Pater Noster*. The same cannot be said, however, concerning his criticism in this passus of other groups, whether lay or ecclesiastical.

Soul's discourse on charity occupies the remainder of the passus, and this is as it should be. The entire process of the Dreamer's education has been leading up to this, and Soul's discussion provides a kind of climax to the whole section of the B-continuation which has the Creation as its setting. Furthermore, as we have seen, the doctrine of *ne solliciti sitis* and patient poverty expounded by Patience in passus 14 must be viewed in the context of the all-inclusive Christian doctrine of charity. Otherwise patient poverty might appear, as in fact it does to many modern readers, to be a kind of futile and groveling acquiescence. Our poet certainly does not regard it in this light, and Soul's discourse on charity makes this perfectly clear. For charity, which is the basis of patient poverty, is also, or should be, the motivating principle for men in all ranks of society, and especially for those in positions of leadership, both worldly and spiritual. This fact explains why Soul's discourse on charity spends little time on pure definition, and much time on criticism of the aristocracy, clergy, and episcopate. The harmonious existence of a Christian society requires that *all* members of that society obey the law of love. This is the message of Soul in passus 15.[44]

The Dreamer initiates the discussion by asking a question (B 15.145–46):

> "What is Charite?" quod I tho. "A childissh thinge," he seide;
>> *"Nisi efficiamini sicut paruuli, non intrabitis in regnum*
>> *celorum;*
> With-outen fauntelte or foly, a fre liberal wille."

In response to this the Dreamer asks where one might find a friend with so free a heart; and he adds (B 15.148–49):

> "I haue lyued in londe," quod I, "my name is Longe Wille,
> And fonde I neuere ful charite bifore ne bihynde!"

To understand this statement we need to have in mind the poet's characterization of the Dreamer. Much of the Creation section of the B-continuation has been devoted to teaching him humility and patience. Such was the purpose of the speech assigned to Trajan; the counsel of Reason; the teaching of Imaginatif; and, of course, the sermon of Patience. Nevertheless, as we have seen, the Dreamer has been slow to absorb these lessons. When he was shown God's Creation, so that he might come to know his Creator through the things that were made, he responded by asking why Reason did not follow men, as he did the animals. When Reason himself rebukes him, the Dreamer wakes up and says, rather grimly, that he at last knows what Do-wel is. Imaginatif asks him of what thing it is, and he replies (11.401–2):

> "Yiwisse, sire," I seide,
> "To se moche and suffre more, certes," quod I, "is Dowel!"

This is spoken in bitterness, and might be paraphrased as follows: I must say that it takes a lot of patience (or endurance, "suffraunce") to see what goes on in this world and yet remain silent. Imaginatif then goes on to explain that if he *had* held his peace, he would have learned more through Reason. And so the teaching of the Dreamer continues. Then in the banquet scene, it will be recalled, he once more reveals his impatience at the behavior of the Doctor. We have already considered this scene, but it is important to remind ourselves of the poet's emphasis there on the Dreamer's *will* as the instrument of his impatience (B 13.77–82):

> "Ac this goddes gloton," quod I, "with his gret chekes,
> Hath no pyte on vs pore; he performeth yuel;
> That he precheth he preueth nou3t"—to Pacience I tolde,
> And wisshed witterly *with wille ful egre,*
> That disshes and dobleres bifor this ilke doctour,
> Were molten led in his maw and Mahoun amyddes!

The teaching which is designed to correct this defect in the Dreamer's will comes in the conversation between Conscience and Clergie at the end of the banquet scene. Clergie has wryly asked Conscience why he wishes to accompany Patience, who is no scholar. To this Conscience replies that he certainly doesn't expect Patience to offer him anything, and then he adds (B 13.190–93):

> Ac the wille of the wye, and the wille of folke here
> Hath moeued my mode to mourne for my synnes.
> The good wille of a wiзte was neure bouзte to the fulle;
> For there nys no tresore therto to a trewe wille.

With these features of the characterization of the Dreamer in mind, we are now in a position to understand his statement about charity. As we know, he has been completely overpowered by his tutors; he is now receptive to the teachings of Soul. At the beginning of the passus he was in a joking mood, and this has provided the transition to his new attitude; now, however, when he asks Soul what charity is, he is perfectly serious. If this is not made clear, as I think it is, by the poet's handling of the Dreamer, then the latter's reply to Soul's initial definition should dispel all doubt (B 15.148–49):

> "I haue lyued in londe," quod I, "my name is Longe Wille,
> And fonde I neuere ful charite bifore ne bihynde!"

That is to say: I have "seen much and suffered more" (B 11.402); I have corrected the defect in my will (B 13.80) and made it over in conformity with that of Patience (B 13.190 ff.); I am now possessed of a will which is long-suffering (1 Cor. 13:4), but I have still not found full charity anywhere!

The fact that the Dreamer is now completely serious is borne out by what he says in the passage immediately following the two lines that we have just examined. Men are merciful to the poor, he says, and will lend where they can expect some return; but true charity, as Paul observes, *is not puffed up, doth not behave itself unseemly, seeketh not her own;* and this I have never seen except as *through a glass, darkly.* Here is a very profound statement indeed. Even Soul, with all his readiness to instruct, might well pause before attempting an answer. Fortunately, however, this is not necessary. The Dreamer very graciously provides him with an opening (B 15.158–59):

> "And so I trowe trewly, by that men telleth of charite,
> It is nought championes fyȝte, ne chaffare, as I trowe."

With this statement Soul is in perfect agreement. At long last we find one of the Dreamer's tutors actually agreeing with him! That's right, says Soul; Charity is no trader or accuser, and he goes on to stress humility, patience, and lack of greed. The Dreamer, meanwhile, seems to enjoy his newly acquired reasonableness. He wants to be helpful. And so he asks (B 15.171):

> "Hath he any rentes or richesse, or any riche frendes?"

Soul is evidently delighted to have this opening. For he now proceeds to show very clearly that Charity indeed is not concerned with wealth, because he has faith in God's promise to provide. Moreover, Charity is a launderer who washes away the pride of the wealthy (B 15.172–88).

When Soul completes this eloquent description of Charity, the Dreamer suddenly exclaims (B 15.189):

> "By Cryst, I wolde that I knewe hym," quod I, "no creature leuere!"

This line represents the climax in the skillful dramatization of the Dreamer's acquisition of a "fre liberal wille." True, he has already claimed that his will "suffereth long" (B 15.148; cf. 1 Cor. 13.4); but in this sudden exclamation he does not merely claim, he spontaneously demonstrates. And it is significant that at precisely this point the poet gives us his final deliberate preparation for the entry of Piers the Plowman into the poem.

The Dreamer's spontaneous desire to see Charity produces the following exchange (B 15.190–94):

> "With-outen helpe of Piers Plowman," quod he, "his persone
> seestow neuere."
> "Where clerkes knowen hym," quod I, "that kepen holykirke?"

"Clerkes haue no knowyng," quod he, "but by werkes and
bi wordes.
Ac Piers the Plowman parceyueth more depper
What is the wille and wherfore that many wyȝte suffreth,
Et vidit deus cogitaciones eorum."

This passage has been variously interpreted. The Latin text quoted
appears to be an adaptation of Matt. 9:4, *And Jesus knowing their
thoughts said, Wherefore think ye evil in your hearts?* Thus the
author would appear to be giving Piers the same ability to know
men's thoughts that Christ possesses in the gospels, and for this
reason several commentators have thought that the poet is in some
way making Piers a "symbol" of Christ himself. I do not believe
this to be the case.[45] The poet has already told us (B 12.62–71) that
humility, patience, and love are the fruit of grace, the gift of God
through the Holy Ghost, and that grace is above both learning and
kynde witte. Learning comes from what we know, kynde witte
from what we see; but anyone who has the grace of the Holy Ghost
*shall not judge after the sight of his eyes, neither reprove after the
hearing of his ears: but with righteousness shall he judge the poor,
and reprove with equity for the meek of the earth* (Isa. 11:3–4). This
is precisely the spiritual quality that Piers possesses: clerks judge
only "by werkes and bi wordes," that is, the sight of eyes and the
hearing of ears; but Piers "parceyveth depper," that is, he has,
through the grace of the Holy Ghost, the ability to judge with
righteousness and reprove with equity. Now it is true that Christ
possesses this ability to the ultimate degree (e.g., Matt. 9:4). But,
as we have seen, our poet has emphasized the supremacy of grace,
not as an impossible ideal, but as a spiritual power which all men of
true charity and humility may possess to some extent, just as all
men can and should imitate Christ.

Furthermore, we have seen that Patience appears in passus 13–14
as the possessor of that humility, patience, and charity which grace
supplies, and in fact proceeds to demonstrate his superiority to
both learning (the Doctor) and kynde witte (Haukyn). Finally,

I have already tried to suggest that Piers is to be the embodiment of Patience, that is, he has grace, plus the spiritual gifts which grace provides. I believe that the passage we are presently considering confirms this. The poet has been moving toward this definition of Piers's character throughout the opening section of the B-continuation.

Soul goes on to point out to the Dreamer that appearances can be deceiving, and that a person's will is what determines whether he has charity (B 15.205-6):

> And that knoweth no clerke, ne creature in erthe,
> But Piers the Plowman, *Petrus, id est, Christus.*

These lines are the climax of the poet's preparation for the entry of Piers at the beginning of the next passus, and they are striking, but their meaning is exactly the same as that intended above by the reference to Matt. 9:4. Piers is Christlike because he possesses grace and the virtues derived therefrom. To suggest Piers's identification with Christ in this sense is perfectly understandable, and differs very little from the statement of Holy Church in the A-text (A 1.86-89):

> For who so is trewe of his tunge, tellith non other,
> Doth the werkis ther with, wilneth no man ille—
> He is a god be the gospel, on ground and on lofte,
> And ek lyk to oure Lord, be Seint Lukis wordis.[46]

But Piers, though he is "like to our Lord," does not "symbolize" Christ. Piers is Piers, the plowman, the ideal representative of the good life, patient poverty personified. This is what he *means* in the poem, statically conceived. I have already suggested his *function* in my discussion (chapter 2, above) of the *Estoire de Piers*. To this we will recur when Piers comes on stage at the beginning of passus 16.

What the poet has accomplished in the introductory section of passus 15 (lines 1-206) is certainly deserving of our admiration, but it is of such complexity that we need to review briefly what it is he has done. Using the Soul (whose appearance at the close of the biblical Creation is traditional) as the spokesman in this final passus devoted to the A-text revisited, our author first dramatizes the reversal of the Dreamer's attitude. The Dreamer is still the Fool, but he is clearly being softened up and made receptive to the teaching that is to come in the remainder of the poem. Furthermore, we have observed that the revision of the Dreamer's attitude assists in the poet's change of tone, brought about by the fact that whereas through Patience he had addressed the impatient commons, through Soul he now addresses the complacent wealthy, including the secular aristocracy, but especially those in the Church. Hence he now uses ammunition taken from the A-text, though at the same time he maintains his belief in the crucial importance of the priesthood in the scheme of salvation. Concerning the theme of charity itself, the central feature of passus 15, we have observed, first, that it is an essential consequence of the doctrine of patient poverty; second, that it is a climax in the Dreamer's education; and, third, that it is a preparation for the biblical drama which is to come, the redemption of mankind through Christ in the Do-bet section of the poem. Moreover, we have seen how the poet, by having the Dreamer ask what charity is, manages very skillfully to dramatize the process whereby the defect in the Dreamer's will is corrected. Finally, Soul's reference to Piers the Plowman identifies him as the embodiment of the poet's ideal, and prepares the reader for Piers's entry at the beginning of the next passus.

Soul's discourse on charity (B 15.207–601) flows logically from what has been summarized above, and we need not consider it in detail. But it will be useful, I think, to indicate the direction of his discourse in a brief summary of it, and to point out the significance of his dramatic peroration (383–601).

Charity, says Soul, is not necessarily to be found among ascetics, some of whom make a display of their self-abasement; in fact it has no necessary connection with any station in life. It may appear in kings or beggars. It once appeared in a friar's frock, but that was long ago, in St. Francis' time. It may appear in the king's council, but not necessarily (B 15.207–38). Soul goes on to define charity, and to cite the examples set by Christ and holy men of old (B 15.247–303). You wealthy men, he says, both in and out of the Church (B 15.304–39), should follow their example. At this point Soul appears to be seized with a sudden melancholy. The contrast between the holiness of life in former times and the corruption and cupidity of his own day evokes in him a somber mood. There is no love between men anymore; we have the appearance of piety, but it is counterfeit. Learning has gone into a decline, and men such as shepherds and shipmen can no longer be trusted to predict the weather. Particularly interesting, I find, is his reference to "wederwise shipmen," who, like shepherds, "wisten by the walkene what shulde bityde." The whole passage has a curiously personal tone (B 15.340–64). Similarly personal and intimate are Soul's reflections on the decline of learning (B 15.365–82). The clergy is poorly educated, and careless about the services of the Church. But, as clerics sing and read on the feast of *Corpus Christi,* "faith alone suffices."

With the words *sola fides sufficit* Soul suddenly shakes off his depression, and begins the peroration that concludes both passus 15 and the entire section of the poem that we have been considering. The main theme of Soul's conclusion is the conversion of the heathen. If it weren't for the cupidity of the clergy, he intimates, perhaps we could convert the heathen (B 15.383–408). After all, the teachers of Holy Church are "the salt of the earth," and they should preserve all people from corruption. *But if the salt have lost his savour, wherewith shall it be salted* (B 15.409–29)? The Apostles converted the world, and there were only eleven of them; why is it that the veritable army of clerics today cannot do as much (B 15.430–43)? Alluding to the parable of the marriage feast, Soul says that although the conversion of the heathen is both necessary and practicable, the clergy excuse themselves, like those who made light of the king's invitation (Matt. 22:5): *But they made light of it, and went their ways, one to his farm, another to his merchandise*

(B 15.444–82). What pope or prelate now performs Christ's command, *Go ye into all the world, and preach the gospel to every creature* (Mark 16:15)? Prelates now reverence the cross on the coin, and glory in the red noble rather than in the cross of Christ. Secular lords would be doing the Church a service should they take their possessions from them! Why don't these prelates who take pride in their honorary titles (Bishop of Bethlehem, Babylon, etc.) go forth and preach the gospel to their heathen charges in these areas (B 15.483–571)? Soul's final summation is an eloquent call for the conversion of the heathen (B 15.572–601).

It is particularly appropriate that Soul ends his discourse on charity with an appeal for the conversion of the heathen. His most effective way of exposing the counterfeit spirituality of his own generation has been to compare it with the genuine holiness of men in the apostolic age, and it is only natural that he should cite their missionary zeal, for this zeal was an inextricable part of the vitality of early Christianity. Perhaps, reasons Soul, a renewal of this zeal might produce a reawakening of the spirituality, the genuine Christian love which the present age so urgently needs.

There is another reason, however, for the appropriateness of the call for conversion of the heathen at this point in the B-continuation. We have now reached the end of the theme of the A-text revisited, and Soul's concluding remarks are the poet's final response to the A-text of *Piers the Plowman*. It will be recalled that Scripture, at the close of the A-*Vita*, refers to the salvation of the heathen, and stresses, in that connection, the importance of the injunction to love God and neighbor. Scripture then concludes (A 11.243–49):

> "That is, iche Cristene creature be kynde to other,
> And sithen hethene to helpe in hope hem to amende.
> To harme hem ne slen hem, God highte us nevere;
> For he seith it hym self, in his ten hestis:
> *Non mecaberis*—'ne sle nought' is the kynde Englisshe;
> For, *Michi vindictam, et ego retribuam.*
> 'I shal punisshen in purcatory, or in the put of helle,
> Eche man for his misdede, but mercy it make.'"

With these trenchant words the vision of the A-*Vita* comes to an end. Soul's last lines at the end of passus 15 contain the B-poet's response to these angry words (B 15.594–601):

> Ac Pharesewes and Sarasenes, Scribes and Grekis
> Aren folke of on faith, the fader god thei honouren;
> And sitthen that the Sarasenes, and also the Iewes
> Konne the firste clause of owre bileue, *Credo in deum patrem*
> > *omnipotentem,*
> Prelates of Crystene prouynces shulde preue, if thei myȝte,
> Lere hem litlum and lytlum [Isa. 28:10] *et in Iesum Christum filium,*
> Tyl thei couthe speke and spelle *et in spiritum sanctum,*
> And rendren it and recorden it with *remissionem peccatorum,*
> > *Carnis resurreccionem, et vitam eternam. Amen.*

This is indeed a sublime answer to the challenge implicit in the A-text. Though the B-poet has spent a great deal of time modifying and correcting ideas expressed in the A-version, it is important to bear in mind that he was also tremendously inspired by what he found there. Without that inspiration the *Estoire de Piers* would never have been written. But there is, at the same time, a fundamental difference in spirit. The God of the A-text is St. Truth; the God of the B-continuation is St. Charity.

Four

FALL AND REDEMPTION

———◄••••►———

In ascending the mountain called Middle-Earth, we have traveled a road with many twists and turns. Our view of the Creation was fleeting, for the poet has been busily engaged in preparing the Dreamer (and the reader) for the drama which he is now ready to present. But we have finally reached the heights, so to speak, and the landscape spread out before us is clear and familiar. The poet shows us a garden, in which there stands a tree. We do not need to be told that the garden is the Garden of Eden and that the tree is the tree of the knowledge of good and evil.[1] The first act of our drama will therefore be concerned with the Fall of Man (B 16.1–166). Then will come the patriarchs and prophets (B 16.167–17.350), the story of the Redemption (B 18), and, finally, the Apostolic Age, continuing down to the poet's own time, in a dramatic conclusion with strong apocalyptic overtones (B 19–20). The reader who has made his way valiantly through passus 11–15 may perhaps exclaim, with Chaucer's friar: "This is a long preamble of a tale!" If so, he will be gratified to discover that, beginning with the Fall, the pace quickens, and our poem rapidly gathers momentum as we descend at last into that familiar plain, the field full of folk in fourteenth-century England.

Students of *Piers the Plowman* have found the latter half of the B-continuation much easier to expound than the first, and for this reason we need not devote as much time to a detailed analysis of the forthcoming biblical drama as was necessary for the Creation. There are, nevertheless, principles of order in the remainder of the B-continuation which the criticism has neglected. One of these is the poet's consistent adherence to the biblical narrative, as it was read and interpreted in medieval tradition; another is the role of Piers, in its literary relation to the more obvious romance elements in the poem; and, finally, there is the Dreamer as Fool, who functions in a very important way at the poem's close. In the ensuing analysis, I shall try to emphasize the importance of these principles for a proper understanding of the remaining passus.

Our poet's treatment of the Fall (B 16.1–89) is undoubtedly the outstanding example of the influence of scriptural tradition in *Piers the Plowman.*[2] It is therefore important to realize that in the Middle Ages the Bible was read allegorically (in the broadest sense), and that by the fourteenth century interpreters were able to expound some scriptural texts on as many as four different levels. The first level, of course, was literal, since any passage, unless it seemed clearly opposed to Christian doctrine, was understood to have a literal meaning. Far more important, however, were the levels of meaning which contained the *sentence,* the doctrinal message which it was the interpreter's responsibility to discover. By the time of our poem, three levels of the *sentence* had been distinguished. One level was the allegorical (in a limited sense), in which the biblical text is expounded with reference to Christ or to the Church in society. Another was the tropological, dealing with the life of the individual (sometimes called the "moral" level). And the third, the anagogical, relates the biblical text to the doctrine of the after-life. Thus the crossing of the Red Sea narrated in Exodus might be viewed, first, as the literal, historical event which took place in the time of Moses; second, allegorically, as baptism, that is, a sacrament of the Church in society; third, tropologically, or "morally," as the cleansing of the individual soul; and, last of all, anagogically, as a crossing over from this life into the next.

Now I have already pointed out that this method of interpreting Scripture has in no way influenced or determined the poetic structure of the B-continuation as a whole, and this should be evident from the analysis of the Creation section just concluded. Yet it is important to have the allegorical method well in mind as we begin an analysis of passus 16, for at this point its use by the poet is clear and unmistakable. His account of the Fall of Man is, in fact, a remarkable example of simultaneous dramatization on the four levels of meaning in scriptural tradition.

Soul remains with the Dreamer long enough to describe the tree in the garden. The root, he says, is Mercy; the middle stock is Pity; the leaves are True-Words, the law of Holy Church; the blossoms are Obedient-Speech and Benign-Looking; and the tree itself is Patience and humble simplicity of heart. And so, through God and through good men, grows charity, its fruit. This is not, of course, the literal tree we find in the Garden of Eden. The poet assumes that we have the literal tree in mind (as we do, once we are aware of the poem's biblical structure), and goes on, appropriately, to let Soul describe it tropologically.[3] Then the Dreamer, reaffirming his sincere desire to know charity, says that he wishes to see this tree and taste of its fruit.[4] Soul tells him where the tree can be found (B 16.13–17):

> "It groweth in a gardyne," quod he, "that god made hym-seluen,
> Amyddes mannes body, the more is of that stokke;
> Herte hatte the herber that it in groweth,
> And *Liberum-Arbitrium* hath the londe to ferme,
> Vnder Piers the Plowman, to pyken it and to weden it."

At this the Dreamer exclaims, "Piers the Plowman!" and swoons for joy.[5] Thus begins the vision which is to contain the first act of the poet's biblical drama: The Fall of Man.

Piers the Plowman has no allegorical role in the Dreamer's vision of the Fall. It is true, as we have seen, that the garden is described in agricultural terms—it is "farmed" by Free Will under Piers's supervision. Moreover, these terms extend into the vision itself, particularly in the description of Piers's care of the tree. But all this is imagery, not allegory.[6] Yet Piers does, of course, have a function: he is a director of the action and an expositor of its meaning. He behaves, in short, exactly as we might expect, once the B-continuation is understood as an *Estoire de Piers*. If we pay attention to what Piers says and do not try to fit him into the allegorical action, the meaning of this vision will be perfectly clear.

Piers comes to the Dreamer and shows him the garden and the tree. The Dreamer notices that three piles, or stakes, are used to support the tree, and asks what they are for. Piers explains that the piles are the Trinity and that they help protect the tree against the World, the Flesh, and the Devil. The first pile, God the Father, defends against the wind of the World (covetousness); the second, the Wisdom of God the Father (that is, the Son), defends against the Flesh (lusts), with the assistance of the individual's prayers, penance, and meditation on the Passion; the third pile, the Holy Ghost, defends especially against the Devil, who is represented as a robber and intruder, but also against all three traditional enemies on condition that Free Will makes use of it. This is a remarkable exposition of the tree on the tropological level, with skillfully integrated imagery from the "farm." Note first that Piers's account explains how, as Soul had said (B 16.9), the fruit of charity grows "thorw god and thorw good men." Man is dependent on God, but must also use his free will. Furthermore, the emphasis on grace is very striking. Yet this is precisely what we should expect to follow from the poet's emphasis on the role of grace in his discussion of humility, patient poverty, and charity in passus 11–15. Finally, of course, the passage reveals the familiar pattern of progressive revelation, God at work in human history (here expounded tropologically), and hence constitutes a further definition of the theme of the B-continuation: Do-wel, Do-bet, and Do-best.[7]

At this point the Dreamer, curious about the piles, asks Piers where they came from (B 16.55–59):

"Ac I have thou3tes a threve of this thre piles,
In what wode thei woxen and where that thei growed;
For alle ar thei aliche longe, none lasse than other,
And to my mynde, as me thinketh, on o more thei growed,
And of o gretnesse, and grene of greyne thei semen."

These piles, which are of even length, grown from one root, and
green of grain, are of course traditional.[8] The poet here alludes to
the story of Seth's journey to Paradise, as it is related, for example,
in the *Cursor Mundi* (1237–1432). Adam sends Seth to Paradise to
obtain the promised oil of mercy (Christ). When he arrives, one of
the cherubim tells him that he may look briefly through the gates.
There Seth sees the Garden, as beautiful as ever, except for a great
tree therein which is dry and bare of bark. It has been this way
since Adam's sin. Its top reaches to the sky and its root down into
Hell.[9] At the top of the tree Seth sees a babe wrapped in swaddling
clothes; at its root he sees his brother Abel. The cherub explains
the meaning of this, and gives him three "kernels" from the tree.
These three kernels represent the Trinity, and Seth is to place them
under Adam's tongue when he buries him. This he proceeds to do
(*Cursor Mundi,* 1417–30):

Þe curnels were put vndir his tonge,
Of hem roos þe 3erdes 3onge,
And sone an ellen hy3e þei wore;
Þenne stode þei stille & wex no more,
Mony a 3eer I liche grene;
Holynes in hem was sene.
Stille stode þo 3erdes þre
Fro Adames tyme to noe;
Fro Noe tym & fro þe flode,
To Abraham, holy & gode;
Fro Abraham 3it stille stode þai
Til moyses þat 3af þe lay.
Euer stode þei stille in oone
Wiþouten waxinge oþere woone.

Here, of course, are Piers's three piles, all of the same length, derived from the same tree, and alike green of grain. But why does

the poet allude to this legend, if he does not plan to use it? The answer to this is to be seen in Piers's reply to the Dreamer (B 16.60–66):

> "That is soth," seide Pieres, "so it may bifalle;
> I shal telle the as tite what this tree hatte.
> The grounde there it groweth, Goodnesse it hiʒte,
> And I haue tolde the what hiʒte the tree: the Trinite it meneth"—
> And egrelich he loked on me, and ther-fore I spared
> To asken hym any more ther-of, and badde hym ful fayre
> To discreue the fruit that so faire hangeth.

What we have here, obviously, is another rebuke to the Fool, not for impatience, pride, or worship of learning, but rather for idle curiosity! What you observe may well be significant, says Piers in effect, but let us not digress. To be brief about it, the ground where it grows is Goodness (Mark 4:8), and the three piles from one tree signify the Trinity. Fortunately, Piers's sharp glance brings to an end the Dreamer's impertinent digression. The poet does not wish to follow Seth on his journey to Paradise.

Piers next proceeds to expound the tree and its fruit on the allegorical level, that is, its *sentence* as applied to the Church in society. There are three "grades" of fruit, representing allegorically marriage, widowhood (continence), and virginity (B 16.67–72):

> "Here now bineth," quod he tho, "if I nede hadde,
> Matrymonye I may nyme, a moiste fruit with-alle.
> Thanne contenence is nerre the croppe, as calewey bastarde,
> Thanne bereth the croppe kynde fruite, and clenneste of alle,
> Maydenhode, angeles peres, and rathest wole be ripe,
> And swete with-oute swellyng; soure worth it neuere."

As we might have expected (cf. B 12.33–40), virginity produces the best fruit of all—angels' pears. Once again the poet emphasizes his disagreement with Wit's exaltation of wedded folk in the A-text.

Thus Soul has introduced us to the tree, and Piers has expounded its meaning on the tropological and allegorical levels. The poet now presents the Fall of Man in a truly remarkable passage (B 16.73–89), giving the action simultaneously on four levels. I quote the passage just as it occurs in the text, except for the terms inserted to designate the levels of meaning.

1. *Literal:*

> I prayed Pieres to pulle adown an apple, and he wolde,

2. *Tropological:*

> And suffre me to assaye what sauoure it hadde.

3. *Allegorical:*

> And Pieres caste to the croppe, and thanne comsed it to crye,
> And wagged Wydwehode, and it wepte after.
> And whan it meued Matrimoigne, it made a foule noyse,
> That I had reuth whan Piers rogged, it gradde so reufulliche.

4. *Anagogical:*

> For euere as thei dropped adown the deuel was redy,
> And gadred hem alle togideres, bothe grete and smale,
> Adam and Abraham and Ysay the prophete,
> Sampson and Samuel and seynt Iohan the baptiste;
> Bar hem forth boldely, no body hym letted,
> And made of holy men his horde in *lymbo inferni,*
> There is derkenesse and drede and the deuel maister.
> And Pieres, for pure tene, that o pile he lauȝte,
> And hitte after hym, happe how it myȝte,
> *Filius,* bi the Fader wille, and frenesse of *Spiritus Sancti,*
> To go robbe that raggeman and reue the fruit fro hym.

Let us briefly review the action that occurs here. As I have already said, the poet does not dwell on the literal story. In the first place, it is not as important as the *sentence;* second, it would detract from the poet's use of the "farm" imagery and the function of Piers; and third, the poet assumes that the reader is familiar with the story and has it in mind. A single line, therefore, suffices for the literal level. But this is made especially clear by the fact that the fruit of the tree, in this line, is called an apple. When the poet wishes to deal with the *sentence,* he refers to the fruit as a pear (cf. B 16.69–72).

The tropological level is also dealt with in a single line in this passage, but the reason for this is immediately obvious. The poet has already expended over fifty lines on tropology. Hence in the action he merely needs to have the Dreamer repeat his desire to know charity, that is, to taste of the fruit of the tree of charity. This serves to remind the reader of the preceding discussion.

True to his function as a director of the action, Piers shakes the tree, and the fruit begins to fall. At this point the "fall" is viewed allegorically, that is, from the point of view of the Church in society. Virginity cries, Widowhood weeps, and Matrimony makes a foul noise (!), so that the Dreamer has pity when Piers shakes the tree, it cries so miserably.

Finally, of course, the Fall is presented on the anagogical level. When the fruits (now the souls of the patriarchs and prophets) drop to the ground, the devil gathers them up and takes them off to Hell, whereupon Piers strikes out after him with the props of the Son and the grace of the Holy Ghost. Surely the meaning here is perfectly transparent.[10] Once we understand Piers's function, then we have no trouble whatever with the *sentence* of this passage, which relates the effect of the Fall on the soul of man after death, and alludes to the coming Redemption, the "oil of mercy" which was promised to Adam.[11]

Immediately following this fourfold depiction of the Fall, the Holy Ghost, represented by Gabriel, speaks to the Virgin, and then the poet gives us a brief account of the life and miracles of Jesus, up to the time of the crucifixion (B 16.90–166). To the reader familiar with literary tradition and the cycle plays, this apparent leap will come as no surprise. In *Cursor Mundi* and the Cornish drama, *Origo Mundi,* the cherub gives Seth such a "foretaste" of the coming Redemption, mentioning the "fulness of time" (*plenitudo temporis* in B 16.93); in the Chester *Creation* Adam prophesies in like manner to Cain and Abel; in the Norwich *Creation,* the Holy Ghost tells Adam the same thing, and then gives him the breastplate, shield, helmet, and sword of Ephesians 6:11–17.[12]

The poet, however, is not merely copying tradition. His prophetic passage is a link which joins the preceding account of the Fall to the forthcoming appearance of the patriarchs and prophets (that is, as represented by Abraham and Moses), and prepares us also for the dramatization of the Redemption in passus 18. The link with the Fall is established by reference to the anagogical fruit of Piers's tree (B 16.93–96). But by far the most important development in this passage is the introduction of the chivalric romance theme, which is woven into the very fabric of the poem, and dominates its imagery from this point virtually to the end of passus 20: Jesus must joust, by judgment of arms, to determine who is to possess the fruit, the devil or himself.

It is important to note that the poet very skillfully accommodates Piers to the Christ-knight imagery (B 16.103–7):

> And Pieres the Plowman parceyued plenere tyme,
> And lered hym lechecrafte his lyf for to saue,
> That thowgh he were wounded with his enemye, to warisshe hym-self;
> And did him assaye his surgerye on hem that syke were,
> Til he was parfit practisoure, if any peril felle. . . .

Students of *Piers the Plowman* have been somewhat taken aback by this passage. How can Piers teach Jesus? But this question arises only if one tries to read Piers allegorically. There is no problem when we understand that Piers is once more being presented as a "director" of the action. But there is one important new development here. In the story of the Fall, the biblical garden and tree were presented with agricultural imagery designed to provide an appropriate background for the entry of Piers into the poem. On the other hand, in the present passage, Piers himself is transformed in order to "accommodate" the Christ-knight imagery. This should not be misunderstood: Piers is still Piers. But he is now playing a new role. Whereas before he was the custodian of the "farm" of Eden, he is now the traditional tutor of the chivalric hero, a role that is perhaps best exemplified in romance by Gornemant de Goort, the tutor of Perceval, "the best knight in the world," in Chrétien's *Conte de Graal* (1305–1698). This metamorphosis has no effect whatever on what Piers "means," for it is simply an accommodation to the poet's imagery. But it is a fine example of how we can expect the plowman to behave in the B-continuation, a perfect illustration of his function in the poet's *Estoire de Piers*.

Upon completion of the prophecy concerning the Redemption, the Dreamer awakens from the inner dream (B 16.167–75):

> And I awaked there-with and wyped myne eyghen,
> And after Piers the Plowman pryed and stared.
> Estwarde and westwarde I awayted after faste,
> And ȝede forth as an ydiote in contre to aspye
> After Pieres the Plowman; many a place I souȝte.
> And thanne mette I with a man, a Mydlenten Sondaye,
> As hore as an hawethorne and Abraham he hiȝte.
> I frayned hym first fram whennes he come,
> And of whennes he were and whider that he thouȝte.

This interlude is designed to prepare us for the biblical pageant which will take us through passus 18, reaching its climax there with the resurrection of Christ. Abraham and Moses, of course, represent the patriarchs and prophets. The Samaritan, however, introduced to complete the poet's triad of Faith, Hope, and Charity, functions impressively as a transitional figure representing the intertestamental period. Although the poet's allegorical reading of the parable of the Good Samaritan is taken from tradition,[13] this use of it in conjunction with the patriarchs and prophets is highly original.

It is not enough, however, simply to recognize the traditional biblical narrative, as modified by the author. We must note also that the centering of attention on Abraham and Moses corresponds exactly to the emphasis which these worthies receive in the cycle plays. Our author exploits this emphasis and, in so doing, strips away the other stories, often included in the cycles for their own sake, in the interest of dramatic compression. More than this, his portrayal of Abraham and Moses concentrates on their allegorical significance and merely alludes to the events in their lives in support of the allegory.

The biblical pageant which we have just considered might easily have become a series of "panels" when converted from dramatic into poetic form. But our poet very skillfully sets his narrative in motion by combining the relatively static pageant with the Christ-knight theme. Thus Abraham becomes a herald, in search of a Knight with the blazon of the Trinity, and Moses becomes one whom this Knight had entrusted with a "writ" at Mount Sinai, which he will "seal" at the Crucifixion. These venerable figures then startle us by stepping down from their pageants, so to speak, and walking with the Dreamer on the road to Jerusalem. The reader not well acquainted with medieval poetry may perhaps be surprised to see Abraham and Moses, dressed in chivalric splendor, walking on the road from Jericho to Jerusalem in order to witness the "tournament" of the Crucifixion. If he regards this device with even the slightest hint of condescension, however, he does so at his own peril. For what we see at work here in *Piers the Plowman* is a highly sophisticated poetic technique, a coalescence of contrasting imagery and symbolism which some literary critics, though not all, seem to think is the "invention" of modern poetry.

The biblical narrative, as we have seen, here defines the poem's structure. The Christ-knight theme, the tournament at Jerusalem, gives the narrative a certain momentum. There is, however, a third factor, of considerable importance in any definition of the form and meaning of the Do-bet section. I refer to the role of the Dreamer himself. He is, of course, still the Fool (who "ȝede forth as an ydiote"), and, overawed by his exotic, Old Testament surroundings, he stares anxiously around, looking for a familiar face—that is, for Piers, the fourteenth-century plowman. On the other hand, his indoctrination is virtually complete, and he can no longer expect the intimate kind of instruction earlier provided by Imaginatif, Conscience, Patience, and Soul. The rest is up to him. The gospel narrative must speak for itself.[14] Most important of all, however, we should observe how the poet depicts the Dreamer's spiritual progress. For the Dreamer, in addition to being a witness to the biblical drama and a pilgrim on the road to Jerusalem, is also moving through Lent to Easter. He meets Abraham, for example, on a Mid-Lenten Sunday; at the beginning of passus 18 he hears the traditional songs in celebration of Palm Sunday; and finally, of course, he awakens at the end of the passus to the sound of church bells ringing the resurrection on Easter morning. This admirable addition to the poem's depth and complexity is not, of course, merely added as a display of virtuosity. Its purpose is rather to delineate the Dreamer's inward repentance, and his spiritual awakening, which will be dramatized at the end of the poem.

It might be objected, however, that my definition of the Dreamer's spiritual progress fails to take into account his response to Moses (B 17.23–46). Your words are wonderful, he says to Moses, but whom should I believe—you or Abraham? For he teaches faith in the Trinity, while you say nothing of this; instead you merely tell me to love God and my neighbor. The Dreamer then decides that he would rather believe Abraham than Moses (B 17.41–46):

> "It is ful harde for any man on Abraham byleue,
> And welawey worse ȝit for to loue a shrewe!
> It is liȝter to leue in thre louely persones
> Than for to louye and leue as wel lorelles as lele.
> Go thi gate," quod I to *Spes,* "so me god helpe!
> Tho that lerneth thi lawe wil litel while vsen it!"

Now to a certain extent it is true that the Dreamer is here acting the Fool, for he is clearly obtuse in his denial of the validity of the Great Commandment, and the poet's satirical purpose in the lines quoted should be obvious. But our author cannot be restricted to a unilateral treatment of the Dreamer. If we try to hold him to this, the result will be a literalistic and hence distorted reading of the poem. For it is evident that in this passage the Dreamer has been "recruited" to play a minor role in the drama. According to the biblical account, Moses, when he was told by God to free Israel from the Egyptians, objected on various grounds that he was incapable of accomplishing this task. One of his objections was this (Ex. 4:1): *But, behold, they will not believe me, nor hearken unto my voice: for they will say, the Lord hath not appeared unto thee.* And as a matter of fact, this particular objection is presented by Moses in the Cornish *Origo Mundi* (1435–40):

MOSES

Lord, they will not believe,
Nor hear my voice,
    Notwithstanding that I speak to them.
Both people small, and people great—
That God has appeared to me,
    Never, never will they believe it.[15]

The Dreamer's questioning of Hope is our poet's dramatization of the skepticism that Moses anticipated. But in addition it paves the way for the Samaritan's explanation of the importance of the teachings of both Abraham and Moses. In view of the multiple function of this passage, therefore, we need not regard it as evidence of the Dreamer's spiritual regression.

The poet's presentation of Abraham, Moses, and the Samaritan includes one other feature that requires comment: his emphasis on the Trinity. We have seen that the Trinity is a topic traditionally associated with the beginning of Genesis, as in the *Cursor Mundi;* but why should it figure so extensively in the section on the patriarchs and prophets? True, the Trinity is customarily associated with Abraham, because Abraham is the representative par excellence of Faith, and because the story of his three visitors (Gen. 18:1 ff.) provides an admirable text for expounding the doctrine.[16] But this fact cannot explain the Samaritan's extensive discourse on the

Trinity. The explanation for such a strong emphasis must involve something other than mere tradition.

There are two reasons, I believe, for the poet's stressing of the Trinity. One is that he is responding once more to what he considered a deficiency in the A-text, where the doctrine of the Trinity receives relatively little attention. In fact, the reference in the A-*Vita* to the carpers who

> . . . telle . . . of the trinite, how two slowe the thridde
> And bringe forth a ballid resoun, tak Bernard to witnesse,

does not leave the reader with a particularly favorable impression of the importance of the trinitarian doctrine. Our poet wants to rectify this state of affairs, so that the reader will have an understanding of what the Trinity really means.

Most important, however, is the fact that the doctrine of the Trinity is an instrument in the poet's continuing emphasis on the necessity of grace. We have seen this emphasis almost from the beginning of the B-continuation (esp. B 12.62 ff.). Grace is the gift of the Holy Ghost which engenders humility, patience, and love. It abases the pride of the learned; it teaches patience to the poor; it redeems the wealthy who might otherwise be harsh and unkind to beggars who cry at the gate. Grace, instrumented by Free Will, can withstand the combined assault of the World, the Flesh, and the Devil. I do not see how anyone can fail to be impressed by the poet's lyrical praise of grace.[17] It is a major theme in the B-continuation. This is the explanation for the Samaritan's teaching concerning the Trinity. The unforgivable sin is the sin against the Holy Ghost, which extinguishes grace. And when this flame dies, there is nothing left but the darkness of potential damnation. Yet the poet, as we have already suspected, is not simply presenting versified doctrine. There is a special note of urgency in his teaching. For the darkness which he warns against is about to descend on the field full of folk and envelop the ignorant armies of the Peasants' Revolt.

We may now review the Do-bet narrative, from the Dreamer's

encounter with Abraham (Faith) to the resurrection (B 16.176–18.431).

Faith introduces himself to the Dreamer as a herald of arms of Abraham's house, in search of a bold bachelor with the blazon of the Trinity. He then launches into a definition of the Trinity, in which the Holy Ghost is by no means slighted (B 16.188–190):

> The thridde hatte the Holygoost, a persone by hym-selue,
> The liȝte of alle that lyf hath, a londe and a watre,
> Confortoure of creatures: of hym cometh al blisse.

Furthermore, the Father sent the Son to earth to occupy himself here till issue were sprung, that is, patriarchs, prophets, and apostles, the children of Holy Church, and embodiment of charity, the fruit of grace. Faith then goes on to liken the Trinity to the now familiar triad of wedlock, widowhood, and virginity. The power of the Father is matrimony: *Be fruitful, and multiply, and replenish the earth* (Gen. 1:28). The Son resembles the widow: *My God, my God, why hast thou forsaken me?* (Mark 15:34).[18] The "children of charity" are, by implication, virginity (B 16.220–24):

> Thus in thre persones is perfitliche manhede,
> That is, man and his make, and moillere her children,
> And is nouȝt but gendre of o generacioun, bifor Iesu Cryst in
>   heuene,
> So is the Fader forth with the Sone, and fre wille of bothe;
>   *Spiritus procedens a patre et filio;*
> Which is the Holygoste of alle, and alle is but o god.

Faith, as Abraham, goes on to mention his encounter with the Trinity in the form of the three men who visited him, as recounted in Gen. 18.1 ff. More important, however, is his summary of Abraham's signification for the Christian faith. God told him to offer Isaac his son (Christ's sacrifice on the cross); to circumcise him (baptism); and to do sacrifice with bread and wine (communion). The doctrinal function of Abraham is of course traditional; but the audience that our poet is addressing is most likely to have known this doctrine in some such form as we find in the Chester cycle.[19] The three Chester episodes (Melchizedek, circumcision, and the offering of Isaac) provide one more interesting dramatic parallel to our poet's treatment of the biblical narrative.

The final aspect of Abraham which the poet exploits is anagogical. Faith shows the Dreamer the patriarchs and prophets who are in his lap, that is, those who have been carried by the angels to the "bosom of Abraham." With them is Lazarus, the poor beggar (Luke 16:19–31). They are all, however, in the power of the devil, and must therefore await the future Redemption. The Dreamer is moved by this sight (B 16.270–71):

> "Allas!" I seyde, "that synne so longe shal lette
> The myȝte of goddes mercy, that myȝt vs alle amende!"

The Dreamer's exclamation constitutes a skilled dramatic preparation for the Redemption which is to come, echoing the famous words of the prophet Isaiah (Isa. 6:11): *How long, O Lord?*

The Dreamer next sees another figure walking rapidly along the road, and asks him to identify himself and tell where he is going. This new personage is of course Hope, or Moses, who replies by saying that he is in search of a knight who has entrusted him with a commandment and who will seal it on the cross. He refers, of course, as we have noted, to the Great Commandment. But he adds an interesting elaboration which is typical of medieval romance (B 17.15–18):

> And who so worcheth after this writte, I wil vndertaken,
> Shal neuere deuel hym dere ne deth in soule greue.
> For though I seye it my-self, I haue saued with this charme
> Of men and of wommen many score thousandes.

This "charm" reminds us of the prayer, undoubtedly the *Pater Noster,* which the hermit teaches Perceval in Chrétien's *Conte del Graal:* [20]

The hermit counsels him a prayer in his ear, and repeated it until he knew it; and in that prayer there were many of the names of our Lord, for the greatest were there that mouth of man should not utter, if he name them not for fear of death. When he had taught him the prayer he forbade him that in any wise he should say it without great peril.

But the Dreamer, for reasons that we have already noted, is skeptical about Moses' law, and the two of them continue along the road until they see a Samaritan, riding on a mule.

The Samaritan is the most important of the three travelers on the road to Jerusalem. He appears first in an allegorical action based on a traditional interpretation of the parable.[21] Faith and Hope, playing the roles of the priest and the Levite, pass by a man wounded by thieves. The Samaritan, riding on a mule, stops and takes care of the man. He then resumes his journey to the jousts at Jerusalem. The Dreamer overtakes him and asks him why Faith and Hope avoided the wounded man. The Samaritan explains that the man was in such serious need that only the blood of a child born of a virgin could help him. A thief lurks in the wood to attack men, but he dares not approach the Samaritan, who is on horseback (man's flesh). Within three days this thief shall be bound fast with chains. Then Faith shall be forester, and Hope the innkeeper, till the Samaritan returns with salve for all sick men.

This summary makes it clear that the Samaritan's explanation shadows forth the impending Crucifixion, harrowing of Hell, apostolic age, and even the second coming of Christ at Doomsday.[22] This is an elaboration of the traditional signification of the parable, in which the Samaritan is equated with Christ, and it functions as another bit of preparation for what is to come in the poem. On the other hand, the Samaritan has been given a somewhat different role in his relation to Faith and Hope. As the third traveler on the road to Jerusalem, he is Charity personified, that is, he is God's Love, on its way to assume the burden of flesh. Hence he can say, with perfect propriety (B 17.122–23):

> For the barne was born in Bethleem that with his blode shal
> saue
> Alle that lyueth in faith, and folweth his felawes techynge.

The Dreamer next asks the Samaritan whether he should believe Faith or Hope. The Samaritan tells him to obey the teachings of both, and goes on to explain the Trinity, first likening it to a hand and then to a candle. We have already seen the reason for the poet's emphasis on the Trinity here. Both examples stress the seriousness of the sin against the Holy Ghost. The poet's greatest eloquence, however, is reserved for his discussion of the candle, which includes both a stern warning to those who extinguish the flame and a promise of mercy to those who show mercy and thus relight the candle. Most significant of all, the candle flame is given two meanings: it represents the Holy Ghost and, at the same time, *human life itself.* This fact has been duly noted by students of *Piers the Plowman,*[23] but no one, so far as I know, has even attempted to explain why the poet, in discussing the Trinity, should be particularly concerned with murder (B 17.214–16):

> So is the holygost, god and grace with-oute mercy
> To alle vnkynde creatures that coueite to destruye
> Lele loue other lyf that owre lorde shapte.

Then follows the poet's exhortation to rekindle the flame of the Holy Ghost, thus melting the might of Father and Son into mercy (B 17.231–38):

> And as wex with-outen more on a warme glede
> Wil brennen and blasen be thei to-gyderes,
> And solacen hem that may se that sitten in derkenesse,
> So wole the fader forʒif folke of mylde hertes
> That reufulliche repenten and restitucioun make,
> In as moche as thei mowen, amenden and payen.
> And if is suffice nouʒte for assetz, that in suche a wille deyeth,
> Mercy for his mekenesse wil make good the remenaunte.

What does this mean? The tone of this passage and its abrupt appearance in a definition of the Trinity will not allow us to explain it simply as a discussion of the doctrine of *redde quod debes.*[24] Who is to make restitution? And why the emphasis on mercy for those who, though truly repentant, do not have sufficient "assets" to make amends? The whole context in which this passage appears, with its discussion of murder, leads me to conclude that the poet has in mind acts of violence and lawless plundering. Could this part of the B-continuation be dated as late as 1381? If so, our poet is now clearly addressing the impatient poor of the Peasants' Revolt.[25] The tone of Patience's praise of poverty in passus 14 suggested that the poet was attempting to prevent impending violence. Here, however, the Samaritan acknowledges the fact of violence and invokes the might of the Father and the Son in order to bring it to an end.

But the impatient poor are not the only ones to blame for this violence which the poet abhors. The rich must share the blame (B 17.258–64):

> For-thy beth war, ʒe wyse men, that with the worlde deleth,
> That riche ben and resoun knoweth, reuleth wel ʒowre soule.
> Beth nouʒte vnkynde, I conseille ʒow, to ʒowre euene-crystene.
> For many of ʒow riche men, bi my soule, men telleth,
> ʒe brenne, but ʒe blaseth nouʒte; that is a blynde bekene;
> > *Non omnis qui dicit domine, domine, intrabit, etc.*
> *Diues* deyed dampned for his vnkyndenesse
> Of his mete and his moneye to men that it neded.

The threat of damnation is here even more explicit than it was for the poor. Not all the indulgences that the rich can procure will save them if they are "unkynde." They will dwell forever with Dives in Hell.

In addition to the poor and the rich, there appears to be a third class, which completes the poet's trinity of sinners against the Holy Ghost (B 17.271–79):

> For that kynde dothe, vnkynde fordoth, as these cursed theues,
> Vnkynde cristene men, for coueityse and enuye,
> Sleeth a man for his moebles, wyth mouth or wyth handes.

For that the holygoste hath to kepe, tho harlotes destroyeth,
The which is lyf and loue, the leye of mannes bodye.
For euery manere good man may be likned to a torche,
Or elles to a tapre to reuerence the trinitee;
And who morthereth a good man, me thynketh, by myn inwyt,
He fordoth the leuest ly3te that owre lorde loueth.

It is possible, of course, to regard the reference to these "thieves" as
an extension of the Samaritan's earlier exposition of the devil's
attack on men—an elaboration of the parable of the Good Samaritan.
But this merely explains the choice of imagery; it does not explain
the meaning of the passage just quoted. Who are these unkind
Christian men, these harlots, who, for covetousness and envy, slay
a man for his possessions? And what kind of thief is it that kills
with his mouth? Surely these thieves are the friars, who were
accused by their opponents (of whom our author is one) of fanning
the class hatreds that flared into open violence in 1381. In this sense
the friars might be regarded as slaying men "wyth mouth."

The Samaritan closes his remarks, ostensibly defining the Trinity,
with an appeal at once angry and anguished (B 17.284-92):

How my3te he axe mercy, or any mercy hym helpe,
That wykkedlich and willefullich wolde mercy anynte?
Innocence is nexte god, and ny3te and day it crieth,
"Veniaunce, veniaunce! for3iue be it neuere,
That shent vs and shadde owre blode, forshapte vs, as it were;
    Vindica sanguinem iustorum!"
Thus "veniaunce, veniaunce" verrey charite asketh;
And sith holicherche and charite chargeth this so sore,
Leue I neure that owre lorde wil loue that charite lakketh,
Ne haue pite for any preyere there that he pleyneth.

Is there no hope, then, for those who have sinned against the Holy
Ghost? The Dreamer asks this question, and the Samaritan responds: yes, there is, *if* they repent, though this seldom happens.
All things are possible with God, whose mercy is greater than all his
works. But they must make restitution, or, if they cannot pay, then
sorrow will suffice. Sins of the flesh can easily be forgiven; mercy

is readily available to those who are sick; but covetousness and un-
kindness quench God's mercy, for every man has the ability to love
his neighbor. With these words the Samaritan rides off like the
wind toward Jerusalem, and the Dreamer awakes.

In passus 18 the poet presents his final and climactic elaboration
of the three principal features of the Do-bet section. Here the biblical narrative, strongly influenced by the medieval drama, reaches
its climax in the resurrection; the traditional Christ-knight theme,
thanks to the poet's direct knowledge of medieval romance, is
elaborated with striking originality; and, finally, the Dreamer's
spiritual progress culminates in the dramatic ceremony of creeping
to the cross. On all this shines the light of Piers, the ideal representative of *humana natura*. It is small wonder that critics have ac-
claimed this passus as the triumph of our poet's art.

The Fool now wanders, reckless of any woe, until, weary of the
world, he falls asleep and dreams of the celebration of Palm Sunday
(B 18.8–9):

> Of gerlis and of *gloria laus* gretly me dremed,
> And how *osanna* by orgonye olde folke songen.

This is of course descriptive of a traditional Palm Sunday procession; but it is also a feature of the cycle plays, in which children sing
the *Gloria Laus* and adults sing the *Hosanna*,[26] while flowers and
branches are strewn along the way of Christ's entry into Jerusalem.
Next the poet describes Christ's triumphant entry (B 18.10–16):

> One semblable to the Samaritan, and some-del to Piers the Plowman,
> Barfote on an asse bakke botelees cam prykye,
> Wyth-oute spores other spere, spakliche he loked,
> As is the kynde of a knyʒte that cometh to be dubbed,
> To geten hem gylte spores or galoches ycouped.
> Thanne was Faith in a fenestre, and cryde *"a! fili Dauid!"*
> As doth an heraude of armes whan auntrous cometh to iustes.

Here is a remarkable example of the poet's original and highly
effective use of tradition. God's love (the Samaritan) has become
man (Piers),[27] and Christ's entry is now described as a procession

glittering with chivalric splendor, while Faith (Abraham), the herald, proclaims the arrival of the Hero. Faith then goes on to elaborate the romance imagery. Jesus will joust in Piers's arms so that his divine nature will not be recognized (a typical romance motif); he will fight against the fiend, False-doom and Death; and, finally, Death and Life make their respective boasts as to the outcome of the tournament.

The poet's account of the trial and crucifixion of Christ follows the gospel narrative—with traditional additions from the apocryphal gospels—and elaborates the imagery of the tournament. Pilate is seen as the judge of a contest—"Thanne cam *Pilatus* with moche peple . . . To se how doughtilich Deth sholde do, and deme her botheres riȝte." (B 18.36–37). One is reminded of the language of the torturers in the Towneley *Crucifixion:*

> Stand nere, felows, and let se
> how we can hors oure kyng so fre,
>   By any craft;
> Stand thou yonder on yond syde,
> and we shall se how he can ryde,
>   And how to weld a shaft.[28]

It is possible, of course, that the cycle plays and *Piers the Plowman* represent independent developments of the Christ-knight theme. But, in any case, the two are very close at this point.

Following the poet's moving and justly famous description of the death of Christ on the cross, we find the incident of Longinus, the blind soldier who pierced the side of Christ, whose story is told in the apocryphal *Gospel of Nicodemus.*[29] It is worth noting, however, that in the apocryphal story Longinus pierces Christ's side before he dies. In *Piers the Plowman,* following the canonical gospel (John 19:34), Longinus pierces his side after his death. This agrees more closely with the cycle plays, where the thrust of the spear is designed to insure that Christ is actually dead.[30] Furthermore, our poet makes the point that no one dared touch the Lord because of his rank (B 18.75–77):

Ac was no boy so bolde goddes body to touche;
For he was knyȝte and kynges sone, kynde forȝaf that tyme,
That non harlot were so hardy to leyne hande vppon hym.

In the *Ludus Coventriae* this point is emphasized by Pilate:

I charge you All at the be-gynnyng
as ye wole Answere me biforn
that ther be no man xal towch your king
but yf he be knyght or jentylman born.[31]

Returning to *Piers,* our poet describes the Longinus incident forcefully and dramatically (B 18.85–91):

But this blynde bacheler thanne bar hym thorugh the herte;
The blode spronge down by the spere, and vnspered the kniȝtes
    eyen.
Thanne fel the knyȝte vpon knees and cryed hym mercy—
"Aȝeyne my wille it was, lorde, to wownde ȝow so sore!"
He seighed and sayde, "sore it me athynketh;
For the dede that I haue done, I do me in ȝowre grace;
Haue on me reuth, riȝtful Iesu!" and riȝt with that he wept.

One cannot fail to be impressed by the emotional intensity of this passage. It is true that tradition may have led the poet to include this story; it appears in much the same form in most of the cycle plays. But our poet rarely uses tradition for tradition's sake. And it is hard to escape the conclusion that his brilliant dramatization of Longinus' story is an exemplum for those who are guilty of extinguishing the flame of human life.

That Longinus could be used here in the way I have suggested is readily apparent when we recall his role in medieval romance. The famous bleeding lance of the grail procession in Chrétien's *Conte del Graal* was a symbol of the violence that has darkened the life of man from the beginning. "Why does the lance bleed?" This was the question which Perceval was supposed to ask. Why indeed? It has bled, so to speak, ever since Cain slew Abel in the field, and the reason for it is as old as the Fall. Now in the later "exegetical" romances the bleeding lance was specifically associated

with the lance of Longinus, thus producing an intensification of
the mystery of man's inhumanity exactly analogous to that achieved
by our poet in the passage under consideration. But note also that
the poet dramatizes Longinus' repentance. Hence Longinus is a
bright mirror for those sinners mentioned by the Dreamer who are
truly sorry for their sins (B 17.293–98):

> "I pose I hadde synned so, and shulde now deye,
> And now am sory, that so the seint spirit agulte,
> Confesse me, and crye his grace, god, that al made,
> And myldliche his mercy axe, myȝte I nouȝte be saued?"
> "Ȝus," seide the Samaritan, "so wel thow myȝte repente,
> That riȝtwisnesse thorw repentance to reuthe myȝte torne."

That the Longinus incident reflects this concern of the poet will be
substantiated, as we shall see, by his recurrence to the theme of
violence later on in this passus.

The poet now presents the traditional debate of the Four Daughters of God.[32] This famous allegorical debate is based on Psalm
85:10 (A.V.): *Mercy and truth are met together; righteousness and
peace have kissed each other.* It is a dramatization of the paradoxical
relationship of justice and mercy in God's scheme of salvation for
mankind. Conventionally, as in the *Cursor Mundi,* the debate is
introduced as a prelude to the Redemption. In the fifteenth-century
morality play, the *Castle of Perseverance,* the four daughters dispute
over the fate of Mankind's soul. But our poet attaches the debate to
the harrowing of Hell. This is quite original, and accords well with
the warning which he has given concerning the damnation of
sinners against the Holy Ghost. God's mercy is greater than all his
works (cf. B 17.310–12). The whole scene is dramatically conceived.
As Skeat suggests, the poet is surely indebted in some way to
medieval stage tradition.

A transition between the debate of the Four Daughters of God
and the Harrowing of Hell is provided by a wight named "Book," [33]
who describes the miraculous signs accompanying the life of Christ
on earth, and the joy that will come from his resurrection. Then

follows the story of the Harrowing of Hell, in which the poet achieves dramatic compression by omitting the speeches of the patriarchs and prophets at Jesus' approach, and the account of the journey to Paradise after their release. The consternation of the devils is expressed by a dispute between Lucifer and Satan over Christ's right to rescue the condemned souls from eternal pain; the trend of the argument is reminiscent of that of the Four Daughters. When Christ makes his triumphal entry into Hell, the patriarchs and prophets rejoice, and Lucifer is blinded by the light. Guile is beguiled; Lucifer must drink his own poison. Christ then prophesies concerning his second coming and promises to be merciful to his brethren at the Last Judgment.

Near the end of Christ's prophecy occurs another of the poet's references to violence and to the threat of damnation (B 18.382–85):

> And I, that am kynge of kynges, shal come suche a tyme,
> There dome to the deth dampneth al wikked;
> And ʒif lawe wil I loke on hem, it lithe in my grace,
> Whether thei deye or deye nouʒte for that thei deden ille.

By itself, this statement might be viewed simply as a confirmation of the fact that Christ shall come to judge the quick and the dead. But he goes on to say that if the sins of the wicked *are paid for in any way* ("Be it any thinge abouʒt"), then he will be able to grant mercy. That is, if the wicked shall have made restitution, either by "assets" or by "sorrow" (cf. B 17.234–36, 313–14), then, and only then, can he show them mercy. And although holy writ declares that no evil shall go unpunished, Christ says, yet penitent sinners shall be washed clean in purgatory, "And my mercy shal be shewed to *manye* of my brethren." Why not to *all* of Christ's brethren? Here is the reason (B 18.392–93):

> For blode may suffre blode bothe hungry and akale,
> Ac blode may nouʒte se blode blede, but hym rewe.

Those who do not repent of violence and bloodshed will be deprived of Christ's mercy on the Day of Doom.

Lucifer is bound with chains, and Do-bet moves rapidly to its close. Many hundreds of angels harp and sing, and Peace pipes a note of poetry (B 18.409–15):

> "After sharpe shoures," quod Pees, "moste shene is the sonne;
> Is no weder warmer than after watery cloudes,
> Ne no loue leuere, ne leuer frendes,
> Than after werre and wo, whan Loue and Pees be maistres.
> Was neuere werre in this worlde, ne wykkednesse so kene,
> That ne Loue, and hym luste, to laughynge ne brouȝte,
> And Pees thorw pacience alle perilles stopped."

Then Truth and Love (Mercy) embrace, and Righteousness and Peace kiss each other (B 18.422–23):

> Treuth tromped tho, and songe *"Te deum laudamus";*
> And thanne luted Loue in a loude note,
> > *Ecce quam bonum et quam iocundum, etc.*

These lines have been justly admired, but I do not believe that the extent of the poet's achievement in them has been fully appreciated. The reconciliation of Truth and Love operates on at least three levels in the poem. First, it represents the resolution of the paradox of justice and mercy through the Redemption. As such it is the rightful climax of the Do-bet section. But this reconciliation is also related to the undercurrent of blood and violence which we have detected here and there in passus 17 and 18. The song of Peace is both a benediction and a prayer: let there be no more war and woe, let perils cease, and let love and peace turn wickedness to friendship and smiling. Occurring as they do in the context of the resurrection, these lines constitute a powerful appeal to the hostile forces in contemporary England. Finally, the reconciliation of Truth and Love dramatizes the reconciliation of the A and B versions of *Piers the Plowman*. St. Truth and St. Charity are met together. Lest the reader miss this vital point, the poet has Love sing, Behold, how good and how pleasant it is for brethren to dwell together in unity! (Ps. 133:1). We need only recall the ironic context of this verse in the A-version (A 11.190),[34] to realize how different is the spirit in which the same verse is now "luted" by Love.

In the closing lines of passus 18 our attention is directed once more to the Dreamer (B 18.424-31):

> Tyl the daye dawed this damaiseles daunced,
> That men rongen to the resurexioun, and riȝt with that I waked,
> And called Kitte my wif and Kalote my douȝter—
> "Ariseth and reuerenceth goddes resurrexioun,
> And crepeth to the crosse on knees and kisseth it for a Iuwel!
> For goddes blissed body it bar for owre bote,
> And it afereth the fende, for suche is the myȝte,
> May no grysly gost glyde there it shadweth!"

This is indeed an impressive climax. The ringing of the bells, a familiar part of Easter, suggests also the end of the ancient *Sepulchrum* play, where, after the *Te Deum* (sung in our poem by Truth), occurs the instruction:

> *This begun, all the bells chime out together.*[35]

In fact, everything about the closing lines suggests antiquity and venerable tradition. Creeping to the cross was one of the earliest evidences of the dramatic instinct in the Church; the power of the cross over the fiend was of ancient memory; and finally, of course, out of the Easter Mass itself came the *Quem quaeritis* trope, the very heart of the medieval drama.

It is therefore appropriate that in this venerable setting we are now privileged to witness the rebirth of the Dreamer, restored at last to the ancient faith. Lest there be any doubt about the importance of this moment in the Dreamer's spiritual progress, the poet provides him with a symbolic wife and daughter. The result is an impressive tableau: father, mother, and child bowing in reverence before the cross of Christ, living examples of the profound message of Faith (B 16.205-10):

> Adam owre aller fader, Eue was of hym-selue,
> And the issue that thei hadde, it was of hem bothe,
> And either is otheres Ioye, in thre sondry persones,

And in heuene and here one syngulere name;
And thus is mankynde or manhede of matrimoigne yspronge,
And bitokneth the Trinite and trewe bileue.

In this very human way the poet dramatizes the Dreamer's spiritual regeneration.[36]

In passus 16–18 we have witnessed the drama of the Fall and Redemption, "directed" by Piers, the humble plowman, and fitted with the splendid trappings of medieval romance. The *Corpus Christi* pageants have lined the road to Jerusalem, where the tournament between Life and Death is held. In addition we have been led, with the Dreamer, through Lent to Easter—that is, through repentance to spiritual regeneration. Yet in spite of the triumphant conclusion of Do-bet, there is a prophetic undertone of violence and tragedy. Our return to the field full of folk in passus 19–20 is not destined to be a pleasant one. And it is only with the profoundest sense of irony that the poet has given this last section of his poem the title of "Do-best."

Five

THE APOSTOLIC AGE AND APOCALYPSE

This last section of the poem, called "Do-best," extends from the resurrection to the poet's own day. The most obvious features of the poem's biblical structure are to be seen in passus 19. First comes the Ascension (B 19.1–193), then the sending of the Holy Ghost (B 19.194–256), followed by the post-biblical History of the Early Church (B 19.257–330), and finally the apocalyptic Last Judgment (B 19.331–478). Passus 20, of course, is a symphony of themes taken from virtually all that has gone before in the poem, and its setting is the field full of folk; but its structure and its driving momentum are attributable to our poet's use of the book of Revelation (Apocalypse). Thus the last two passus, as we shall see, provide impressive testimony to the fact that the B-continuation, from beginning to end, from Genesis through Revelation, is a poem not merely indebted to, but actually based on, the Bible.

The biblical narrative of passus 19 is so famous and its use by the poet is so complex that it will be necessary for us to digress briefly in order to understand the multiplicity of the poet's materials and his method of procedure. The Ascension, for example, is so intimately associated with liturgy, homiletics, theology, the church calendar, and the drama—not to mention other aspects of religious life and literature—that it would be folly to try to explain what the poet is doing at the beginning of passus 19 in terms of any one of these categories. The same reservation holds, of course, in varying degrees, for the entire B-continuation; but it is especially appropriate in passus 19, and we need to pause for a moment to consider its implications. The Ascension provides us with a perfect subject for analysis.

The opening lines of passus 19 set the stage for what is to come, and actually describe the Ascension (B 19.1-14):

> Thus I awaked and wrote what I had dremed,
> And diȝte me derely and dede me to cherche,
> To here holy the masse and to be houseled after.
> In myddes of the masse, tho men ȝede to offrynge,
> I fel eftsones a-slepe, and sodeynly me mette
> That Pieres the Plowman was paynted al blody,
> And come in with a crosse bifor the comune peple,
> And riȝte lyke in alle lymes to owre lorde Iesu;
> And thanne called I Conscience to kenne me the sothe.
> "Is this Iesus the Iuster?" quod I, "that Iuwes did to deth?
> Or it is Pieres the Plowman! who paynted hym so rede?"
> Quod Conscience, and kneled tho, "thise aren Pieres armes,
> His coloures and his cote-armure, ac he that cometh so blody
> Is Cryst with his crosse, conqueroure of Crystene."

Before we attempt to consider these lines in detail, it will be well, first, to establish the fact that they do indeed describe the Ascension. One of the best evidences of this can be found in the dramatization of the Ascension in the Cornish *Resurrection* (2487-2630). The play consists primarily of a dialogue between Jesus and nine angels, and the time is the Ascension into heaven. I quote only a portion of the dialogue: [1]

THIRD ANGEL.

> Who is he that hath come from the earth, red
> As blood, head and shoulders,
>   Legs and feet?
> I am astonished at the one of human kind!
> So swiftly as he hath come here,
>   An angel doth never approach.

FOURTH ANGEL.

He from Edom hath come;
To a thousand devils if he caused not grief,
    A wonder is to me;
For I swear that this is
That same Son who went hence;
    He is the King of Joy.

FIFTH ANGEL.

Who canst thou be,
When thy clothing is so red,
    In the kingdom of heaven?
For I know certainly, one of human kind,
Unless through the full Godhead,
    Stands not here.

JESUS.

I am a King, who have done battle
To bring Adam and all his seed
    From evil plight.
The King I am of joy,
And the victory was gained by me
    In arms of red.

    .   .   .   .

Fitting it is that red should be
My habergeon, which was turned
    From dark to light,
All the length of my skin scourged,
So that deep in my flesh were pierced
    Many thousand holes.

The mention here of Christ in red arms (Cornish *yn arvow ruth*)
and the habergeon (Cornish *hobersen*) may simply be common-
places of the Christ-knight theme, but these touches correspond
nicely to the red arms and "cote-armure" of Piers.

On the other hand, the general method of representing the
Ascension as we see it in the Cornish play is quite traditional. The
Chester *Ascension,* for example, though briefer than the Cornish

version, and lacking the Christ-knight imagery, has a similar dialogue between Christ and the Angels: [2]

ANGELUS TERTIUS.

Why is thy Clothing now so redd?
thy body blody and also heade?
thy Clothes also all that bene lead,
lyke to Pressors of wyne?

IHESUS.

for the Devill and his power,
that mankynd brought in great Dangere,
through death on Crosse and bloud so clear,
I have made them all myne.
These bloudy dropps that you may see,
all they freshe shall resarved be,
till I come in my maiesty
to Deme the last day.

Several plays in the Chester cycle, however, including the *Ascension,* are indebted to the *Stanzaic Life of Christ,* a fourteenth-century English poem based on the *Legenda Aurea* and Higden's *Polychronicon.* [3] This poem contains an elaborate discussion, including six points relating to the Ascension itself, and nine "fruits" of the Ascension (8669–9532). One of the points discussed involves the manner of Christ's Ascension, under which is mentioned the questioning of the angels, including "whi is thi huling now so rede/ and thi clothes opon the/ like wyne-pressores on lenth and brede,/ and al blody opon to se?" (8993–96). But of course the *Stanzaic Life* itself is, in this passage, based on the *Legenda Aurea,* in which the angels ask the same questions and get the same answers. [4]

Thus the representation of the Ascension that we find in the Cornish play is also to be found in the Chester *Ascension,* the *Stanzaic Life of Christ,* and the *Legenda Aurea.* All of these refer to the redness of Christ's apparel, and the reasons therefor. Moreover, all of these texts cite an important passage from Isaiah 63:1–3: *Who is this that cometh from Edom, with dyed garments from*

*Bozrah? this that is glorious in his apparel, travelling in the great-
ness of his strength? I that speak in righteousness, mighty to save.
Wherefore art thou red in thine apparel, and thy garments like him
that treadeth in the winefat? I have trodden the winepress alone. . . .*
Hence it can be seen that the questions of the angels are traditional,
allegorical elaborations of this passage (and other passages as well),
applied to the Ascension. Nor is this use of the biblical verses limited
to the texts which we have considered. The *Legenda Aurea,* for
example, cites St. Denis on "the Hierarchy of holy angels" (Pseudo-
Dionysius, *De coelesti Hierarchia*); and it is therefore likely that
our poet could have had access to any one or more of the numerous
forms of this Ascension tradition.[5]

Finally, it seems likely that our poet did in fact go beyond the
medieval drama for suggestions affecting his treatment of the Ascension. This is evident in his use of Piers himself. We saw in the
passage quoted (B 19.1–14) that Christ is described as wearing
"Pieres armes," and we know that Piers is used by the poet to
represent *humana natura.* Hence one meaning of this passage is
that Christ ascends to heaven manifesting his Human Nature
(Piers). He descended to earth as God; he ascended to heaven as
man. The plowman imagery makes this clear. And it is confirmed
by the fact that the dignity of man is, according to the *Legenda
Aurea,* one of the nine fruits of the Ascension:[6]

> A great dignity have we gotten when our nature is lift up unto the right
> side of the Father. . . . And of this S. Leo saith in a sermon of the Ascen-
> sion: This day the nature of our humanity hath been borne above the height
> of all puissances unto where as God the Father sitteth. . . .

The Chester *Ascension* does not bring out this fact, and our
poet therefore knew of it from some other source.[7] But this need
not have been the *Legenda Aurea.* He may have known it as a
commonplace of homiletics, theology, or scriptural tradition—or
all of these combined.

This digression has taken us far from the poem, but it has been
useful, for it shows us the danger of assuming that the poet's

dramatizations, however much they may resemble the cycle plays, are exclusively derived from stage tradition. There is, moreover, a further indication that the poet here exploits the biblical narrative in a more complex fashion. The Dreamer tells us (B 19.1–5) that he fell asleep in the midst of the Mass, when men went to the offering. It is quite possible that the poet is utilizing the symbolism of the Mass, or perhaps other liturgical features specifically associated with the Ascension. Indeed, as we shall see, Conscience's discourse on the names of Christ is—in a sense—a sermon on the Ascension. And when the poet next describes the Sending of the Holy Ghost (B 19.194 ff.), Conscience tells the Dreamer to sing *veni, creator spiritus,* a hymn traditionally associated with Pentecost. The Dreamer says (B 19.206–7):

> Thanne songe I that songe, and so did many hundreth,
> And cryden with Conscience, "help us, god of grace!"

Clearly the Dreamer is but one in a congregation of hundreds who are participating in the services of the church, while the poem, following the church calendar, continues to unfold the corresponding biblical narrative. The modern reader can scarcely imagine the impact that this portion of *Piers the Plowman* must have had on its fourteenth-century audience.

The "Ascension sermon" on the names of Christ delivered by Conscience fits very well into the tradition that we have just considered. Indeed, one might say that Conscience's "text" is the third question of the angels: *Quis est iste rex glorie?* . . . that is, *Who is this King of glory? The Lord of hosts, he is the King of glory* (Psalm 24:10, A.V.). But we have now reached the limits of tradition. For the sermon of Conscience (if we may call it that), though to a certain extent traditional, contains the poet's own teaching, and, like most good sermons, it has an important bearing on contemporary affairs.

In response to the Dreamer's question ("Why calle ȝe hym Cryst?"), Conscience launches into a threefold explanation of the names (B 19.26–193). First of all, Jesus was knight, king, and conqueror. He became a knight when he was baptized by John the Baptist; he became a king by virtue of his teaching and healing; and he became a conqueror through his victory over death. The example of his suffering should guide us and help us avoid falling into sin (26–64). Next the poet restates these three phases in Jesus' life by elaborating the chivalric imagery and adding to it the names Jesus, Son of David, and Christ, together with the familiar triad Do-wel, Do-bet, and Do-best. As a child he was called Jesus, a name before which every knee shall bow (as did the three kings, allegorically explained), but during this time he was neither king nor conqueror, and only when he turned water into wine did he begin to "do wel" (65–119). As a man he was called Son of David, for it was during this time that he worked miracles and healed the sick, and thus commenced to "do bet" (120–35). But it was not until his victory over death, revealed in his resurrection, that he became known as Christ, and began to "do best" (136–93). This last part of Conscience's discourse includes a review of the events of the passion and resurrection, similar to Christ's summation in the Cornish version of the Ascension (2571–2606).

Apart from tradition, then, what is the reason for this extended discourse on the names of Jesus? Its purpose is clearly revealed, I think, in Conscience's concluding remarks on Do-best (19.177–85):

> And whan this dede was done, Dobest he tauȝte,
> And ȝaf Pieres power, and pardoun he graunted
> To alle manere men, mercy and forȝyfnes,
> Hym myȝte men to assoille of alle manere synnes,
> In couenant that thei come and knowleche to paye,
> To Pieres pardon the Plowman, *redde quod debes.*
> Thus hath Pieres powere, be his pardoun payed,
> To bynde and to vnbynde bothe here and elles-where,
> And assoille men of alle synnes, saue of dette one.

Conscience then concludes by saying that Christ shall come again to judge the quick and the dead. From the evidence of the lines

quoted, however, we can see that the real emphasis is this: Christ
did best when he granted Piers the power to bind and loose. Now
Piers, in this context, obviously represents Peter, and, by extension,
the priesthood of Holy Church, to whom a portion of this power is
delegated. Furthermore, the only true pardon is that forgiveness of
sins which the priest is empowered to grant—but only on condition
that the penitent pays what he owes. We have already encountered
this emphasis on restitution, *redde quod debes.*

But the way in which Conscience stresses the spiritual jurisdiction
of the Church in the world, the power to bind and loose here and
now, suggests that the poet is also in some measure responding to
contemporary attacks on the temporal power of the Church. Of
course in defending the Church he is not motivated by materialistic
interests, for we have had occasion to see how sharply he criticizes
covetousness among the clergy. But he does believe strongly in the
necessity of the priesthood in the scheme of salvation, and some of
the current attacks on the power of the Church may have seemed
to him to strike at the very heart of this belief. An excellent example
of such an attack can be seen in the words of the knight, arguing
with a clerk, in the anonymous fourteenth-century satire, *Dialogus
inter Militem et Clericum.* I quote from the translation of John
Trevisa: [8]

Myles. Ich haue herde of wise doctors þat we schal distingue twey di-
uerse tymes of Crist: oon of his manhed and anoþer of his power & mageste.
Þe tyme of his manhed was from þat he toke flesch & blode anoon to his
passioun. Þe tyme of his power & maieste was & is after þe resurreccioun,
whanne he seide: "Al power is ʒeuen to me in heuene & in erþe." . . .
Peter was ordeyned Cristes vicarie, for þe state of his manhed & nouʒt for
þe state of his blisse & maieste. He was nouʒt made Cristes vicarie in
doyng þat Crist doþ now in blisse; but for to folowe hym in his doyng
þat he dide here on erþe. Þanne he ʒaf his vicarie þat power þat he vsed
here in erþe, depliche. & forto preue þis by Holy Writt, y take witnesse of
Crist & of Holy Writt as þou dost. Lo! Crist seide to Pylat: "My kyngdom
is nouʒt of þis world." Also he seiþ þat "he come nouʒt to be serued, but
to serue oþer men." Luce 12 °. And oon seide to Crist: "Maister say to my

broþer þat he departe heritage wiþ me." Crist answerde & seide: "Man who haþ made me juge to departe bitwene ȝou?" Luce 12 °. Lo! þou herest openlich þat Crist was nouȝt juge & deler ouer temporalte. . . .

The knight continues in this cynical vein, allowing the clerk no real reason for being, and leaving religion little or no place in human affairs. But the important thing to note is that his argument rests on a distinction between Christ's manhood and his majesty, and the assertion that Peter's power was limited to that of Christ's manhood. Our poet's discussion of the names of Jesus is a direct response to this kind of argument. *Redde quod debes* is of course fulfillment of the law of love, and is therefore fundamentally a spiritual imperative.[9] But spiritual and temporal affairs are not separate and distinct realms. *Ergo,* a spiritual command may well have a visible consequence in the material world, and such is indeed the case with *redde quod debes.* In this sense, says our poet, the Church does have a very real and highly important power in temporal affairs.[10]

The poem next describes the sending of the Holy Ghost (B 19.194–256), following the account given in Acts 2:1–4, with the addition of the gifts of the Holy Ghost adapted from 1 Cor. 12:4 ff. The hero of this story is Grace. When he first appears, Conscience tells the Dreamer to kneel. It is Grace who distributes the gifts of the Holy Ghost and who delivers the prophetic exhortation at the end of the scene. To the reader who has perceived the emphasis on Grace at every crucial juncture of the B-continuation, this development will come as no surprise. Grace provides the "treasure" for man to live by and the weapons with which man may fight against Antichrist and his followers. Each man is granted the skill necessary for a particular trade or vocation; hence there should be no discord among the members of the body of Christ.[11]

The poet's exposition of the History of the Early Church (B 19.257–330) is a good illustration of the process of allegorization which we find in the later romances. The continuator takes the "matter" of existing tradition, and gives it his own "sense." [12] The romance writer, for example, may construct a composite *aventure,* derived from narrative incidents of earlier romances, in such a way as to give the new story a clearly allegorical meaning. Thus in Malory's version of the Holy Grail, the Castle of Maidens episode becomes a romance form of the Harrowing of Hell.[13] Similarly, our poet in the B-continuation of *Piers the Plowman* takes the "matter" of Piers's plowing of the half-acre from the A-text, and gives as its "sense" the history of the Church. His materials, therefore, are agricultural, and not chivalric; but his method is exactly analogous to that observable in the tradition of "exegetical" romance. The result is a very skillfully constructed allegorical action. Piers has a team of four oxen (Matthew, Mark, Luke, and John), and four "stottis" (Augustine, Ambrose, Gregory, and Jerome). He sows the seeds of the cardinal virtues, and harrows them with the Old Law and the New. He builds a barn, Unity, or Holy Church, in which to store the grain when it is harvested. Finally, Grace devises a cart called Christendom (B 19.326–30):

> And whan this dede was done, Grace deuised
> A carte, hyʒte Cristendome, to carye Pieres sheues;
> And gaf hym caples to his carte, Contricioun and Confessioun,
> And made Presthode haywarde, the while hym-self went
> As wyde as the worlde is with Piers to tulye treuthe.

Thus ends the poet's admirable sketch of the history of the Church: *Go ye into all the world, and preach the gospel to every creature* (Mark 16:15). One is reminded of the eloquent appeal, at the end of passus 15, for the conversion of the heathen. Piers and Grace now set out together in order to accomplish this task.[14]

We have now reached the field full of folk once more, and it is significant that at precisely this point begins the poet's use of the book of Revelation. For this reason it will be well to review briefly the ways in which the poet uses this last book of the Bible, and the extent to which his use of it is qualified by extra-biblical literary tradition.

First of all, be it noted that the poet clothes his apocalyptic narrative in the trappings of chivalry. The imagery of the tournament is effectively exploited, especially in passus 20, and it may well be, as Skeat has suggested,[15] that the author was familiar with the thirteenth-century French *Turnoyement de l'Antechrist,* although his evident familiarity with romance itself would be sufficient to account for the use of this motif. Moreover, the tournament imagery ultimately gives way to the concept of the siege. Antichrist leads an army, composed of the Sins,[16] in an attack on Unity, or Holy Church. But the lines are not clearly drawn. This army invades the field full of folk, and the result is one of two things: it overcomes some of the folk, who then join the ranks of Antichrist; it drives others into Unity, that is, into Holy Church. We should also note that the characters engaged in this action are clearly identified by the poet. His use of the Apocalypse is not narrowly polemic. Antichrist is Antichrist, that is, Satan, the deceiver, in the book of Revelation (e.g., 12:9). He does not stand for someone whom the poet has in mind but does not name. He is himself.

In addition to the army of Antichrist, however, there is another fighting force in the field. I refer to Kynde (Nature), Elde (Old Age), and Deth. These combatants must be sharply distinguished from Antichrist's army, for they are arrayed *against* Antichrist, and function as the defenders of Unity.[17] They respond to Conscience's call for assistance. Indeed, these grim champions of Holy Church are the counterparts in our poem of the Four Horsemen of the Apocalypse (Rev. 6).

Thus it is clear that the poet uses the book of Revelation extensively, and with great freedom and effectiveness. But he also exploits apocalyptic tradition outside of the Bible itself. Particularly noticeable is the influence of the drama; to illustrate, let us examine the closing scene of passus 19, for this scene is a remarkable adaptation of the Last Judgment, as it was conventionally represented on the medieval stage.

As soon as Piers sets out to till truth throughout the world, Pride, with a great army of sins, comes and boasts to Conscience that he will destroy the seeds of the virtues sown by Piers and corrupt Unity, so that no one will know Christian from heathen. Then Conscience calls all Christian people to come into Piers's barn, and Kynde Witte orders them to dig a moat, which is filled with tears of contrition. The defenders are now ready for the expected siege. I care not, says Conscience, if Pride comes now! But at this point something goes wrong. The commons object to Conscience's insistence that they pay what they owe before receiving Communion. A brewer says that he does not intend to "hakke after holynesse." Conscience warns him that unless he lives by the teaching of justice he will be lost, life and soul. Suddenly a new spokesman puts forth his head (B 19.407–10):

> "Thanne is many man ylost," quod a lewed vycory,
> "I am a curatour of holykyrke, and come neure in my tyme
> Man to me, that me couth telle of cardinale vertues,
> Or that acounted Conscience at a cokkes fether or an hennes!"

This "lewed vycory," who is, I am sure, our poet thinly disguised, goes on to point out the shortcomings of cardinals, the pope, and the commons, and offers a prayer for their amendment. Particularly interesting is his devout hope for the betterment of society (B 19.422–25):

> And thow, Conscience, in kynges courte, and shuldest neure
> come thennes,
> And Grace, that thow gredest so of, gyour of alle clerkes,
> And Pieres with his newe plow and eke with his olde,
> Emperour of al the worlde, that alle men were Cristene!

This is the poet's final positive statement concerning the ideal society that he envisions.[18] The pope is imperfect; unlike the pope, Piers works for the betterment of both the righteous and the wicked. When the vicar finishes speaking, a lord laughs and says that he will employ the virtue of fortitude (i.e., brute force) to exact his rents. And, finally, a king remarks that he can justly take what he needs without asking anyone's permission—hence he can be houseled without making restitution. Conscience cautiously agrees, but adds that the king must rule his realm reasonably. The passus concludes with the poet's humorous reference to himself in the role of the "lewed vycory" (B 19.477–78):

> The vyker hadde fer home and faire toke his leue,
> And I awaknend there-with and wrote as me mette.

In view of his severe criticism of the Pope, we might at first suppose that the "vicar" was well advised to make his excuses and leave the scene in a hurry. Actually, however, such criticism of popes as we find in *Piers the Plowman,* although severe, is by no means unprecedented. Dante's *Divine Comedy* immediately comes to mind. But more pertinent to the passage in our poem just considered is the *Papa Damnatus* of the Chester play, *The Last Judgment* (173–88):

PAPA DAMNATUS.

> Alas! Alas! Alas! Alas!
> now am I worse then ever I was;
> my Body the soule agayne hase,
> that longe hath bene in hell.

> To geather they be, now is no grace,
> defyled they be before thy face,
> and after my death here in this place,
> in payne ever to dwell.

> Now Bootles is to aske mercy;
> for lyvinge, highest in earth was I,
> and Conning, chosen in Clergie,
> but Coveteousnes did me care.

> Also Silver and Simonye
> made me Pope unworthy;
> that burnes me now full bitterly,
> for of Blis I am full bare.

The cyclical versions of *The Last Judgment* customarily include the separating of the sheep and the goats; *Bonus* prays for God's mercy, and *Malus* bewails his fate. The Chester play, however, is more graphic in its treatment of this subject. In the cast of characters are a pope, emperor, king, and queen, all saved; but also a pope, emperor, king, queen, justice, and merchant, all damned. Our poet uses this motif from the drama with great effectiveness. For it is important to remember that in the terms of our poem the pope, cardinals, king, lord, and commons are not yet damned or saved. They are being weighed in the balances, but it is not yet too late. For the reader who is sensitive to the poet's apocalyptic overtones, and who is also familiar with the Last Judgment as presented on the medieval stage, this passage has a great dramatic intensity. The storm clouds gather as the pope commands Christians to kill each other, the cardinals live in luxury, and king, lords, and commons cynically take what they can get. The lightning clenches for the stroke.[19]

In the final passus of the B-continuation the Dreamer, now awake, meets with a person identified only as "Need." Couldn't you excuse yourself, says Need, as did the king, lord, and commons? After all, if you are governed by temperance, it is no sin for you to get your sustenance by sleight when you are hungry. Need goes on to deliver an elaborate discourse on this subject, winding up with the assertion that Christ himself was willfully poor, and that the Dreamer should therefore not be ashamed to beg and be needy. In view of what the poet has said about patient poverty (esp. B 14.49–59), this is certainly strange teaching. All students of *Piers the Plowman* are indebted to R. W. Frank, Jr., for first pointing out that Need's speech is modeled on the specious arguments of the friars in defense of their theoretical poverty.[20] We have already had occasion to observe our poet's antimendicant point of view (e.g., B 11.59–102), and Need's speech prepares us for the B-continuation's ending with a powerful indictment of the friars.

When Need's argument is concluded the Dreamer falls asleep,

and the final vision begins. Antichrist storms into the field full of folk and overturns the crop of truth. In this destructive work he is now assisted, not merely by abstract sins, but by friars and religious; in other words, those members of contemporary society who have succumbed to him and joined his army. The convent bells ring as everyone comes out to welcome Antichrist. Meanwhile, the poet tells us, there are a few "fools" who heed Conscience's advice to come into Unity and help defend it against the onslaught of Belial's children.

Conscience cries out to Kynde for assistance, and thus begins the driving attack of the "Three Horsemen," Elde, Kynde, and Deth, against the army of Antichrist. The poet heightens the effectiveness of this scene by identifying the destructive power of these personifications with the Black Death, which was ravaging England in the second half of the fourteenth century; for the pale horse of Death was at that time a terribly familiar sight. The shattering impact of these democratic destroyers on the army of Antichrist is reported with grim humor. The lord that lived after lust (Rev. 18:9) cries out for help (B 20.91–93):

> "Al-arme! alarme!" quod that lorde, "eche lyf kepe his owne!"
> And thanne mette this men ar mynstralles myʒte pipe,
> And ar heraudes of armes hadden descreued lordes.

Elde, Kynde, and Deth apparently have no regard for chivalric decorum.

But the folk who survive the initial onslaught do not seem to have learned their lesson. Sinners abandon themselves to lechery and luxurious living. This is, as we know, one of the historical consequences of the plague in our poet's day; but it is also a phenomenon observed in Revelation (9:20–21): *And the rest of the men which were not killed by these plagues, yet repented not of the works of their hands, that they should not worship devils, and idols of gold, and silver, and brass, and stone, and of wood: which neither can see, nor hear, nor walk: Neither repented they of their murders, nor of their sorceries, nor of their fornication, nor of their thefts.* This theme the poet develops at considerable length in a passage which contains some of his most effective satire (B 20.105–81).

The poem ends with a grim account of the storming of Holy Church. Worldly priests, siding with Covetousness in the army of Antichrist, begin the attack. Conscience cries for help from Clergie (learning), and this brings on the friars, the real villains of the narrative.[21] Conscience is reluctant to admit them to Unity, and warns them to imitate Francis and Dominic in holiness and love. But the friars preach that all things should be in common, and corrupt the sacrament of penance with easy confession. Meanwhile, some of the defenders of Unity, wounded by Hypocrisy, are impatient with the painful plasters applied to their wounds by Contrition. They call for the friars. At first Conscience is opposed to this (B 20.316–19):

> "We han no nede," quod Conscience, "I wote no better leche
> Than persoun or parissh-prest, penytancere or bisshop,
> Saue Piers the Plowman, that hath powere ouer hem alle,
> And indulgence may do, but if dette lette it."

But then he gives in and admits a friar,[22] who proceeds to apply soothing plasters to the wounded. The army of Antichrist now renews its attack, and Conscience cries out for Contrition to keep the gate (B 20.375–77):

> "He lith and dremeth," seyde Pees, "and so do many other;
> The frere with his phisik this folke hath enchaunted,
> And plastred hem so esyly, thei drede no synne."

To this Conscience replies (B 20.378–84):

> "Be Cryste," quod Conscience tho, "I wil bicome a pilgryme,
> And walken as wyde as al the worlde lasteth,
> To seke Piers the Plowman, that Pryde may destruye,
> And that freres hadde a fyndyng, that for nede flateren,
> And contrepleteth me, Conscience; now Kynde me auenge,
> And sende me happe and hele til I haue Piers the Plowman!"
> And sitthe he gradde after grace, til I gan awake.

The poem thus ends with the search for Piers, and a prayer for Grace. The two are, in fact, now one: for Piers the Plowman is the custodian of Grace, the key to the salvation of man. The siege has resulted in the defeat of Unity, which Conscience is now forced to abandon in quest of Piers the Plowman, who alone can destroy Pride and restore Holy Church. Thus the poem's ending is not without hope, but in Conscience's cry for vengeance there remains the threat of Judgment.

But there is one feature of passus 20 which we have not considered, and which mitigates the severity of the poem's conclusion. I refer, of course, to the conversion of the Dreamer (B 20.182–212). The actual process of this conversion, as we have seen, has been under way since the beginning of the B-continuation, but its completion is not dramatized until the last passus. The Dreamer finds himself caught in the center of the conflict between the defenders of Unity and the army of Antichrist. Suddenly he sees Elde, Kinde, and Deth heading straight toward him. Elde overruns him and leaves his head bald (B 20.185–87):

> "Sire euel-ytauȝte Elde," quod I, "vnhende go with the!
> Sith whanne was the way ouer mennes hedes?
> Haddestow be hende," quod I, "thow woldest haue asked leue!"

Elde's "assault" on the Dreamer is next amusingly described. I can't escape the feeling that the poet here owes something to that famous description of old age, senility, and death in the twelfth chapter of Ecclesiastes.[23] *Remember now thy Creator in the days of thy youth, while the evil days come not, nor the years draw nigh, when thou shalt say, I have no pleasure in them.* Elde scorns the Dreamer and attacks him (20.188 ff.):

> "ȝe! leue lordeyne!" quod he, and leyde on me with age,
> And hitte me vnder the ere, vnethe may ich here;

(and all the daughters of musick shall be brought low . . .)

> He buffeted me aboute the mouthe, and bette out my tethe,

(and the grinders cease because they are few . . .)

> And gyued me in goutes, I may nouȝte go at large.

(and fears shall be in the way . . .)

> And of the wo that I was in, my wyf had reuthe,
> And wisshed ful witterly that I were in heuene.
> For the lyme that she loued me fore, and leef was to fele,
> On nyȝtes namely, whan we naked were,
> I ne myght in no manere maken it at hir wille,
> So Elde and she sothly hadden it forbeten.

(and the grasshopper shall be a burden, and desire shall fail. . . .)

When Elde has completed his assault, the Dreamer looks up and sees Kynde passing by and Deth drawing near. Now thoroughly frightened, he cries out to Kynde (20.201–2):

> "Loo! Elde the hoore hath me biseye,
> Awreke me, if ȝowre wille be, for I wolde ben hennes."

Kynde tells the Dreamer to go into Unity and there learn some craft. And when the Dreamer asks what craft is best to learn, Kynde tells him to learn to love. Finally, the Dreamer asks (20.208):

> "How shal I come to catel so, to clothe me and to fede?"

The Fool! The whole poem, from beginning to end, has been designed to answer that question. God will provide. But the difference here, of course, is that the Dreamer is now fully prepared to accept the answer. And so he comes into Unity, there to join those other "fools" who are still resisting the onslaughts of Antichrist. In the midst of this confused struggle, with its ominous threat of Doom, we have seen one man take the ridiculously simple step necessary for salvation. The "foolishness" of God surpasses the wisdom of men.

Six

———◆•••◆———

We have now examined the literary structure of the B-continuation, and have seen its relation to the A-text. But the B-poet did not merely attach his poem to the A-text; for there is considerable evidence of revision, A having been expanded from about 2,500 to about 3,200 lines in the corresponding passus of B. Furthermore, it is evident that the *Visio* and *Vita* of A are now treated as one poem, which in turn is joined to the B-continuation in such a way as to show that the poet wishes us to regard the whole poem, prologue and twenty passus, as a single work. Any study of the literary relations of the A and B texts of *Piers the Plowman,* therefore, must inevitably take into account the changes made by the B-poet in that portion of the text where the two versions run parallel.

But what are these changes? The answer to this question is by no means self-evident. For one thing, there is as yet no modern text of the B-version based on a critical study of all the manuscripts, and hence what looks like a revision in B may in fact be nothing more than an aberration of the nineteenth-century edition. This danger, fortunately, is not as great in Skeat's B-text as it is in his A and C texts. But it is very likely that our understanding of the B-text will be considerably facilitated when the new edition of *Piers the Plowman* is published.[1] On the other hand, we can avoid some

[165]

pitfalls by using the critical edition of the A-version which was published in 1952.[2] Hence I do not believe that the proposed analysis will be seriously impeded by defects in existing editions of the poem.

There is, however, a more serious problem involved in determining the B revisions of A, one which I fear will remain even after the publication of the new edition of all three texts. I refer to the presence in the B-version of textual irregularities that appear to have existed in the original from which all extant B manuscripts are derived. Several passages in the B-text, though they show no sign of purposeful revision, nevertheless differ from the A-text in remarkable ways. In some, the order of lines is jumbled; in others, lines or half-lines are skipped, and "fillers" are lifted from an adjacent passage and inserted, somewhat repetitiously, to plug the gap; elsewhere, passages of considerable length are omitted entirely, for no discernible literary reason. What is particularly striking about these irregularities is the fact that in many cases the A-text contains a repetition of word or phrase in adjacent lines which explains how the errors occurred. Such errors, in fact, are clearly scribal and should not be attributed to the poet himself. I therefore exclude them from the present literary analysis of the B-revision.[3]

Before beginning our analysis it will be well to review briefly the general nature and scope of the B-revision. We have already seen that the poet expands the A-text by about seven hundred lines. But it is interesting to note that his method of procedure differs in the two parts—or rather the two poems—of the A-text. The *Visio* is left virtually intact, and the revision of it is accomplished mainly by the insertion of new passages which, in some cases, are over one hundred lines long. The most extensive of these additions occurs in the prologue (B prol. 95–209), a passage which includes the famous Rat Parliament. But there are, also, a passage containing a mystical prophecy by Conscience and further refutation of Meed (B 3.297–349), a confession of Wrath, since this sin was not represented in A (B 5.134–87), an addition to the confession of Covetousness (B 5.232–303), another prefixed to the confession of Sloth

(B 5.392–448), and, finally, at the end of the confession scene, a closing prayer by Repentance (B 5.485–516).

On the other hand, our poet seems to have been more inclined to revise, cut, or even omit entirely parts of the *Vita* section of A. Wit's discussion of Inwit, fools, and helpless children (A 10.49–75) is thoroughly revised (B 9.59–91), and his definition of Do-wel, Do-bet, and Do-best is virtually replaced by a new one (B 9.92–106). The final definition of the triad in A (A 11.179–215) is almost completely rewritten (B 10.230–330). The poet, in short, appears to have been dissatisfied with many of the ideas expressed in the *Vita*.

One important feature of the B-revision is that it contains allusions to contemporary affairs in England in the late 1370's. An example of this is of course the Rat Parliament scene, which scholars have used in establishing the date of the B-text. A detailed review of the problem of dating would be out of place in the present analysis. But since we have suspected that there are possible allusions to the Peasants' Revolt in the B-continuation, it will be well to consider briefly whether or not the B revision of A contains any confirmation of this suspicion.

Considerable attention has been devoted in recent years to the problem of determining the date of the B-text.[4] And it is interesting to note that the tendency in modern scholarship, particularly the independent studies of Huppé and Bennett, has been toward accepting a date later than 1376–77, the period to which the composition of B has been traditionally assigned. One argument in support of a later date is based on the identification of the "cat," which the rats wanted to bell, as John of Gaunt. Hence the composition of the Rat Parliament scene would have to be after the death of Edward III in June, 1377, though how much later than this it would be difficult to say. But other evidence suggests that the date must at least be later than 1377. Bennett argues persuasively that the B-poet refers to the Great Schism of 1378 in his criticism of cardinals, very likely those French cardinals at Avignon who "presumed" to elect a pope (B prol. 107–9):

[167]

> Ac of the cardinales atte Courte that cauȝt of that name,
> And power presumed in hem a pope to make,
> To han that power that Peter hadde, inpugnen I nelle.

Surely this refers to the election of the antipope, Clement VII, and we must therefore conclude that these lines were written toward the end of 1378, if not later. Moreover, if Bennett is correct, the date of at least part of the B-text may be as late as 1381. He finds evidence for this in our poet's denunciation of the pope in a passage in the B-continuation (B 19.426–27, 439–42) which we have already considered. These lines, Bennett argues, are intended as criticism of the true pope, Urban VI, who is referred to as *the* pope (B 19.439), in contrast to Clement VII, who is presumably the one referred to as *a* pope (B prol. 108). Hence the poet clearly recognizes Urban as pope, though he feels free to criticize him for his warlike efforts against his enemies. Bennett concludes:

> Urban's proclamation of a crusade against the schismatics, in March 1381, must have caused [the poet] as much distress as the Schism itself. . . . [These lines] *may* have been written in the period between the proclamation of the crusade and the Peasants' Revolt, which is only grimly foreshadowed in the poem.[5]

Thus we see that the B-text has been dated, though with some hesitation, as late as March, 1381. And I suspect that scholars have been unwilling to assume a later date only because they have failed to perceive any reference to the Peasants' Revolt in June of the same year.[6] But could it not be that the very tensions created by the Revolt precluded an open reference to it? We should not demand, after all, that the poet refer explicitly to the Revolt itself. With this in mind I think we can see that the references to murder as a quenching of the flame of life (e.g., B 17.203–92) may well reflect the poet's deep distress at the violence and bloodshed of 1381.

Is there any evidence of the poet's concern over the Peasants' Revolt in the B-revision of A? I believe that there may be, though of course nothing can be cited as a direct allusion to the event.

Surely it is possible to read Conscience's ecstatic prophecy of the time when swords shall be beaten into plowshares (B 3.297–327) as relevant to this period. More telling, however, is the poet's softening of several passages that deal with violence. I refer, for example, to his revision of A's account of Saul's mission against the Amalekites (A 3.241–52; B 3.262–75), and his euphemistic paraphrase of Envy's desire to murder his neighbor (A 5.84; B 5.103).[7] Finally, one passage seems to me particularly suggestive of the Peasants' Revolt and highly reminiscent of the poet's criticism of violence in the B-continuation. This passage occurs in the B-poet's expansion of Hunger's advice on feeding the needy and poor (B 6.225–30):

> And alle maner of men that thow myȝte asspye,
> That nedy ben, and nauȝty, helpe hem with thi godis,
> Loue hem and lakke hem nouȝte, late god take the veniaunce;
> Theigh thei done yuel, late thow god y-worthe:—
>   *Michi vindictam, et ego retribuam.*
> And if thow wilt be graciouse to god, do as the gospel techeth,
> And biloue the amonges low men, so shaltow lacche grace.

Since Hunger is here referring to those who are genuinely in need, one might well ask, What is the vengeance which God is to take? And what is the evil which the needy have done? Surely this is advice directed at those who were advocating severe reprisals against the rebellious peasantry. As such it corresponds precisely to the poet's plea for the relighting of the flame of the Holy Ghost in the B-continuation (B 17.217 ff.).

Turning now to a more general survey of the B-revision, we need, first of all, to see whether the B-poet's criticism of the various ranks of society differs from that found in A, and whether this criticism accords with what we have found in the B-continuation. One of the first things that strikes the reader of the B-revision is the extent of its satirical horizon. King and pope (B 5.49–52), cardinal (B prol. 100–111), knight (B 6.47–51), archdeacon (B 2.172–76), and pardoner (B 5.648–49)—all receive attention from the poet. We even find some advice for beggars (B 7.71–88), though this passage seems less knowledgeable in its handling of the problem of begging and poverty in general than is the case in the A-text (cp. A 7.109–307; 8.67–88). There is, for example, no suggestion in A that needy beggars should solace themselves by reading the Lives of the Saints. Most significant, however, is the fact that the B-poet's satirical treatment of certain groups in the revision differs sharply from what we find in A, while at the same time it accords well with the attitudes and criticisms which we have already noted in the B-continuation. These differences are particularly evident in the reviser's treatment of lawyers, friars, the religious, and bishops.

Lawyers receive their share of criticism in the revision (B 4.31–43, 149–70), but an occasional passage appears which, while critical, seems to me more hortatory than satirical (e.g., B 4.171–81). The poet wishes to criticize the legal profession, but he seems more alert to its importance in the scheme of things, and he apparently does not wish to leave unmodified the severe and trenchant criticism of lawyers which we find in A. Most important, he will not condone the blanket condemnation of them on the grounds that they are learned men. Men of law had least share in Truth's pardon, according to A, "for lettride thei ben alle" (A 8.45). The B-poet cuts this sardonic statement out of the text in his revision.

In view of the villainous role of the friars in the continuation, it is not surprising to find that our poet expands on their deficiencies in the B-revision. One of the many criticisms of the friars introduced near the end of the poem was that parishioners, out of shame, went to friars for confession instead of to their parish priest (B 20.277–91). To this idea the B-poet recurs more than once in his revision of the confession of the Deadly Sins. Envy, for example, says that he would be confessed, if he dared for shame (B 5.91). Wrath tells us that he was at one time a friar who wished to please lords (B 5.141–42):

And now is fallen ther-of a frute, that folke han wel leuere
Schewen her schriftes to hem than shryue hem to her persones.

[170]

Sloth indulges himself at the expense of religious observances (B 5.416–18):

> And vigilies and fastyng-dayes, alle thise late I passe,
> And ligge abedde in lenten, an my lemman in myn armes,
> Tyl matynes and masse be do, and thanne go to the freres.

Other practices of the friars are also condemned (B 5.263–73), and an occasional line is inserted (e.g., B 6.74) to remind us of their shortcomings. They preach at St. Paul's out of pure envy of clerks (B 10.71–77), and, like itinerant minstrels, enjoy making themselves at home at other men's expense (B 10.92–93). But one of the most interesting of the poet's additions regarding the friars occurs at the beginning of the *Vita* section (B 8.14–17):

> For thei ben men on this molde that moste wyde walken,
> And knowen contrees, and courtes, and many kynnes places,
> Both prynces paleyses and pore mennes cotes,
> And Do-wel and Do-yuel, where thei dwelle bothe.

Now it is possible that this should be taken at its face value; but the mention of Do-wel and Do-yuel, and, in fact, the whole ironic A-context in which these lines occur, lead me to think that the poet is here imitating the tone of the A-version and that he is making an ironic effort to be fair to the friars. This interpretation is confirmed, I believe, by a revision he makes at the end of this scene. In A, the Dreamer takes his leave of the friars (A 9.50–52):

> "I bekenne the Crist, that on the crois deighede."
> And thei seide the same—"Save the fro myschaunce,
> And yive the grace on this grounde in good lif to ende."

The delightful touch of the last line, with its veiled invitation to the Dreamer to let the friars dispose of his estate (cf. B 11.52–83), is typical of the detached manner in which the satire on friars is handled in the A-text. This detachment, however, is too much for the B-poet, who revises the lines quoted so as to permit the Dreamer to hope for the reform of the friars (B 8.59–61):

"I bikenne the Cryst," quod he, "that on the crosse deyde."
And I seyde, "the same saue ʒow fro myschaunce,
And ʒiue ʒow grace on this grounde, good men to worthe."

Our poet senses the strategic advantage of imitating the relatively impersonal criticism of friars in the A-text, but, although he attempts a similar restraint, he is never entirely successful. His pronounced antagonism toward the friars will not allow it.

Another class that is subjected to criticism in the revision is the religious. But the form this criticism takes is quite distinct from that of the friars, and it is much less severe by comparison. Wrath, for example, in the confession scene, says that he has been among monks, but that he often fails in his purpose there, and is severely disciplined. Occasionally, he says, when wine is served in the evenings, he is able to tell tales of wickedness about the brethren (B 5.169–81). Aside from this confession of Wrath, there is but one other significant addition dealing with monks, and that appears in a passage containing the famous prophecy concerning the abbot of Abingdon, inserted near the end of the last passus of A (B 10.306–30). The prophecy itself, of course, accords well with our poet's conviction that the wealth and possessions of the Church are a form of spiritual poison.[8] Particularly interesting, however, is the intimate picture we get of one of these lordly religious at dinner (B 10.310–11):

And but if his knaue knele, that shal his cuppe brynge,
He loureth on hym and axeth hym, who tauʒte hym curteisye?

This stands in sharp contrast to the more general, "public" view of the religious that we find in A (A 11.208–13). The B-poet has evidently broken bread with some of these men.

But by far the most dramatic change wrought by the B-reviser in his criticisms of society is effected by his emphasis on the shortcomings of bishops. We have already had occasion to note that the A-text is almost totally lacking in criticism of the episcopate, and that the world of high religious office lies beyond the horizon of the A-poet. Such is clearly not the case in the B-text. Not only do we find criticism of the lordliness of bishops (B 4.124–25), but our poet even seems reluctant to acknowledge their function as correctors of the priesthood, a function stressed in Truth's pardon to bishops in A (A 8.13–19; cp. B 7.13–17).

The reason for this attitude toward bishops appears in part to be the poet's scorn for their life of ease and complacency. Bishops are evidently among those wealthy lords who pay jesters to entertain them while the poor cry at the gate (B 10.79–91). Severe criticism of this kind is very striking, especially if the reader recalls the deferential treatment of bishops in A, where they are the "rose" of the triad, supported by the "brier" of the clergy and the "root" of the commons. This entire simile is removed by the B-poet, and the passage which replaces it includes sharp criticism of the episcopate. But even this passage pales when compared with Clergy's definition of Do-best in the last passus of the revision (B 10.256–90). This is truly a remarkable example of the B-poet's hostility toward bishops. In effect what Clergy says is, Let him who is without sin reprove; in seeing the mote in thy brother's eye, do not overlook the beam in thine own; physician, heal thyself! Surely our poet is a man who has felt the sting of a bishop's reproof, or, what is more likely, for some other reason has a personal antagonism toward a particular prelate. Especially striking in this connection are Clergy's remarks, amplifying his advice to bishops to heal themselves (B 10.272–73):

> For goddis worde wolde nou3t be loste, for that worcheth euere;
> If it auailled nou3t the comune, it my3te auaille 3owseluen.

Surely this is a pointed and ironic personal allusion. And, strange as it seems,[9] the passage may possibly refer to the words of Thomas Brunton, Bishop of Rochester, popular champion of the poor and an important figure in governmental affairs. In one of his sermons (no. 101), according to Sister Mary Aquinas Devlin, he attacks the evils of English society and says that "he is discouraged, for although he has preached continually for ten years in his diocese, he has not seen one person rise effectively from sin." [10] The lines quoted above (B 10.272–73) certainly appear to be a direct response to this observation. Bishop Brunton's sermon was delivered at Cobham, probably on July 22, 1382. As we have seen, there is nothing to prevent the supposition that at least part of the B-text may have been written during this time.

But why should the B-poet be angry with Brunton? The two men had many ideas in common.[11] One possible explanation is that the bishop was present at and assented to the condemnation of John Wyclif in May, 1382,[12] shortly before he delivered the sermon referred to above. It is to be doubted that the B-poet assented to all the teachings of the famous Oxford reformer; but Wyclif's influence on the poem (e.g., B 15.513 ff.) has long been recognized, and Brunton's acquiescence in the condemnation must have been a bitter disappointment to many of the reformer's friends, since both Wyclif and Brunton had often attacked the same evils in contemporary society. It is therefore quite possible that our poet is thinking of the condemners of Wyclif, especially the bishop of Rochester, when he says (B 10.284): "For-thi, ȝe corectoures, claw-eth her-on, and corecteth fyrst ȝow-seluen."

There is evidence elsewhere in *Piers the Plowman* to suggest that the poet's expression of hostility toward bishops is occasional, rather than a blanket condemnation. I refer to a passage added to the original B-text in passus 15,[13] where the poet cites, as a model for all bishops, St. Thomas à Becket, Archbishop of Canterbury, who was martyred in 1170. He then adds (B 15.554–56):

> Holy cherche is honoured heyȝliche thoruȝ his deynge;
> He is a forbysene to alle bishopes, and a briȝt myroure,
> And souereyneliche to suche that of Surrye bereth the name.

Skeat sensed that this was a personal allusion, and I think he was right: the bishop "who bears the name of Syria," and who, as these lines suggest, imitated the example of St. Thomas, was almost certainly Simon Sudbury, Archbishop of Canterbury, murdered by a mob in London at the height of the Peasants' Revolt in June, 1381.[14] The tribute to Sudbury is especially significant when we recall that it was this archbishop who, despite considerable pressure, managed to avoid a condemnation of the teachings of John Wyclif. We may conclude, therefore, that the B-poet's criticism of bishops is of a very special order, and that a careful reading of this criticism reveals he may well be taking sides in the controversies raging around Wyclif during the period 1378–82.

From the poet's treatment of the various ranks and offices of society in the fourteenth century we must now turn to consider briefly a more general question regarding the structure of the B-revision. Is there any evidence of preparation early in the B-text for what is to come later on in the continuation? Fortunately, an affirmative answer to this question has been provided by Nevill Coghill, in his interesting lecture on the pardon of Piers Plowman.[15] Hence it will not be necessary to go over this ground again. But there are a few "foretastes," as Professor Coghill aptly calls them, hitherto unnoticed, which deserve mention. Some of these are little more than hints of what is to come. The Dreamer's perverse reaction to the reasonableness of the animals, for example, dramatized in the B-continuation (B 11.315–66), is briefly foreshadowed in the B-revision of the *Vita* (B 8.52–56); and a faint hint of the B-poet's alteration of the meaning of Do-wel is likewise provided (B 8.125–26). More extensive are the additions which point toward the Creation (B 9.33–47) and the later treatment of the Trinity (B 10.230–48).

From the point of view of literary method, however, the most interesting change comes at the very end of the A-text. The original conclusion of the A text was (A 11.301–3):

> Souteris and seweris, suche lewide jottis,
> Percen with a *pater noster* the paleis of hevene,
> Withoute penaunce, at here partyng, in-to the heighe blisse.

[175]

But the B-poet changes this to read (B 10.460–64):

> Souteres and shepherdes, suche lewed Iottes,
> Percen with a *pater-noster* the paleys of heuene,
> And passen purgatorie penaunceles at her hennes-partynge,
> In-to the blisse of paradys for her pure byleue,
> That inparfitly here knewe and eke lyued.

And he goes on for ten more lines to point out that clerks of Holy Church often wish they knew nothing but *Pater Noster* and creed, for those in positions of responsibility can fall deeper into sin than ignorant men. At one time I resented this watering down of A's dramatic ending, but of course it should have been obvious that the B-poet had no choice. His firm belief in the value of learning demanded that something be done to blur the effect of A's sharp condemnation of it, and his revision of the ending of the *Vita* admirably serves this purpose. The reader is now prepared for Imaginatif's defense of learning (B 12.72 ff.), and the change in the first line from "seweris" to "shepherdes" forecasts the argument in support of learning based on the appearance of both shepherds and the Magi at Christ's birth in Bethlehem (B 12.141–55). The delicacy with which the poet manages the transition from the A-text to the B-continuation is indeed worthy of our admiration.

There is, finally, one other aspect of the B-revision of A which we need to consider, and that is the extent to which the revised text throws light on the character, position, and interests of the B-poet himself. It will be recalled that the continuation, with its defense of learning, and its affirmation of the necessity of the priesthood in the scheme of salvation, tends to support the idea that the author himself may have been a ranking member of the secular clergy. The B-revision, as we shall see, confirms this impression to a remarkable degree.

It should first be understood that our poet is no clerical apologist. The B-version of *Piers the Plowman* abounds in criticism of the priesthood, and some of the most severe passages occur in the revision. Priests are worldly and lacking in devotion (B prol. 95–99).

They get into controversies with the friars, and become so wrathful that they lose all spirituality (B 5.143–52; cp. B 11.84–102). Especially reprehensible is their ignorance. Here the difference between the A and B texts is very striking. In the former, a priest is made the symbol of learning in the pardon scene, and then condemned on that basis in the *Vita*. In the B-text, however, priests are condemned for precisely the opposite reason. We have seen them reprimanded for their ignorance in the continuation (e.g., B 11.289–308); and it is therefore not surprising that we also find this same criticism in the revision, appropriately inserted as an addition to the confession of Sloth (B 5.422–28). Finally, the B-poet adds a very interesting critique of the priesthood near the end of the *Vita* (B 10.390–413). He takes as his text the verse used ironically in A: *The scribes and the Pharisees sit in Moses' seat* (Matt. 23:2). Learned men and clerks, he says, often fail to practice what they preach. God grant that the teachers of Holy Church do not perish like the carpenters who built Noah's ship! And he concludes (B 10.411–13):

> At domes-day the diluuye worth of deth and fyr at ones;
> For-thi I conseil ȝow clerkes, of holy cherche the wriȝtes,
> Wercheth ȝe werkes as ȝe seen i-write, lest ȝe worth nauȝt ther-inne.

Severe as this passage is, with its threat of damnation, its tone can be clearly distinguished from the criticism of all the other ranks which we have considered. Particularly instructive is the comparison between the teachers of Holy Church and Noah's carpenters. Just as the carpenters were necessary for Noah's salvation, so are curates necessary for the salvation of "Christ's own beasts." Thus the function of the secular clergy is exalted, while the plowmen and shepherds extolled in the A-text become the dumb animals taken into Noah's ark! Yet at the same time the lesson is plain: the carpenters were drowned in the waters of the flood; the clergy are in danger of drowning in the lake which burneth with fire and brimstone.

Besides the additions which contain direct criticism of the secular clergy, the B-poet inserts passages which reflect priestly interests and concerns. An outstanding example of this is his revision of the confession scene in passus 5. We have already had occasion to observe the poet's dissatisfaction with this scene in our analysis of the confession of Haukyn (B 14), where the role of the confessor (Patience) is given the attention that the author felt it deserved. Similarly, in the revision of A's confession scene, the role of the confessor (Repentance) is given much greater emphasis. Covetousness, for example, is examined by Repentance in a dialogue containing both penetrating satire and high comedy (B 5.232–303). At the same time, this passage stresses the importance of restitution (*redde quod debes*) and the greatness of God's mercy, both of which, as we have seen, are of the utmost importance in the B-continuation.

Another such addition is to be found near the end of Glutton's confession (B 5.371–85). Repentance orders Glutton to make explicit confession of his sins (dramatized at the tavern in the A-text), and, when he does so, Repentance observes (B 5.385): "This shewyng shrifte . . . shal be meryte to the." Surely this is the language of the confessional. In A, the confession of the Deadly Sins is public and dramatic; in B, it is private and admonitory. By this shift in emphasis our poet calls attention to the importance of the priesthood in the sacrament of penance, and simultaneously prepares the reader for the necessity of restitution which is to be stressed in the continuation. The whole scene is then brought to an end with a prayer by the confessor (Repentance) for the forgiveness of sins, and a preview of the Redemption, admirable preparation for the biblical drama which is to come. Thus the B-version of the confession scene is a perfect illustration of our poet's skill in revision, as well as a confirmation of his firm belief in the importance of the priesthood.

To say that the B-poet considered the priesthood necessary for man's salvation, however, is perhaps merely stating the obvious. It is true that there were some angry men of the time who might minimize the importance of the secular clergy in the manner of the A-text of *Piers the Plowman,* but surely the majority of people recognized the necessity and importance of their sacramental function. In order to see how the B-revision reveals the touch of a priestly author, therefore, we need to look for evidence of a more distinctive kind.

One of the evidences of clerical authorship in the B-revision is what might be called a kind of hypersensitiveness in the poet's modification of some of the anticlerical passages in A. It will be recalled that one of the criticisms which seem to have haunted the B-poet especially is the denunciation of avaricious chaplains (A 1.153–73), which reaches a sarcastic climax in these lines (A 1.169–71): [16]

> Ye curatours that kepe yow clene of your bodies,
> Ye ben acumbrid with coveitise, ye conne not out crepe,
> So harde hath avarice haspide yow togideris!

Now we know that the B-poet is unsparing in his criticism of the covetousness of priests; but these merciless lines must have seemed too all-embracing. He therefore revises them very slightly (B 1.193–95):

> Many curatoures kepen hem clene of here bodies,
> Thei ben acombred with coueitise, thei konne nouʒt don it
>   fram hem,
> So harde hath auarice yhasped hem togideres.

Thus we see that many curates, though not all, are encumbered with covetousness, and that this covetousness is a serious problem ("thei konne nouʒt don it fram hem"), and is not something to be laughed at ("Ye conne not out crepe").

Similar evidences of the poet's concern for a truer expression of the priestly life are to be found scattered throughout his revision. When the A-text cites courtesy as a desideratum of the clergy, B reiterates the need for the eradication of covetousness (B 4.119). A's ironic condemnation of "clerkis and kete men" (A 11.56) becomes "clerkes and other kynnes men" (B 10.69). Such minor revisions are not carried to extremes, nor does the poet blunt the sharp point of every satiric reference to priests in the A-text with a dogged pedantry, but enough of these minor changes occur to testify to the reviser's painful awareness of the A-poet's denunciation of the secular clergy.[17] No such evidence of revision exists with respect to the other groups of contemporary society satirized in the A-text.

Another striking difference between the A and B versions of *Piers the Plowman* can be seen in their respective treatments of marriage. It will be recalled that the position of marriage is considerably lower in the B-continuation than it is in A. The poet's revision of Wit's discourse is, as we might have expected, in complete accord with this devaluation of matrimony. Whereas in A God is pleased first and foremost with true wedded folk (A 10.127 ff.), in B we find that although those who marry do well, nevertheless we should remember that wedded folk have their heaven on earth (B 9.107–17). It is of course impossible to say whether this attitude toward marriage supports the hypothesis of clerical authorship. But it is interesting to note that the B-poet seems largely dependent on A's discussion of marriage (A 10.135–98), and can add no satirical touches of his own in amplification of the joyless and jangling couples so colorfully depicted in the A-text. In fact, such additions as we do find in B are typical pastoral admonition, with an orientation quite different from that of A (B 9.158–59):

> For goode shulde wedde goode, though hij no good hadde;
> "I am *via et veritas*," seith Cryst, "I may auaunce alle."

This pastoral tone is frequently evident in the B-revision of the *Vita* (e.g., B 9.74–78).

One of the most interesting passages, in its revelation of the B-poet's attitude toward marriage, occurs near the end of the discussion of wedded folk just considered (B 9.177–83). This passage, moreover, seems written almost as a direct reply to an earlier one in A (A 10.87 ff.), in which Wit advises the Dreamer to remain in his present status (Do-wel), and not covet to climb. This A-passage appears in Wit's definition of the triad, which is immediately followed by the praise of wedded folk (A 10.127 ff.). We have already speculated on the possible biographical significance of this (chapter 1), and it is not difficult to see Wit's subsequent praise of marriage as having a direct relation to his advice to remain in the status of the commons (Do-wel). With this is mind, the B-passage sounds very much like a direct reply to A's argument for marriage (B 9.177–83):

> And euery maner seculer that may nouȝt continue,
> Wysly go wedde and war hym fro synne;
> For leccherye in likyng is lymeȝerde of helle.
> Whiles thow art ȝonge and thi wepne kene,
> Wreke the with wyuynge, ȝif thow wilt ben excused.
> *Dum sis vir fortis ne des tua robora scortis;*
> *Scribitur in portis: meretrix est ianua mortis.*

This advice is, of course, derived from St. Paul (1 Cor. 7:9), but its tone is unusual and distinctive. Surely these are the words of a practicing celibate! Note particularly the ironic use of the word "wisely." I am reminded of the confirmed ascetic, who once remarked that he supposed men got married because they were afraid to sleep alone at night.

It is possible, although I do not insist on it, to find confirmation of the poet's attitude toward marriage in a certain suggestion of antifeminism observable in the B-text. We have already noted this phenomenon in the B-continuation, attested, for example, by the antifeminist turn in the poet's development of the *de casibus* theme (B 12.47–52). Similar touches are evident in the B-revision of A. Lot was encumbered by women as well as wine (B 1.32–33); Lady Meed defends lechery as well as writing in windows (B 3.51–58); and nun, abbess, and prioress are mercilessly condemned in the confession of Wrath (B 5.153–68). Particularly striking is the classification of widows and maidens with fools and madmen (B 9.66–73). The poet evidently felt a need for authoritative support here, for he adds (B 9.71–73):

[181]

Of this matere I myȝte make a longe tale,
And fynde fele witnesses amonges the foure doctours,
And that I lye nouȝt of that I lere the, Luke bereth witnesse.

The poet evidently feels that this wave of the hand is sufficient for the reader to recognize his authorities, yet scholars have had trouble identifying them.[18] Perhaps we can never be sure; but I suspect that number one in this hypothetical list is Jerome, *Against Jovinian,* that famed treasury of antifeminist arguments used with such ironic effectiveness by the Wife of Bath in the *Canterbury Tales.*

Last of all, there are, in the B-revision of A, occasional passages that seem to be highly personal reflections or allusions. We have observed passages of this type in the B-continuation, and it is therefore not surprising to find similar lines inserted by the B-poet in his revision. Such, for example, is the meditation on sin in the revised *Vita* (B 10.431–41) which, though it anticipates the argument of Peace in the continuation (B 18.204–27), is nevertheless very similar in tone to the gloomy meditation of Soul (B 15.340 ff.). More significant, however, are the insertions which confirm the impression that our author is familiar with and sympathetic toward the wealthy, especially secular lords. Of course it is true, as with the priesthood, that the poet severely criticizes the rich (B 10.24–31, 78–91), and affirms patient poverty as the ideal (B 10.337–44); but although he frequently echoes A's attitude (e.g., A 8.162 ff.), he sometimes reveals in his revisions that, unlike A, he can exhort the wealthy in a very intimate way (B 10.361–63):

It shal bisitten vs ful soure, the siluer that we kepen,
And owre bakkes that moth-eten be, and sen beggers go naked,
Or delyte in wyn and wylde foule, and wote any in defaute.

It should be understood that the poet does not necessarily imply that he himself is wealthy when he refers to "the siluer that we kepen." On the other hand, these lines clearly exhibit the rhetoric of the corrector who diplomatically includes himself among those who are in need of correction. Our poet, in short, is here admonishing rich lords in a very friendly and personal manner.

The B-poet's familiarity with and respect for wealthy lords is quite evident in his revision. Even where he follows and develops A's criticism of the rich, he will occasionally introduce modifications of language which reveal his sensitive reaction to the severity of A's condemnation. The A-text, for example, reads (A 11.61):

> For now is iche boy bold, and he be riche . . .

Note especially the satiric, disrespectful use of "boy" as applied to the wealthy. The B-poet revises this line as follows (B 10.101):

> I haue yherde hiegh men etyng atte table . . .

We are inevitably reminded here of the poet's similar modification of A's satirical lines on avaricious chaplains (A 1.164 ff.).

In addition to the evidence of respect for the wealthy, the B-revision likewise contains lines and passages revealing our author's familiarity with the way of life of secular lords. Students of *Piers the Plowman* have long been impressed by his description of life in the medieval castle (B 10.94–100):

> Elyng is the halle vche daye in the wyke,
> There the lorde ne the lady liketh nouȝte to sytte.
> Now hath vche riche a reule to eten bi hym-selue
> In a pryue parloure for pore mennes sake,
> Or in a chambre with a chymneye, and leue the chief halle,
> That was made for meles, men to eten inne;
> And al to spare to spille that spende shal an other.

But what has apparently been overlooked is the extent to which further passages in the revision attest the poet's interest in other, less well-known aspects of the life of the secular aristocracy. The religious, for example, "steleth lordes almesses" (B 10.298), and take land which the lord should rightfully pass on to his heirs (B 10.312–13).[19] One other passage of this kind is particularly interesting. It occurs in the poet's expansion of Wit's discussion of Kynde (A 10.27–37; B 9.26–47), which, as we have seen, prepares us for the Creation section of the B-continuation. Here the B-poet pauses to comment on the text, *Dixit, et facta sunt,* and offers the following analogy (B 9.38–40):

> Riȝte as a lorde sholde make lettres, and hym lakked parchemyn,
> Though he couth write neuere so wel, ȝif he had no penne,
> The lettres for al the lordship, I leue, were neuere ymaked.

Thus it can be seen that the B-revision is of great value, both in confirming our reading of the B-continuation and in providing additional hints about the background, station, and interests of the author. In summary, the B-revision of A confirms our suspicion that the poem may not have been completed until some time after the Peasants' Revolt; reveals a shift in emphasis in its criticism of the ranks of society; prepares us in various ways for developments to come in the B-continuation; and, finally, offers further evidence in support of the hypothesis that our author is a ranking member of the secular clergy, and a man intimately acquainted with the life of wealthy lords.

Seven

ABOUT THE AUTHOR

Readers familiar with the conventional biography of "William Langland," putative author of *Piers the Plowman,* will have observed that this biography accords not at all with the inferences we have drawn concerning the author of the B-text in our analysis of the poem. One reason for this is the fact that the poet's life has been reconstructed largely from the character of his Dreamer. Now it should be recognized that the role of the dreamer-narrator, or "fallible first person singular," as Professor Donaldson so aptly terms it,[1] is used with great flexibility in medieval literature, so that it would be a mistake rigidly to exclude the Dreamer in *Piers* from any discussion of the author. As a matter of fact, we have seen this very flexibility operative in the B-continuation. In the section dealing with *Spes* (Moses), for example, the Dreamer is used briefly as an "extra" in the biblical drama (B 17.23–46); and in the first passus of the continuation, he serves as a spokesman for the author (B 11.71 ff.).

On the other hand, to suppose that the behavior of the Fool-Dreamer is in any way intended to depict the actual life of the author is, to say the least, extremely rash. Yet this supposition is rampant in *Piers Plowman* criticism. The highly respected arguments of R. W. Chambers are absolutely dependent on it.[2] It is not my purpose to discuss this question here. I will merely state my belief that the biography of William Langland, reconstructed from the literary character of the Dreamer, has perhaps done more to prevent an accurate reading of *Piers the Plowman* than any other single thing in the stormy history of criticism of the poem. Let us hear no more about Long Will walking the streets of London and refusing to reverence wealthy lords and ladies.

At the same time, however, though the methods of the Langland biographers are open to criticism, their motivation in seeking to know the author, to identify him, is understandable and above reproach. Our study of the literary relations of the A and B texts of *Piers the Plowman* has shown, I believe, how insistently the personality of the author, of whichever version, thrusts itself upon the reader. The B-text, particularly, reveals to us a learned man, a member of the secular clergy, a fearless opponent of corruption in and out of the Church, a friend of the aristocracy, and a relentless opponent of the friars. The question ought not to be resisted: Who is this man?

Of course it may be that we will never certainly identify the author of any of the versions of *Piers the Plowman*. But I suspect that the B-poet, at least, was in all probability a man very much like John Trevisa, Vicar of Berkeley and chaplain to Thomas Lord Berkeley in the second half of the fourteenth century.[3] Little is known of Trevisa's early life, but the name, of course, is Cornish (*Trev-isa, Trev-issa,* "the lower town"); it is generally assumed that his family was from Cornwall and that Trevisa himself was born there around 1342. We know that he died in 1402. The two most distinctive facts in the life of Trevisa are, first, that he was a student at Oxford and, second, that he was Vicar of Berkeley in Gloucestershire.

There is considerable evidence concerning Trevisa's residency at Oxford.[4] He was at Exeter College from Lent, 1362, until the winter of 1365. During the period 1369–78 he was a Fellow of Queen's, and was expelled from that college in 1378, apparently as the result of a controversy between the provost and a group of the scholars, including Trevisa.[5] This expulsion, however, was apparently not permanent, for records indicate that he subsequently paid room rent for the years 1382–86 and 1394–96. The fact that Trevisa was Vicar of Berkeley is likewise well attested, but the date of his accession to that office is not certain.[6] He was not ordained priest until June 8, 1370.[7] In any case we know that he was chaplain to Thomas IV (1368–1417) for the rest of his life, and was, in all probability, buried in his own parish church of St. Mary the Virgin, Berkeley, in 1402. One other fact is worthy of note: Trevisa also held a nonresident canonry in the Collegiate Church of Westbury-on-Trym, in Gloucestershire.[8]

John Trevisa is known to students of English literature almost exclusively as a translator. Perhaps one of the earliest of his works, though the date is not known, was his translation of the *Defensio Curatorum,* a sermon delivered before the pope by Richard Fitzralph, Archbishop of Armagh, which contains a severe indictment of the friars.[9] Fitzralph suffered defeat in his controversy with the friars, and died in 1360, but his arguments continued to provide ammunition for the defenders of the secular clergy in the following decades, as *Piers the Plowman* reveals.[10] Another work translated by Trevisa, the anonymous *Dialogus inter Militem et Clericum,*[11] is a witty satire in which a knight attempts to persuade a clerk that the church should have no control over temporalities. Trevisa seems also to have been responsible for a prose translation of the *Gospel of Nicodemus,* preserved in two manuscripts, one of them with notes by the indefatigable John Shirley.[12]

One of the most important of Trevisa's works is his translation of Ranulf Higden's *Polychronicon,* an omnibus history mentioned above in my analysis of the B-continuation. Higden's original Latin text, together with the translation by Trevisa and another by an anonymous fifteenth-century translator, appears in the nine-volume edition published in the Rolls Series, 1865–86. We can only guess when Trevisa began this impressive task; but we know—for he tells us himself—that he completed it in 1387.[13] The only other work of comparable scope is a translation of the *De Proprieta-tibus Rerum* of Bartholomew Anglicus. This appears to have been the last of Trevisa's accomplishments, for he informs us that he completed it in 1398. One other work, however, may have been completed during this period, and that is his translation of the *De Regimine Principum* of Ægidius Romanus. Reference should also be made, finally, to two traditions frequently mentioned in accounts of the translator's life. One is that he had the Apocalypse inscribed on the roof and walls of his chapel in Berkeley Castle; the other is the curiously persistent belief that he made a translation of the Bible.[14]

The known facts of John Trevisa's life are not inconsistent with what we have deduced concerning the author of the B-text of *Piers the Plowman*. He is a learned man, a priest, and his position as chaplain to the renowned and influential Thomas Lord Berkeley accords well with what we have seen to be the attitude of the B-poet toward the rich. He is not subservient, but his advice to wealthy lords is often formulated in very diplomatic terms. Furthermore, as we have seen, he occasionally gives us intimate glimpses of aristo-cratic life. One is reminded particularly of the simile, referred to in the preceding chapter, that describes the lord who, lacking his pen, cannot write letters, for all his lordship.

Similarly, the fact that Trevisa was a fellow of Queen's College, Oxford, during the stormy period of the Wycliffite controversy, is in agreement with the echoes of that controversy observable in the B-text. Unfortunately we do not know as much as one might wish about Trevisa's life at Oxford, but we may be sure that he was not so fully occupied with his studies as to be unaware of the storms raging around him there during the time of his residency. We have already seen that he was involved in at least one dispute with the provost, though we know only that he and his colleagues were dis-missed "for their unworthiness" (*exigentibus demeritis*) and were accused of refusing to restore to the provost certain charters, books, jewels, etc., in their possession.[15] It is apparently impossible to determine whether this affair was simply an administrative quarrel, or whether it was generated by the larger issues (e.g., Wyclif, the friars) then being debated in the university.[16]

Besides the general relevance to the B-text of Trevisa's life at Berkeley [17] and Oxford, one other feature of his biography is of interest in relation to the poem. Trevisa is known to have traveled on the Continent, specifically in Germany and Savoy, as he himself tells us in one of his additions to the text of the *Polychronicon*.[18] Now students of *Piers the Plowman* have noted references in the B-version to places in Europe, as, for example, Pampiloun (B 17.252) and Rochmadore (B 12.37), and efforts have been made to explain some of these references so as to square them with the prevailing notion of the humble station of the author.[19] The unspoken assumption seems to be that the poet is unlikely to have been on the Continent, and that these place names must have some relevance to England, or London in particular. This may be all there is to it. But I must confess that I am intrigued by Covetousness' (or Haukyn's) admission that he can't be comforted by mass or matins while his servants are overseas at Bruges or in Prussia (B 13.392 ff.). And who is the "penaunt for his synnes" (B 4.133) who should be permitted to bear silver overseas? What is the basis of the B-poet's interest in "wederwise shipmen" (B 15.349 ff.)? [20]

Interesting as such questions may be, however, they cannot be considered apart from Trevisa's translations, and hence we must now try to determine the extent to which these works can shed light on *Piers the Plowman*. Scholars have already made use of Fitzralph's sermon against the friars in explicating the B-continuation, and on this point I have nothing to add. The common interests of the B-poet and the translator of Fitzralph should be obvious enough. Similarly, Trevisa's prose translation of the Gospel of Nicodemus is consonant with the B-poet's interest in the Harrowing of Hell, dramatized in B passus 18. Perhaps this is all that can be said.[21]

Concerning the alleged translation of the Bible it is difficult to speak, because we don't know whether Trevisa actually made one or not. I certainly doubt that he made an independent translation of his own at the request of Thomas Lord Berkeley. Possibly he was one of the translators of the earlier Wycliffite Bible at Oxford in the 1370's. Whatever may be the truth of this, however, we have seen that the B-poet is quite familiar with the Bible, and that he uses it, not merely as a treasury of texts designed to illuminate doctrine, but as a history of the unfolding of God's plan for the salvation of man. The B-continuation is, in fact, based on the Bible, from Genesis to Revelation. Hence we can conclude, I think, that if Trevisa did indeed translate the Bible this fact would not be in-consistent with what we know about the B-poet's use of it.[22] The same can be said of the Apocalypse inscribed on the walls and ceil-ing of Berkeley chapel. We are reminded of the importance of the Apocalypse in the last two passus of the B-continuation.

Of course it is difficult, in discussing Trevisa's translation of Fitzralph, the Gospel of Nicodemus, and perhaps the Bible, to do anything more than indicate areas of general interest. Fortunately, however, we have considerable evidence concerning his particular views, on many subjects, in his translation of Ranulf Higden's *Polychronicon*. In this translation Trevisa inserted numerous com-ments of his own, usually prefixed by his name, and varying in length from one sentence to rather long paragraphs, designed to explicate, correct, or comment on the Latin text of Higden. Some of these "Treuisa" insertions merely confirm our impression concern-ing the translator's general interests; others offer noteworthy parallels to the B-text of *Piers the Plowman;* and a few reveal in a very intimate way certain attitudes and opinions of Trevisa which seem very close to those which we have associated with the B-poet.

It will be well, first, to cite a few passages from the *Polychronicon* which indicate the range of Trevisa's general interests, and, at the same time, illustrate the incisiveness and the occasional trenchant irony of his style. In Book I, chapter 24, Higden tells about the two philosophers, Praxitellus and Fibia, who walked naked in Rome.

When the Emperor asks them why they do this, they explain that it is because they have forsaken all things. At this point Trevisa inserts one of his comments (I, 227–29): [23]

> *Treuisa.* Þe firste poynt of þis doynge and answere techeþ þat who forsakeþ all þyng forsakeþ all his cloþes; and so it foloweþ þat þey þat beeþ wel i-cloþed and gooþ aboute and beggeþ and gadereþ money and corn and catel of oþer men forsakeþ nouȝt al þing.

The ironical reference to the friars in this passage should be obvious enough.[24]

In another passage in the first book, Higden mentions St. Patrick's Purgatory. Whoever suffers the pains of that purgatory, he reports, shall never suffer the pains of Hell, unless he die finally without repentance. Here is Trevisa's comment on this (I, 363):

> *Treuisa.* Þei þis sawe myȝt be sooth, it is but a iape. For no man þat dooþ dedely synne schal be i-saued, but he be verrey repentaunt, what sommeuer penaunce he doo; and euery man that is verray repentaunt at his lifes ende of al his mysdedes, he schal be sikerliche i-saued and haue þe blisse of heuene, þey he neuere hire speke of Patrik his purgatorie.

In Book III, chapter 12, Higden sets forth the views of the philosopher Zeno, including his belief that the soul dies with the body. Again our translator departs from his text (III, 217):

> *Treuisa.* I wolde a wiseman hadde y-seie his water, and i-held it in his þrote þey it were a galoun.

Trevisa seems to have had reservations about the spirituality of the religious. This opinion shows up frequently in his additions. At one point Higden describes the reform of the Church by King Edgar, and tells how this king removed "clerks that lived in outrage," and put monks in their place (VI, 463):

> *Treuisa.* In þat, save reverens of Edgar, he was lewedlich i-meoved, while þere were oþer clerkes þat lyvede wel i-now.

Higden also refers to the fact that, when Odo was appointed Archbishop of Canterbury, he became a monk in order to conform to tradition and to receive the honor of this high office in a holy manner (VII, 5):

> *Treuisa.* Odo was lewedliche i-meoved þerfore to make hym a monk, ffor Crist, ne non of alle his postles, was nevere monk nor frere.

Later on in Higden we read the story of Paternus, a monk, who predicted the burning of his monastery, and, when the time came, burned to death in the fire "for love of martyrdom" (VII, 205):

> *Treuisa.* In þat doynge Paternus the monk semeþ a lewed goost, þat kouþe not y-knowe þe cause and þe circumstaunce of verray martirdom; for þere is no verrey ma[r]tirdom bot it be by meynteninge of truþe and wiþstondynge of wrong and of synne. Bote God graunte, ȝif it is in his wille, þat Paternus be nouȝt i-dampned for his blynde devocioun.

Finally, Higden tells how Archbishop Baldwin advanced the fortunes of the secular clergy at the expense of monks, and expresses surprise that the Archbishop, who was himself a monk, would prefer men of more imperfect life, secular canons, instead of men of more perfect life. And he adds: "For somtyme holy princes and bisshops in Englond wolde nouȝt have to menye of suche manere clerkes, and ȝeve hem choys wheþer þey wolde leve here benefice oþer chaunge hir lyf and goo into religioun." To this Trevisa replies as follows (VIII, 127–29):

> *Treuisa.* It semeþ þat Baldewyn was wel avised þat Crist was heed of holy cherche, and his apostles hyȝe bisshopes, and non of hem alle was noþer monk noþer frere; and so it myȝte seme þat he knewe wel þat oþer clerkes were more profit þan evere was monk oþer frere. Bote for it is i-seide þat þe clerkes hadde choys wheþer þey wolde leve her benefice oþer goo into religioun, of þat choys it myȝte seme grete wonder; for it semeþ þerby þat þey schulde leve her benefice how it evere were; for ȝif þei ȝede nouȝt into religioun þey schulde leve her benefice, and ȝif þey ȝede into religioun þe[y] moste leve þe benefice by þe rule of religioun, oþer þey spekeþ oþerwise of religioun þan alle men in comyn speche wolde mene, and so it semeþ more wonder of þat wonder þan of his menynge. But me wolde wondre þat Baldewyn, þat was a monk, wolde nouȝt flatre wiþ monkes, but helde oþer clerkes more holy þan monkes syth he knew the degre of eyther.

Perhaps the examples given above will be sufficient to indicate Trevisa's general interests, opinions, and mode of expression in his additions to the *Polychronicon* translation. There are, however, other passages which are more directly and specifically related to *Piers the Plowman*. The story of the poisoning of Holy Church by the donation of Constantine, for example, referred to in the B-continuation (B 15.519–23), is also to be found in Higden's *Polychronicon* (V, 131):

> Perfor it is i-write þat whann Constantyn hadde i-made þat ȝifte to chirches, þanne þe olde enemy (*hostis antiquus*) cryde openliche in þe ayer, "Þis day is venym i-hilde and i-schad in holy chirche." Perfore Ierom in vitis patrum seiþ, "Seþþe holy chirche encresede in possessiouns it haþ decresed as in virtues."

In the poem, of course, the speaker is an angel, whereas Trevisa, following Higden, identifies him as the "olde enemy." [25] There is no comment on the story at this point in the translation. On the other hand, Trevisa later refers back to this story in a very interesting insertion. Higden, describing the reforms of King Edgar, tells how the king punished the corrupt clergy by awarding the prebends of the churches to their vicars. But these same vicars, he points out, after they were made parsons, lived in greater outrage than their predecessors had. Here Trevisa breaks in (and it is perhaps significant that he does not sign his name) with the following observation (VI, 465–67):

> and now for þe moste partie monkes beeþ worste of alle, for þey beþ to riche, and þat makeþ hem to take more hede aboute seculer besynesse þan gostely devocioun; þerfore, as it is i-seide bifore in 4°. libro in þe 26 capitulo, by Ierom, seþþe holy cherche encresede in possessiouns hit haþ decresed in vertues. þerfore seculer lordes schulde take awey the superfluyte of here possessiouns, and ȝve it to hem þat nedeþ, or elles whan þey knowen þat, þey beeþ cause and mayntenours of here evel dedes, seþþe þey helpeþ nouȝt to amende hit while it is in hir power, what evere covetous preostes seyn. For it were almesse to take awey þe superfluite of here possessiouns now, þan it was at þe firste fundacioun to ȝeve hem what hem nedede.

This is very similar to the B-poet's comment, immediately following his reference to the poisonous donation of Constantine (B 15.524–29):

> A medecyne mote ther-to that may amende prelates,
> That sholden preye for the pees; possessioun hem letteth,
> Take her landes, ʒe lordes, and let hem lyue by dymes.
> If possessioun be poysoun, and inparfit hem make,
> Good were to dischargen hem for holicherche sake,
> And purgen hem of poysoun or more perile falle.

There is evidence that Trevisa devoted some thought to the problem of the righteous heathen, whose fate was the subject of considerable discussion in the fourteenth century. A Benedictine monk, Uthred of Boldon, clashed with the friars on this subject at Oxford, and it would be surprising if Trevisa had no opinion on this hotly debated issue.[26] His additions to the *Polychronicon* offer no formal discussion of the subject, but two insertions are related to it. One of these is Trevisa's brief comment on the story of the Roman Emperor Trajan. After mentioning some examples of Trajan's admirable qualities, Higden remarks: "For so greet riʒtwisnesse it semeþ þat Seint Gregorie wan his soule out of helle." At this point Trevisa subjoins the following terse reply (V, 7):

> *Treuisa.* So it myʒte seme to a man þat were worse þan wood, and out of riʒt bileve.

At first glance it would appear that Trevisa is denying the tradition that Trajan was saved. But this would surely be a strange opinion in the fourteenth century. On the other hand, it seems more likely that he is merely denying that "Seint Gregorie wan" Trajan's soul out of Hell. The implication seems to be that Trajan was saved by his great righteousness, and not by St. Gregory's prayer.[27] This is exactly the position of the B-poet in his version of the story (B 11.135–64),[28] where we read that Trajan was saved "nouʒt thorw preyere of a pope, but for his pure treuthe."

Yet how can the poet thus ignore the entire sacramental system of

Holy Church and still remain orthodox? Students of *Piers the Plowman* have debated this point, and R. W. Chambers,[29] for example, has suggested that the poet is far ahead of his contemporaries in his thinking about the salvation of the heathen. On the other hand, T. P. Dunning[30] is surely right in questioning the idea that the author of *Piers the Plowman* is either unorthodox or even heterodox in his belief. But no one, so far as I know, has been able to detect precisely the sense in which the poet is able to hold his belief about the righteous heathen and still be considered orthodox. And this is no wonder; for the B-poet does not tell us how he arrived at his opinion.

Trevisa, although he does not discuss the righteous heathen directly, nevertheless does have something to say about the possibility of bringing souls out of Hell. His comment occurs immediately following Higden's assertion that the soul of King Edwin was delivered out of Hell by the prayers of St. Dunstan (VI, 461):

> *Treuisa.* Here take hede, Cristene men, of þe menynge, for þe wordes beeþ perilousliche i-sette; þerfore haveþ mynde now of tweie manere helles; in þe oon was Adam, Abraham, Isaac, and Iacob, and oþere holy forfadres þat deide tofore Crist. Into þat helle Crist aliȝte after his passioun, and brouȝte wiþ hym þens þe holy fadres þat þere were. Þe oþer helle is a place for hem þat beeþ and schal be i-dampned for everemore; who þat comeþ in þat helle schal nevere after be saved noþer come out of peyne. But as me seiþ in comyn speche þat a þeef is delyvered from hongynge and from þe galowes þeyȝ he come not þere, ȝif he is delyvered out of here power þat wolde lede hym to þe galewes and honge hym þeruppon, so in som manere menynge he þat is delyvered out of þe fendes power þat wolde brynge hym in helle, is delivered out of helle, þeyȝ he come nouȝt þere. So meneþ þe prophete in þe sawter, and seiþ: "Þou hast delyvered my soule out of þe lowere helle."

It seems to me that this explanation can perhaps shed some light on the treatment of the righteous heathen in *Piers the Plowman*. First be it noted that the B-poet is perfectly orthodox, both in his acceptance of the fact of Trajan's salvation and his austere refusal to permit Imaginatif to declare openly that the righteous heathen in general are saved (B 12.278–93). Also, the poet feels at liberty to state his own opinion concerning the basis of the salvation of Trajan and any other heathen who may be with him in Paradise. This he proceeds to do in the speeches of both Trajan and Imaginatif, giving his explanations a characteristic ethical rather than sacramental emphasis. But however determined he may be to deny the importance of St. Gregory's prayer in effecting the deliverance of Trajan, he cannot ignore this very striking feature of the story. Hence he skillfully uses the prayer as a means of illustrating his all-important doctrine of Grace (B 11.141–5).

What I have just described is characteristic of the poet's handling of the entire story of Trajan. His integrity will not permit him to ignore any part of the story simply because it is not easily accommodated to his belief. The same is true of his handling of Trajan's escape from Hell. The Emperor, who had "broken oute" of Hell, was dead and damned to dwell in "pyne," and all the learning under Christ could not "cracche" him from Hell; but, in response to Gregory's "bone," he is brought from "bitter peyne." The poet is clearly walking a tightrope. In view of what I have already said about his use of Gregory's prayer, we can immediately see his purpose in referring to it as a "bone": the ambiguity of the term serves as an escape hatch in his interpretation of the story.[31] What may not be so obvious, however, is the fact that the words referring to Trajan's deliverance from Hell ("broken oute," "pyne," "cracche," "bitter peyne") possess the same ambiguity.[32] The poet seems unwilling to state flatly that Trajan was actually *in Hell,* except that, like the condemned thief who escapes the gallows, he "is delivered out of helle, þeyჳ he come nouჳt þere." This is the basis of the poet's deliberate and *visible* ambiguity, and lends point to the statement that Trajan "tilde nouჳt depe in helle,/That owre lorde ne had hym liჳtlich oute" (B 12.210 f.). Such an interpretation is confirmed, I believe, in Imaginatif's review of the case (B 12.280 ff.), where the emphasis is on Trajan's salvation, and no mention is made of his being "in Hell." Thus the poet very skillfully solves a difficult theological problem, while at the same time he stresses the ethical rather than the sacramental significance of the story. Trevisa's "tweie manere helles" has been of great value in helping us to understand the B-poet's treatment of the Emperor Trajan.

Some years ago Mildred Marcett pointed out that there seems to be a reference in *Piers the Plowman* to Friar William Jordan, notorious controversialist and an antagonist of Uthred of Boldon at Oxford.[33] The reference occurs in the satire on the Doctor who stuffs himself at the dinner table while expounding the nature of the good life. The Dreamer is indignant over the Doctor's behavior, and exclaims (B 13.83–84):

> I shal Iangle to this Iurdan with his Iust wombe,
> To telle me what penaunce is, of which he preched rather.

The pun on "jurdan" (chamber pot) and "Jordan" (i.e., William Jordan) is now generally accepted. It is the only known reference to Jordan outside of the literature of the controversy itself. Did John Trevisa know William Jordan? He was at Oxford both before and after the peak of the controversy between Boldon and the friar (1366), and one might suppose that he would at least be aware that an argument was going on. As a matter of fact, it is possible to interpret one of Trevisa's additions to the *Polychronicon* as a reference to Jordan. In the midst of a description of Paradise, Higden pauses to observe that when we say Paradise is as high as the moon we are using a device known as hyperbole. Here Trevisa inserts his own example of this rhetorical device (I, 77):

> *Treuisa.* So we preiseþ a worldely man Iordan or Iohan, and seiþ þat he was þe beste man þat eure was; and ȝit he was neuere so good as Crist. So in wordes þat sotil men wole deuyne, his menynge [is] trewe and good.

To the reader acquainted with Trevisa's incisive style, the words "and ȝit he was neuere so good as Crist" have that razor-like irony which he frequently employs. If the worldly man named Jordan to whom he refers is Friar William Jordan, then the irony is quite understandable.

Thus we have seen that there are many close parallels between Trevisa's additions to the *Polychronicon* and the B-text of *Piers the Plowman*. But one further question ought to be asked: Was Trevisa acquainted with the A-text? Without some kind of explicit statement on Trevisa's part, of course, this question is difficult to answer. Yet there are two of his insertions which suggest that he may have been familiar with it. One of these passages occurs in the midst of a long speech in the *Polychronicon* by Pope Gregory VI, who is attempting to justify his shedding of the blood of thieves. Whoever shortens the life of such a one, argues Gregory, is actually doing him a favor, for the thief is thereby prevented from doing more wickedness, for which he would have to suffer more pain. Trevisa evidently could not stomach this argument, for he breaks in with a warning to the reader (VII, 525):

> *Treuisa.* Here war of the develes argument and of gyle. For be a man neuer so evel, ʒett he may amende, while he is alyve, and so dide Paul and Marye Maudeleyn, and many othere, and so Crist meneth in the gospel in the ensaumple of whete, and of eure, that som men clepeth darnel.

One is reminded of the Dreamer's ironical discussion of the penitent thief at the conclusion of the A-text, and particularly of these lines (A 11.279–84):

> Thanne Marie the Maudeleyn, who mighte do wers?
> Or who dede wers thanne David, that Urie destroyede?
> Or Poule the apostil, that no pite ne hadde,
> Cristene kynde to kille to dethe?
> And arn none, for sothe, so sovereyne in hevene,
> As thise that wroughte wykkidly in world whanne thei were.

As we have seen, this is a *reductio ad absurdum,* and I am unaware of any comparable use of Mary Magdalen, David, and Paul in the commentaries or exempla. Yet I suppose we should allow the possibility that the idea might occur to various individuals independently.

The other passage which suggests that Trevisa may have known the A-text of *Piers the Plowman* occurs in Book VII, chapter 7 of the *Polychronicon*. Higden tells how a certain Earl Roger had himself made a monk before he died, in order to "have som socour." Trevisa comments as follows (VII, 355):

> *Treuisa.* A wise man wolde wene þat eorle Roger hadde as moche mede of þat he was a monk, as Malkyn of here maydenhood, þat no man wolde have, and nouȝt a deel more.

The reader familiar with the A-text will recall its denunciation of the rich, and especially this homely but incisive comment (A 1.157–58):

> Ye ne have no more meryt in masse ne in oures
> Thanne Malkyn of hire maidenhod, that no man desirith.

Trevisa changes "desirith" to "wolde have," but otherwise the second line quoted from A is preserved intact, complete with alliteration.[34]

One other work by Trevisa, interesting in its relation to *Piers the Plowman,* is his translation of the *Dialogus inter Militem et Clericum.* Near the beginning of this satire Trevisa inserts a lengthy note commenting on the argument of the knight and the clerk over the extent of the Church's power in temporal affairs. We have already had occasion to refer to this argument in analyzing the B-continuation (chapter 5, above). It will be recalled that the knight argues that there are two "times" of Christ: the time of his manhood and the time of his power and majesty. His point is, of course, that the Church's power is limited to the time of Christ's manhood, that is, the imitation of his life on earth. Christ said that his kingdom was not of this world, and hence the Church should keep out of temporal affairs. Trevisa breaks into the knight's argument with the following comment:[35]

> *Treuisa.* Here takiþ hede of þe knyȝtes menying & of þe clerkes menyng also. For þe wordes beþ nouȝt fulle chambred. For al þe tyme of Cristes manhed, þat was tofore his passioun, was tyme of his myȝt, power, & maieste. For bifore his passioun he turned water into wyn; & heled blynde, & lame, & many maner seke men; & hadde þe see, & wynde, & weder, & fendes attondaunt to his heestes; & fedde fyue þousand of men wiþ fyue loues of

breed & lefte twelue cupes of relef; & rered men from deþ to lif; & ȝaf his
disciplis myȝt & power ouer alle þe deueles & fendes; and schewide of his blis
to Petre, James, & Ioon; & ȝede vppon þe see in grete tempest of weder & of
þe see. Also whanne he sent his disciplis to fecche hym þe asse to ride on into
Jerusalem, he seide: "Ȝif eny man seiþ ouȝt to ȝow, seiþ þat þe lord
haþ to do þerwiþ"; & in his ridyng he was worschiped as a Kyng, & somme
spradde cloþes in his wey & somme bowes; & þanne was þe prophecie fulfilled,
seiþ: "Douȝtres of Syon, lo! þi kyng comeþ to þee, meke & mylde, sittyng
vppon an asse." Also in a tyme he drof biggers & sillers out of þe temple as
lord & kyng. Also his lore was in myȝt & power, & he dide al þis & many
oþer grete dedes bifore his passioun; þanne before his passioun was tyme
of his power & of his myȝt & after his passioun was & is tyme of his
manhed. For after his passioun Seynt Steuene seyȝ hym in his manhed
stonde in þe fader riȝt side [Acts 7:56].

Trevisa's comment here is formulated specifically as a reply to the
argument of the knight. Yet in spite of this the passage is an admirable summary of the Ascension sermon of Conscience on the
names of Christ (B 19.1–193).

An examination of all of John Trevisa's work would be out of
place in our study of the literary relations of the A and B texts of
Piers the Plowman; nor have I attempted any such examination. Yet
enough has been said, I think, to indicate how close are the ties between Trevisa and the poem. There remains but one other question.
Did Trevisa write alliterative poetry? I am not aware of any evidence that he did. Trevisa's reputation is based entirely on his work
as a translator; he is one of the "fathers of English prose." But there
is one feature of his prose style seldom mentioned in the conventional tributes to his name, and that is its alliteration. This trait
shows up most clearly in his original work, where he is not inhibited
by the requirements of translation. I quote the opening lines of the
dedicatory epistle prefixed to his translation of the *Polychronicon:* [36]

The Epistle of mee Sr John Trevisa Chapelain unto lord Thomas of
Berkeley upon the translation of Polichronicon into our English tongue.
Wealth and worship To my worthy and worshipfull lord, Sr Thomas
lord of Berkeley; I John Trevisa your preest and bedeman, obedient and
boxom to worke your will, holde in herte, thenke in thought, and meen in

mynde, your needfull meninge and speech That yee spake and said, that you would have English translation of Ranulphus of Chesters books of Cronikes, Therefore I will fond to take that travell, and make English translation of the same bookes, as God granteth mee grace; for blame of backbiters will I not blin, for envy of enemyes, for evill spitinge and speech of evill speakers, will I not leave to doe this deed; for travell will I not spare comfort I have in medefull makeing and plesinge to God, and in knowing that I wote that it is your will. . . .

To be sure, prose that alliterates is common enough. But it is worth observing that Greenwood, whose judgment was untroubled by the impingement of other issues, regarded the presence of alliteration in Trevisa's prose as unusual, if not actually strange: [37]

> [Trevisa] had, too, a fine onomatopoeic taste: Higden's *boatus et garritus* ("talk of peasants") becomes a "wlafferynge, chiterynge, harrynge and garryge grisbayting"; and to this sense of sound is, no doubt, owing the alliteration to which, though southern by birth and education, he was certainly addicted—a curious trait in a prose writer.

I have tried to show the ways in which Trevisa resembles the author of the B-text of *Piers the Plowman*. But the question should be faced: was he in fact the author of the B-text? At first glance the answer would seem to be, No, he wasn't. The poem is nowhere attributed to him, nor is there a shred of direct evidence connecting his name with it. Instead we have some rather definite attributions of authorship: William (or Robert) Langland (or Langley), John Malvern, "Willelmus W.," and the son of Stacy de Rokayle. I have already given my opinion concerning the literary origin of "Long Will"; but what of the others? No one, so far as I know, has been able to explain how all these names could become attached to *Piers the Plowman*. Perhaps they are merely wild guesses. On the other hand, it may be that they all have a common denominator.

It is possible to argue, though by no means with certitude, that the names John Malvern, "Willelmus W.," and the son of Stacy de Rokayle, have one thing in common, and that is their connection with Higden's *Polychronicon*. A John Malvern wrote a continuation to Higden's work.[38] William of Wykeham, Bishop of Winchester (if his name was intended, however implausibly, by the attribution to "Willelmus W."), figures in a continuation of the *Polychronicon,* and is known to have presented to Winchester College a copy of Higden's work, which included a continuation to the end of the reign of Edward III.[39]

The identification of "William de Langlond" as the son of Stacy de Rokayle occurs as an entry at the end of a C-text manuscript of *Piers the Plowman* in Trinity College, Dublin. In a recent and valuable study of this entry, E. St. John Brooks has demonstrated the importance of studying the attribution of authorship in the context of other materials added, apparently by the same writer, at the end of the Dublin manuscript.[40] These materials amount to a list of historical events in England covering the period 1265–1348, but are concerned primarily, as Brooks points out,[41] with the tragic life of Edward II, who was deposed and then murdered at Berkeley Castle in September, 1327. The profusion of entries in these annals concerning detailed events of Welsh history leads Brooks to locate the compiler of this list in Abergavenny, South Wales. I believe this is correct. But from what source was the list compiled? Brooks believes that the source may have been a *Brut*-continuation (covering the period 1282–1332), but then is forced to admit that the list includes events, notably the first occurrence of the plague (1348), which go beyond the *Brut*-continuation. As a matter of fact, the annals at the end of the Dublin manuscript stop precisely where the received text of Higden's *Polychronicon* ends.[42]

Why should the Stacy de Rokayle entry appear with a list of historical events related primarily to the career of Edward II? Brooks offers the following explanation:[43]

Writing of these events [the insurrection of Llewellyn Bren in 1315] which so nearly concern the history of the Despensers, writing about them on a blank page at the end of a manuscript of *Piers Plowman,* it was only natural that the writer should record what he knew, or claimed to know, of the author's parentage—that he was a son of a tenant of the Despensers.

Thus a writer in South Wales compiles a list of events relating to Edward II, and, since these events include reference to the fortunes of the Despensers, he adds what he knows of the author's father, a tenant of the Despensers in Oxfordshire. I do not think that this is very likely. On the other hand, there may be some significance in the fact that the annals of the Dublin manuscript appear to have been compiled at Abergavenny in South Wales, that they deal with events related to Edward II, and that they end with the last entry of the *Polychronicon*. First, Abergavenny is not far from Berkeley (as compared, say, with Shipton-under-Wychwood, Oxfordshire); second, Trevisa was certainly interested in Edward II, and, as one passage in the *Polychronicon* indicates,[44] he was sensitive about the report that the king was murdered in Berkeley Castle; and third, of course, Trevisa translated the *Polychronicon*. Unfortunately, I am not able to explain precisely the significance of these facts. Did the writer of the Dublin annals compile his list from a version of the *Polychronicon?* Relatively few of the more than one hundred manuscripts of Higden's text have been studied. When all of these manuscripts have been examined, therefore, *it may be* that one of them will be found to contain the Welsh additions which distinguish the Dublin annals, and *it may be* that this supposed manuscript will also include that information on the son of Stacy de Rokayle from which the Dublin attribution seems partly derived.[45]

If, therefore—and this is a big "if"—John Malvern, "Willemus W.," and the son of Stacy de Rokayle can all be related in some way to Higden's *Polychronicon,* what does this mean? It is rash to speculate, but I will be rash. If the author of the B-text were known to have been connected in some way with the *Polychronicon* (translated it, continued it), then the various attributions that we have considered might be regarded as efforts to guess the author's name on the basis of partial or misleading information. But if this is the case, then knowledge of this connection must have died out at the time of or shortly after Trevisa's own death; otherwise someone (John Shirley, for example) sooner or later might well have attributed the poem to Trevisa.

But if Trevisa is the author of the B-text, why should he have been reluctant to disclose his name? Fortunately, this question is answered for us by the Dreamer [46] in the first passus of the B-continuation (B 11.85–86):

> "Wherfore lourestow?" quod Lewte, and loked on me harde.
> "Ʒif I durste," quod I, "amonges men this meteles auowe!"

Of course the Dreamer and Lewte are here discussing the moral question involved in the B-continuation's condemnation of the friars, and they eventually conclude that it is proper for the "dream" (i.e., the poem) to be "avowed" (i.e., written). But the poet evidently decided that the practical consequences of "avowing" his author-ship might be severe, and in this decision he may have been in-fluenced by the earlier condemnations of such opponents of the friars as Uthred de Boldon and Archbishop Fitzralph.

Let us now return to the question, Was John Trevisa the author of the B-text? Is it not possible that he simply belongs to the same "school of thought" as the B-poet, or that he has only read the poem and been influenced by it? This would seem to be a possibility, even if the B-text is dated as late as 1382, for his translation of the *Poly-chronicon* was not completed until 1387. On the other hand, how-ever, there is one thing about Trevisa which leads me to believe that he *may* have written the B-text: he was a Cornishman. How ex-tensively was the Cornish language known outside of Cornwall itself? In short, how many lettered men of the "school of thought" represented by *Piers Plowman* B were acquainted with the Cornish language? I suspect there were very few. Yet we have seen (chapter 3, above) that the B-poet's description of the animals in his Creation scene (B 11.332–53) is almost certainly derived from the Cornish *Origo Mundi*. This fact, coming as it does on top of all the other evidence, seems to me to tip the scales in favor of Trevisa's author-ship.[47]

Throughout this discussion I have considered Trevisa only in rela-tion to the B-text. Could he also have written A? It is my opinion that he could not. My doubts are based mainly on my reading of the literary relations of the two texts, especially that portion of the B-continuation where the poet is "revisiting" the A-text (chapter 3, above).[48] It seems to me that if the two versions were by the same man, Imaginatif (for example) would display more confidence in his understanding of A's meaning. Similarly, the long speech apparently assigned to Trajan would, I think, employ less "di-plomacy" if the author were engaged in correcting his own views.[49] Both the A and B texts are, of course, profoundly religious in outlook, and both contain incisive criticisms of English society in the fourteenth century. Also, since the later version was inspired by its predecessor, the two poems are intimately related to one another. But here the resemblance ends. The A-text, with its praise of the essential spirituality of the commons and its angry condem-nation of learning and wealth, gives aid and comfort to those desirous of revolutionary action against the social order, as John Ball perceived. The B-text, however, calls for a revolution, not of society, but a revolution within the individual. And while these two classic views of man and society are perhaps not ultimately irrecon-cilable, they nevertheless stand in significant opposition in the A and B texts of *Piers the Plowman*.[50]

The exploration of the authorship problem in this chapter should not be allowed to obscure the fact that the most important need in *Piers Plowman* criticism today is the literary analysis of the text itself. Indeed, it will be long, I suspect, before this profound work has yielded its full harvest of meaning. At the same time, a serious effort to identify its maker(s) would be a worthy tribute to the poem which Dr. Tillyard[51] has rightly called the "English epic of the Middle Ages."

NOTES

———◆•••◆———

CHAPTER ONE

1. T. P. Dunning, *Piers Plowman: An Interpretation of the A-Text* (London, 1937); D. W. Robertson, Jr., and B. F. Huppé, *Piers Plowman and Scriptural Tradition* (Princeton, 1951); E. T. Donaldson, *Piers Plowman: The C-Text and Its Poet* (New Haven, 1949). Other studies are mentioned in the following pages when they relate to my analysis of the A-*Vita*. It is a pleasure to record my indebtedness to all these scholars, including the ones with whom I am forced to differ occasionally in matters of interpretation.

2. R. W. Frank, Jr., *Piers Plowman and the Scheme of Salvation. An Interpretation of Dowel, Dobet and Dobest* (New Haven, 1957), p. 1. Although Frank affirms his belief in single authorship (p. 5, n. 9), his analysis of the B-text is remarkably free of Langland harmonistics, i.e., question-begging appeals to the other versions in support of his interpretation of B. As a result his exposition of the "scheme of salvation" in the B-*Vita* is generally convincing, and I shall be surprised if his main conclusions are ever successfully challenged, though modifications will undoubtedly be made.

3. Cf. Thomas A. Knott and David C. Fowler, *Piers the Plowman. A Critical Edition of the A-Version* (Baltimore, 1952), p. 240, for the MS readings. I quote from this edition throughout the following analysis of the poem. The text of the *Vita* appears on pp. 128–47. The editions by W. W. Skeat (EETS OS 28, 38, 54, 67, 81, London, 1867–84, and the *Parallel Texts,* 2 vols., Oxford, 1886) are still valuable for the study of all three versions of the poem, but will undoubtedly be superseded by the new edition of A, B, and C now being prepared under the general direction of Prof. George Kane of the University of London. The first volume of this new edition has just recently been published: George Kane (ed.), *Piers Plowman, The A Version* (University of London: Athlone Press, 1960).

4. Cf. Knott and Fowler, *Piers the Plowman,* Appendix I, pp. 148–50, 170 (note to line 117), and 252 (variant readings); also pp. 20–28 (on text). The late Prof. R. W. Chambers (*MLR* VI [1911], 302–23) made it clear that he was, in the beginning, undecided about the extent of John But's authorship of passus 12. He added one more suggestion concerning the place at which But's composition may have begun, but I find his remarks on the quality of passus 12 especially pointed (pp. 319 f.): "But the whole twelfth passus is quite short: including Butt's undoubted addition it contains only 112 lines. Why may not the whole of it be John Butt's end? Butt was clearly a person of no great ability, who possessed the knack of writing tolerable alliterative verse. The lines summarized above (XII, 1–54), with their strongly imitative cast, are what we might expect from such a writer. There is no chronological difficulty; for the fact that there is a phrase and an idea common to this twelfth passus of A and to the B-text does not prove it earlier than B. It would be conceivable that Butt put together this twelfth passus from one or two vague recollections of the B-continuation and by more deliberate borrowing from the eleventh passus of A, which lay before him." I find this a very judicious statement, which my own reading of the text confirms. Nevertheless, Chambers later seems to have swung over to the view that our poet wrote at least part of passus 12 (*Man's Unconquerable Mind* [London, 1939], p. 131): "If, as we are nearly all agreed, this conclusion [passus 12] is at least in its opening the work of the author of the immediately preceding *passus,* it proves that the poet really was at a loss for an answer to be put into the mouth of Clergy or Scripture or Reason." (Chambers argues from the colophon at the end of the *Visio* that the absence of an allegorical character "Reason" in the *Vita* indicates incompleteness; but cf. Dunning, *Piers Plowman: An Interpretation of the A-Text,* p. 171.) Of course everyone should have the right to modify or change his opinions in the course of years, especially Chambers in this case, since in the earlier article he had not committed himself in either direction. But the context of his later remarks, just quoted, makes it clear that Chambers is intent on showing that the A-text "suddenly ends" and "breaks off sharply" (p. 129), a view which would seem to gain striking support from passus twelve, if we were to concede the supposition that there is a break within the passus at some point before John But gives us his name.

5. P. xxv. Of course Skeat later changed his mind, as a result of the exciting discovery of the complete "John But" passus in MS R. Cf. pp. 137*–44* at the end of the EETS edition of 1869. These pages were

designated for insertion in the edition of A (1867). See Skeat's note, pp. 142* ff., and also the *Parallel Text* edition (1886), II, ix, 164–65. These early opinions about the text cannot, of course, be decisive; at best they reveal, I think, the extent to which extratextual and extraliterary considerations can affect one's judgment as to the authenticity of the twelfth passus.

6. Dunning, *Piers Plowman: An Interpretation of the A-text,* pp. 168–69. Father Dunning does not commit himself to the view that the twelfth passus is actually spurious. He later offers an explanation of its meaning based on the possibility that part of it may, after all, be genuine (pp. 182 ff.), though the most that he will concede is: "It bears every appearance of being, as Dr. Chambers has suggested, an afterthought on the part of the poet—if, indeed, it be genuine at all" (p. 182).

7. R. W. Frank, Jr., *Piers Plowman and the Scheme of Salvation,* p. 57. In a footnote (2) Frank cites R. W. Chambers, *Man's Unconquerable Mind,* pp. 130–31.

8. This is substantially the position of R. W. Chambers. See note 4, above; also *MLR,* VI (1911), 318–19. I have cited only early and late comments, but this theme runs through much of his *Piers Plowman* criticism. My complete respect for Professor Chambers' universally recognized achievements in English studies conflicts not at all with my belief that in this particular matter he is in the wrong. It should be said that many of the critics who have adopted his views concerning the A-text (e.g., Frank, mentioned above) nevertheless do not follow Chambers in his stress on the biographical (cf. Frank, *Piers Plowman and the Scheme of Salvation,* pp. 57–58).

9. For a recent example of the idea that the author (in this case, of all three versions) lacks the ability to organize, see Elizabeth Suddaby, "The Poem *Piers Plowman,*" *JEGP,* LIV (1955), 91–103, especially p. 98: "In spite of all that has been written of the essential clarity and coherence of the theme of *Piers Plowman,* it is very often a clarity and coherence apparent more in analysis than at the time of reading." On Miss Suddaby's behalf it should be said, first, that at the time her article appeared what she says about the success of criticism in defining the poem's theme was generally true (I assume she refers primarily to the efforts to solve the problem of organization by reference to the "three lives"—cf. R. W. Frank, Jr., *Piers Plowman and the Scheme of Salvation,* pp. 6 ff.); and, second, it should be pointed out that she has great respect for and appreciation of the poet's attention to esthetic effects, of which she cites a number of judicious examples. On the other hand,

E. T. Donaldson, whose study of the C-text is referred to above (note 1), has a different point of view (*Piers Plowman: The C-Text and Its Poet,* p. 72): "The poem may, incidentally, contain a number of one-line gems, but if we spend our time admiring these, instead of trying to grasp the broad significance, there is something wrong with our perspective, and A, B, or C would probably not have much patience with us." Both of these critics have made abundantly clear their genuine admiration for *Piers the Plowman* as a great literary work, yet it is apparent that their critical approaches to the poem are inexorably opposed. For my part, at least as far as the A-text is concerned, I can accept neither position as valid. Rather I will maintain—until proved wrong—that the author of the A-version has absolute control over both his poem's theme and its esthetic form. And we are destined to learn, I think, that this is also true of B. A few years ago I tried—though, it is to be feared, without notable success—to make clear what seems to me the fact that certain irregularities in the B-text (and some in C as well) can be objectively demonstrated by textual analysis to be scribal corruptions, not chargeable to the poet himself (*MP*, L [1952], 5–22). Surely it is more profitable for the critic, whether textual or literary, to base his criticism on the assumption that the poet is both thematically and esthetically competent than it is to approach him with even the slightest feeling of condescension or apology.

10. Cf. "The Authorship of Piers Plowman," *JEGP*, IX (1910), 404–20. A more detailed exposition of his theories is to be found in *Charakterentwickelung and ethisch-theologische Anschauungen des Verfassers von Piers the Plowman*, Leipzig, 1900.

11. *Ibid.*, p. 405.

12. *Ibid.*, p. 416. Professor Chambers refers favorably to this argument in *MLR*, VI, 319, n. 1.

13. Dunning, *Piers Plowman: An Interpretation of the A-Text,* cited above, note 1. An article by George Winchester Stone, Jr., appeared in *PMLA*, LIII (1938), 656–77. A summary and discussion of the contents of the *Vita* occur on pp. 667–73. In such a relatively brief study, of course, it is difficult to get much below the surface of a poem as rich as *Piers the Plowman*. Yet many of Professor Stone's remarks, especially on the poet's satirical effects, are original and pointed. Simply as a matter of general emphasis, I believe the first of his three disagreements with Father Dunning should be given considerable weight (p. 656, n. 1), where Professor Stone believes the theme of the poem involves the question, "What must I do to save my soul?"

14. The discussion of the *Vita* occurs on pp. 167–82. See also the admirable discussion of the ideological background for the Dreamer's rejection of learning, pp. 185–86. The extent to which I disagree with or depart from Dunning's interpretation can be seen (below) in my analysis of the *Vita*.

15. R. W. Frank, Jr., "The Pardon Scene in Piers Plowman," *Speculum*, XXVI (1951), 317–31. Cf. also Frank, *Piers Plowman and the Scheme of Salvation*, pp. 24–33. Frank is of course concerned primarily with the B-text, and he is interested in showing how Piers's use of the *ne solliciti sitis* theme foreshadows developments to come in *Dowel* (B-text). Hence in certain respects my interpretation of the scene will occasionally differ from his. But in the main I fully accept his views and offer the following interpretation as proof that they are confirmed by a close reading of the A-text.

16. Cf. *MLN*, LXVII (1952), 534–36.

17. This has often been cited as a slip on the author's part, corrected in the B-text, where "pope" is changed to "treuthe." I do not believe it to have been a slip. It is possible, however, that not every reader of the A-text would catch the poet's irony. Two A MSS attempt to eliminate reference to the pope. Instead of "pope" MS D reads "people" and W reads "Piers."

18. Cf. John Lawlor, "Piers Plowman: The Pardon Reconsidered," *MLR*, XLV (1950), 449–58. There is much that is very stimulating in this article. Note especially his discussion of "the contrast between Truth and Liar" (p. 451). But I feel that he has not fully apprehended the emphasis of the pardon scene. "But now with ruthless force comes a question that perhaps the reader had never dreamed of asking. *How* good is Piers?" (p. 450; italics by Lawlor). This seems to me a post-Reformation reading of the poem. That Piers falls short of "be ye perfect" is true; but this is not the poet's primary concern here, dramatically speaking; to read the pardon scene in this way is to throw the whole *Visio* out of focus. It should perhaps be added to what I say above that my purpose in citing Job is not to suggest any specific indebtedness of the poet, but merely to point out that Piers's twofold reaction to Truth's message is in conformity with a traditional pattern of religious experience (Job 42:5–6; cf. also Isa. 6:1–5).

19. Cf. R. W. Frank, Jr., *Piers Plowman and the Scheme of Salvation*, p. 33: "What Piers says here is the merest hint, a preparation for the fuller development to come in *Dowel*, especially at its climax, the scene with Haukyn." Frank is of course dealing strictly with the B-text; but

since B in this passage agrees closely with A, I do not see how he can suppose that the poet had difficulty with the resolution of A, and yet had been able to make "preparation" at this point for a development in B (B XIII) that does not come into being until after the poet had presumably resolved his literary difficulties (cf. Frank, *ibid.,* p. 58).

20. Notice also that Piers "proveth himself" what he has taught (6.85–87). Cp. 4.107–8, 5.33–36.

21. As Father Dunning points out (*Piers Plowman: An Interpretation of the A-Text,* p. 154), the poet shows that he is quite aware of the function of indulgences. To what Dunning says about this I might add that the poet seems to feel that, in any case, pardons are of no use to humble folk who have "here penaunce and here purgatorie upon this pur erthe" (8.88; cf. also 11.303). Pardons are for the rich (8.162 ff.).

22. There is evidence that not every reader was alert to the poet's irony. For "be pure resoun" the A MSS TH₂ChD have "before resoun"; one MS, M, has "be poure resoun." The B-text changes the line to read, "And how the prest impugned it with two propre wordes" (B 7.147), and "And how the prest preved no pardoun to Dowel" (B 7.168). The line occurs twice in B; cf. *MP, L* (1952), 5–22, especially 19 and n. 14.

23. Contrast the methods of D. W. Robertson, Jr., and B. F. Huppé, *Piers Plowman and Scriptural Tradition* (see note 1 above), with those of R. W. Frank, Jr., *Piers Plowman and the Scheme of Salvation* (see note 2 above). Cf. also Frank, "The Art of Reading Medieval Personification-Allegory," *ELH,* XX (1953), 237–50, for an excellent review of the problem and further references. It will be obvious that I agree with Frank's definition of the nature of the allegory in *Piers* as it applies to A. But I do have some reservations about its application to the B-text, especially to parts of the B-continuation, where it seems to me Robertson and Huppé provide a valuable corrective.

24. That is, in the *Visio,* for example, personifications (Meed, Wrong, Liar) rub elbows with real people (the king, friars, clerks, etc.) in the allegory. Thus one function of the personifications in the scene at Westminster (passus 3 and 4) is to act as "tracers" which illuminate the moral issues involved in the literal action. "Theology," however, in 2.79 ff., simply states what theology teaches, and in this way resembles the personifications of the *Vita.* On the other hand, as Frank has pointed out ("The Art of Reading Medieval Personification-Allegory," note 23 above), the tower and the dungeon of the prologue

are symbols, something quite different in form and function from the usual materialized abstractions of the main allegory.

25. *Ibid.,* see note 10 above.

26. *Ibid.,* p. 170.

27. It should not be inferred that I am accusing the poet of dismissing "Clergie" without a hearing. On the contrary, the *Vita* reveals clearly that he gave much penetrating thought to his subject. All I am saying is that before he wrote the first line of the *Vita* (as the art of the poem shows), he had made up his mind, decisively, about the value of learning. I cannot see that there is any "activity of the poem itself, bringing to the poet, in the act of telling, new relations and significances." (John Lawlor, "The Imaginative Unity of Piers Plowman," *RES,* VIII [1957], 125). But in all fairness it should be pointed out that Lawlor is here considering the B-text, where the phenomenon to which he refers does, I think, appear, e.g., in B 11.274–310, 12.175–85, 14.132 ff., 15.340–82.

28. Cf. R. W. Frank, Jr., *Piers Plowman and the Scheme of Salvation* (see note 2 above), pp. 3–4, 48–49. Frank rightly stresses the importance of the interlude in the "real world" of the poem in its relation to the dream which follows. What he says about the function of the interlude here involving the friars, however, is affected by the fact that he is looking ahead to the meaning of the entire first dream in the Dowel section of the B-version (B 8.70–13.1). And since, as I believe, the attitudes expressed in the A and B texts differ considerably with respect to the issues raised in the *Vita,* Frank does, I think, distort the intent of the Dreamer's encounter with the friars (cf. especially pp. 48 f.). He allows occasional "flashes" of irony, but insists that the scene as a whole, and especially the friar's sermon, should be taken seriously. The scene does have a serious purpose; yet I cannot agree that the friar's sermon in itself has any direct bearing on the thematic structure of the following vision. (Lines 8.14–17 in B—not represented in A—might possibly suggest that the revision was intended to soften the satirical effect of the original portrait, though I suppose they could as easily be understood to be an intensification of the satire; cf. B 11.54–102.) But Frank is certainly right in pointing out that the poet is making use of the friars' "formidable reputation for learning in England in the fourteenth century."

29. As Dunning observes, *Piers Plowman: An Interpretation of the A-Text,* p. 173.

30. Cf. Matt. 23:1–12, especially 6–10. The poet is very fond of this passage, e.g., 10.116 (Luke 14:11), 11.219. For word play in *Piers* consult B. F. Huppé, *"Petrus Id Est Christus:* Word Play in *Piers Plowman,* the B-text," *ELH,* XVII (1950), 163–90. I cannot find that Huppé anywhere cites the striking example given above, though he seems to regard the friars as satirically portrayed. He suggests (p. 165) a play on the similarity of the words *faire* and *fer* in 9.70 (=B 8.79), and remarks: "The Friar's confidence in his knowledge of the life of perfection is ironically pointed in the approximate rhyme of *faire* and *fer."* But this is Thought speaking; or, if Huppé means that the words are intended to reflect back on the friars (or constitute a pun on *frere?*), then his reading seems overly subtle. But he cites many other valuable examples of word play.

31. Cf. R. Quirk, "Langland's Use of Kind Wit and Inwit," *JEGP,* LII (1953), 182–88; also Frank, *Piers Plowman and the Scheme of Salvation,* p. 47, n. 1.

32. It may be true that uses of *kind wit* (="kynde knowyng") and *wit* in *Piers the Plowman* show "the unity of and at the same time the distinction between the *vis cognitiva* (which corresponds to the *vis aestimativa* in animals) and the *ratio particularis"* (Quirk, "Langland's Use of Kind Wit and Inwit," p. 185). But while I agree that the poet uses his terms with admirable precision (and this is Quirk's very real contribution in the article cited), I must add that we will still misread the poem if we fail to realize that "kynde knowyng" places a strong emphasis on the simple, uncomplicated nature of the understanding as opposed to the more complicated mental machinery required for "sotilyng." This is the sense in which the phrase is used by Holy Church (1.129–31). "Kynde knowyng" is but one of the poet's many effective instruments used in distinguishing between "lewid and lettrid," and is to him far more important than "conceyvyng wordis."

33. R. W. Frank, Jr., *Piers Plowman and the Scheme of Salvation,* has, I think, disposed of the theory that the "three lives" govern the structure of the B-text. His argument as it relates to the A-text, however, is not so clear (especially pp. 39, 41). The definition of the triad in A does not of course envision the active, contemplative, and "mixed" lives (though these lives can be applied to it); but against Frank's observations I would point out that the basic definitions of Do-wel, Do-bet, and Do-best are adhered to consistently throughout the A-text *Vita,* and that the poet makes his meaning perfectly clear. Frank urges that in A, particularly passus 10, Do-best is omitted in two cases and is used obscurely

(p. 39). But the alleged obscurity he cites (A 10.210–12) is the *summary* of a complete and crystal-clear definition, re-enforced by two metaphors (the castle and the rose), which can be seen to extend all the way through passus 10; and the allegation concerning omissions simply is not true (see below). The *culorum* of this is that it is dangerous to ignore context, though I suspect that Frank has been misled, in his analysis of A, by paying attention to the wrong context, that is, he is "hearing footsteps" of the B-version (cf. p. 39, n. 9).

34. Robertson and Huppé (*Piers Plowman and Scriptural Tradition,* pp. 104 f.) take this as a reference to the friars, though they apparently include the earlier idealistic description of lines 77–80. Concerning the sudden shift from the ideal cleric it should be noted once again that Do-bet includes *all* categories of "clerks" in the broadest sense of that term, whether priest, monk, or friar, and that the poet uses the term "Do-bet" to apply to any of these he may wish to discuss in a given definition. Once we understand the nature of this device, there can be no difficulty in following the admirable satiric turns and twists in the *Vita,* of which the above passage is but one example. This sudden and often violent juxtaposition of the ideal and the corresponding reality is one of the author's trademarks (cf. the *Visio,* where it can be seen almost constantly), and it reveals the genuine depth and complexity of his satiric vision. In many ways the poet reminds one of the Old Testament prophets, with his fierce indignation, his emphasis on ethical conduct as against sophisticated evasion of it, and his frequent use of irony. A perfect model for his juxtaposition of ideal and reality (though I do not claim that this *was* his model) can be seen in Isaiah, chapter 2, where verses 1–5 represent the ideal, and verses 6–8 the reality.

35. Robertson and Huppé (*Piers Plowman and Scriptural Tradition,* pp. 104 f.) refer to the *Glossa Ordinaria* (PL 114, 567) and Peter Lombard (PL 192, 75) on 2 Cor. 11:19, clearly showing that the commentators understood Paul to be ironical here. But, in my opinion, their statement that Thought, and hence the Dreamer, failed to understand the fraudulence of the friars grows out of a misapprehension of the whole tone of this passage. On the other hand it is only fair to point out that they are interpreting these lines in the context of the B-version, which, though at this point very close to A, introduces elsewhere changes that inevitably affect the way the whole *Vita* in B is to be read.

36. Cf. Knott and Fowler (*Piers the Plowman* [see note 3 above]) p. 166, note to 9.90–100.

37. The B-text is more explicit. In place of A 10.14–15, B has (9.14–16):

> Dobest is aboue bothe, a bisschopes pere;
> That he bit, mote be do, he reuleth hem alle;
> *Anima* that lady is ladde bi his lerynge.

But I think it is clear that in A the poet is stressing the *servus* aspect of both Do-bet and Do-best. This is confirmed by Wit's subsequent emphasis on sufferance and humility (see below). The revision in B, stressing the episcopal authority (and echoing A 9.86, 11.194), seems to run counter to Wit's emphasis in A.

38. Cf. R. Quirk, "Langland's Use of *Kind Wit* and *Inwit*," *JEGP*, LII (1953), 182–88. Quirk demonstrates convincingly that the poet clearly distinguishes between Conscience and Inwit (Conscience is Inwit in action). His general conclusion should be noted (p. 188): "The familiar cognate expressions he chose admirably demonstrated the close relation between the concepts thus designated, and at the same time the elements bore meanings in general usage which must have made the specialized senses he intended readily comprehensible to his contemporaries." This statement applies beautifully to the passage just considered. In view of the poet's dim view of learning as a way to salvation, it is well to keep in mind that he has a perfect grasp of things intellectual. He is by no means passing judgment on something he knows not of. This fact will likewise be important for an understanding of what the poet says at the end of the *Vita* (see below).

39. Skeat suggests (*Parallel Texts,* II, xxxvii): "It thus appears that he had received the tonsure, but probably had only taken minor orders, and, being a married man, was hardly in a position to rise in the church." This statement is based, of course, on such evidence as all three texts might seem to afford. As far as the A-text is concerned, the passage quoted above seems to suggest that the poet may not even have taken minor orders. But Wit's statement is very cautiously worded, and it is difficult to draw even a tentative conclusion from it.

40. G. W. Stone, Jr., makes this point, *PMLA,* LIII (1938), 669.

41. Cf. Knott and Fowler, *Piers the Plowman,* p. 168, note to line 179.

42. Here I interpret line 198 to mean: "those men (the clergy) were endowed for the purpose of aiding beggars in distress" (cf. 11.185–87). Alternatively, the line may mean: "those men (the clergy, particularly the regulars) were endowed lest they become trouble-making beggars," in which case the latter reference would be to the actual condition of

the friars, who were not endowed and could not legally have "posses-sions," and who therefore ran about like beggars, confessing ladies (11.199–200; and cf. *Canterbury Tales,* General Prologue, 215 ff.). In-cidentally, it should be obvious that the poet regards good works—feed-ing and clothing the poor, etc.—as an important responsibility of all the clergy.

43. "Then spake Jesus to the multitude, and to his disciples, saying, The scribes and the Pharisees sit in Moses' seat: all therefore whatsoever they bid you observe, that observe and do; but do not ye after their works: for they say, and do not" (Matt. 23:1–3). This is one of the poet's favorite passages in the Gospels. See note 30 above. The relevance of this quotation to the poet's theme of *preach and prove* should be obvious enough. It is his standard indictment of the learned.

44. *Canterbury Tales*, Gen. Prol., 62–63. One must of course refrain from judgments about Chaucer's personal opinions on this or any other matter; I am here referring only to the tranquillity of his poetic utterance.

45. This is the view of Dunning, *Piers Plowman: An Interpretation of the A-Text,* p. 179. Cf. also Knott and Fowler, *Piers the Plowman,* p. 169, note to line 250.

46. It is certainly true that modern critics, except Dunning, seem not to have understood either the form or the meaning of the poet's conclusion; but I have tried to give reasons for this. One is the insistent tendency to read the poem as autobiography; another is the fallacy of reading the A-text with one eye on developments that come later in B. There are other reasons. Skeat's editions of the text have quotation marks around lines 11.250–303, erroneously suggesting that these lines are in dialogue form, and add a part of the John But passus (though suppressing the last few lines), in which conversation resumes in such a way as to suggest that it had never stopped (strange, if the work of the original poet). Finally, the failure of critics to perceive the intimate way in which the *Vita* grows out of the *Visio* (the *lettrid* vs. *lewid* conflict) has blinded them to the exact parallelism of 8.127–81 and 11.250–303. Although the two parts of the A-text are certainly two dif-ferent poems, in both form and content, their intimate relationship is striking. I believe, with Father Dunning (*Piers Plowman: An Interpre-tation of the A-Text,* p. 3), that "the *Visio* and the *Vita* in A are the work of the same writer."

47. 11.250 ff. The Dreamer's reference to knowing "witterly in herte" corresponds exactly to the "kynde knowyng" which he failed to obtain

from the friars (9.48). See note 32 above, and recall the spirited words
of Holy Church (1.129–30):

> "Thou dotide daffe," quath heo, "dulle arn thi wittes!
> It is a kynde knowyng that kenneth in thin herte. . . ."

The Dreamer means that in spite of his pursuit of learning ("for
nought I have walkid"), through Thought, Wit, Study, Clergie, and
Scripture, he has not obtained a natural, simple knowledge of the good
life, the kind of knowledge that actually enables you to live that life,
rather than merely talk about it.

48. Compare the same kind of rhetorical development in the poet's
exploitation of the pardon motif, 8.1–94.

49. Mark 13:9, 11 (Vulgate): "Tradent enim vos in conciliis, et in
synagogis vapulabitis, et ante praesides et reges stabitis propter me, in
testimonium illis. . . . Et cum duxerint vos tradentes, nolite praecogi-
tare quid loquamini; sed quod datum vobis fuerit in illa hora, id loqui-
mini; non enim vos estis loquentes, sed Spiritus Sanctus." In the B
and C texts (B 10.442 ff., C 12.274 ff.) the whole passage is softened;
reges is restored to the quotation, *steteritis* is rendered "come bifor," and
the reference to priests is eliminated.

50. Observe the Swiftian use of "lewide jottis" (St. Augustine's
ydioti). The poet gives satiric expression to his unmistakable admiration of the humble poor by calling them, in effect, "stupid dolts." "Ye
wise, suffrith the unwise with yow for to libbe."

CHAPTER TWO

1. The book by Robertson and Huppé, *Piers Plowman and Scriptural
Tradition* (Princeton, 1951), is of particular value. D. W. Robertson,
Jr., has likewise published a variety of articles on the importance of
Christian doctrine and scriptural tradition in medieval literature. All
of these articles are valuable, especially in their exposure of a tendency
toward condescension in much modern criticism of the literature of the
Middle Ages. Robertson's scholarship, his profound knowledge of and
respect for medieval thought, are, I think, having a salutary effect in
the field of medieval studies.

2. Ed. Richard Morris, London, 1874–78 (EETS OS 57, 59, 62, 66,
68).

3. Ed. Churchill Babington and Joseph R. Lumby, Rolls Series, London, 1865–86 (9 vols.).

4. Cf. Hardin Craig, *English Religious Drama of the Middle Ages* (Oxford, 1955), pp. 168 ff.

5. Alfons Hilka (ed.), Der *Percevalroman* (Halle, 1932); a more recent edition is that by William Roach, *Le Roman de Perceval* (Textes Littéraires Français; Geneva, Switzerland: Librairie Droz, 1956). An excellent English translation is Robert W. Linker, *The Story of the Grail* (Chapel Hill, N.C.: The Book Exchange, 1952). For a recent interpretation of the poem's religious theme, see the study by David C. Fowler, *Prowess and Charity in the Perceval of Chrétien de Troyes* (University of Washington Press: Seattle, 1959).

6. Perceval, 1173: *Mout griés chose est de fol aprandre.*

7. R. W. Frank, Jr., *Piers Plowman and the Scheme of Salvation. An Interpretation of Dowel, Dobet and Dobest* (New Haven, 1957), p. 14.

8. Cf. Malory's *Morte D'Arthur*, XVII, 5 ff. E. Vinaver (ed.), *The Works of Sir Thomas Malory,* (Oxford, 1954), pp. 710 ff.

CHAPTER THREE

1. This does not exclude the possibility that they are one and the same person.

2. B 11.208 reads, "For-thi lakke no lyf other, though he more Latyne knowe." The antecedent of "he" is not clear. Perhaps the ambiguity is intentional—"let us not have recriminations from either side." My paraphrase is intended to suggest that this line may be a delicate reproof, a hint that the A-poet may be jealous of learned men.

3. Skeat assumed that these lines were spoken by Lewte, and punctuates accordingly. Others have thought that they are the words of the Dreamer himself. R. W. Frank, Jr., however, argues convincingly against the latter proposal (*Piers Plowman and the Scheme of Salvation. An Interpretation of Dowel, Dobet and Dobest* (New Haven, 1957), p. 60, n. 1): "The speech, however, expresses ideas and doctrines which the Dreamer, at this moment of his education, has not mastered. The purpose of the speech, I believe, is to *teach* the Dreamer these doctrines."

4. Skeat, *Parallel Texts,* II, xxxvii.

5. Compare the tone of A prol. 65–79, especially where the Bishop's seal is sent "to disseyve the peple" (76). The purpose of the passage dealing with the ignorance of priests (B 11.289–310) is to forestall an obvious rebuttal from the friars. If the friars are corrupt (B 11.5–102), then priests are ignorant. The poet acknowledges this before the opposition has a chance to point it out.

6. *Cursor Mundi,* 683–98:

Þese beestis were so meke in dole
Wiþouten hurtyng þei ȝeoden hole;
Among þe wolues lay þe shepe,
Sauely myȝte þei to gider slepe.
Þe hound harmed not þe hare,
Ny no beest souȝte oþere to forfare;
Bi þe deer þat now is wilde
As lomb lay þe lyoun mylde;
Þi gripe also biside þe bere.
No beest wolde to oþere dere;
Þe scorpioun forbare his tonge
Fro beestis þat he lay amonge;
Al maner þinge in dyuerse wise
ȝalde to Adam her seruise.

7. Edwin Norris (ed. and trans.), *The Ancient Cornish Drama* (Oxford, 1859 [2 vols.]). The original text of the passage quoted in translation reads as follows (Vol. I, p. 10):

ADAM

yt'hanwaf bugh ha tarow
ha margh yw best hep parow
    the vapden rag ymweres
gaver yweges karow
daves war ver lavarow
    hy hanow da kemeres

lemyn hanwaf goyth ha yar
a sensaf ethyn hep par
    the vygyens den war an beys
hos payon colom grvgyer
swan bargos bryny ha'n er
    moy drethof a vyth hynwys

Adam then goes on to name the fishes: porpoises, salmons, congers, ling, and cod. The text and translation quoted above do not agree exactly with Norris' edition. The reason for this is that I have been able to correct Norris' text by consulting the fresh collation of the original MS made by R. Morton Nance and A. S. D. Smith, as well as their unpublished edition of the *Ordinalia* in unified Middle Cornish. I am indebted to Mr. E. G. R. Hooper for permitting me to use his copy of Norris, containing the collations, and to the Royal Institution of Cornwall for allowing me to make use of their recently acquired Nance MSS.

8. The word that Norris translates "fowl" is Cornish *yar,* "hen," glossing Latin *gallina,* as he indicates in his notes (II, 205) and glossary (II, 431).

9. The Cornish word is *colom,* from Latin *columba.*

10. See Skeat's note to B 11.349, *Parallel Texts,* II, 177.

11. In an appendix to Norris' edition of the Cornish drama, E. H. Pedler gives his opinion concerning the date of the plays (II, 506): ". . . these writings cannot well be assigned to a period much later than the last quarter of the thirteenth century." Norris himself, however, considers the plays to be of the fourteenth century (II, 437). E. K. Chambers, *The Mediaeval Stage* (London, 1903, 2 vols.), says that the date cannot be earlier than the fourteenth century (II, 433), but does not specify how early. From the evidence of *Piers the Plowman* (B 11.332–53) it would seem that the Cornish *Origo Mundi* must be dated at least sometime earlier than 1378–82. For a more detailed consideration of the problem, see my forthcoming article, "The Date of the Cornish Ordinalia."

12. George England (ed.), *The Towneley Plays,* London, 1897 (EETS ES 71), p. 8, ll.234–39.

13. Lib. II, cap. iii, ed. Babington, II, 217. With B 11.323–24 compare the following (*ibid.*): "he haþ neiþer pees ne reste, but werre and stryf wiþ ynne." The general idea of man's unreasonableness is similarly expressed in Alanus de Insulis, *De Planctu Naturae,* prose iv (cf. C. S. Lewis, *Allegory of Love,* p. 160, n. 2). But *Piers Plowman* scholars have begun to realize that we must look to the "common repositories" of the poet's own time (R. W. Frank, *Piers Plowman,* p. 2, though I cannot agree with Frank's assessment of the poet's education; e.g., cf. B 15.373–77).

14. This is a turning point in the development of the Dreamer, just as is true of Perceval in his encounter with the wretched maiden (3778–3811).

15. Lines B 12.57–59 are in MSS R and F only. This appears to be one of those cases where these MSS preserve lines lacking in the archetype of all other copies of the B-text. Repetition of a word at the end of lines 56 and 59 (soules, soule) will perhaps explain this. Cf. E. T. Donaldson, "MSS R and F in the B-Tradition of Piers Plowman," *Transactions of the Connecticut Academy of Arts and Sciences,* xxxix

(September, 1955), 177–212; especially pp. 205 f. and p. 206, n. 65. The entire passage discussed above (B 12.33–60) is the subject of an interesting and valuable investigation by Morton W. Bloomfield, "Piers Plowman and the Three Grades of Chastity," *Anglia,* 76 (1958), 227–53. Bloomfield clearly shows, I think, that the passage which I have simply called *de casibus* (B 12.41–52) is based on a *Minnesklaven* topos, listing victims of lechery (especially Solomon, Samson, Aristotle, Hippocrates, and Virgil). This is a compelling identification, in spite of the difficulties presented by certain of the names (Lucifer, Job, Alexander), since the passage follows hard upon a discussion of the three grades of chastity. But while the list of names in context suggests the *Minnnesklaven* topos, the point which the poet wishes to make does not seem to be at all concerned with lechery (B 12.46): "Catel and kynde witte was combraunce to hem alle"—an idea which is again urged at the end of the passage (B 12.57–60).

16. D. W. Robertson, Jr., and B. F. Huppé, *Piers Plowman and Scriptural Tradition* (Princeton, 1951), p. 152, stress the traditional association of the shepherds in Luke with the modern clergy. But I think the poet clearly identifies the clergy here with the Magi (as Robertson and Huppé indicate, p. 153); the shepherds, on the other hand, are associated in the poet's mind with Kynde Witte. This is, indeed, an excellent example of the poet's "diplomacy" in his revision of the ideas expressed in the A-text.

17. The poet's insistence on the reputable quality of Christ's birthplace (B 12.147–48), which Skeat calls "a strange version of the Bible narrative" (*Parallel Texts,* II, 183), is no doubt a further criticism of the friars, whose representation of Christ's humble birth is inevitably associated with their defense of theoretical poverty and begging. It also seems to agree with Luke 2:7 as translated in the earlier Wycliffite Bible (ed. Forshall and Madden, IV, 148): "And sche childide her firste born sone and wlappide him in clothis, and puttide him in a cracche, *for ther was not place to him in the comyn stable*" (italics mine).

18. Lines B 12.152–53 are in RF only. Donaldson ("MSS R and F in the B-Tradition of Piers Plowman"; see note 15 above) lists this as a case of accidental omission (p. 206, n. 67). It may be; but the lines strike me as an authentic authorial revision.

19. I do not understand the apparent equation here of clerks and kind-witted men. In B 12.66–155 the two are clearly opposed. Cf. especially 12.109–10.

20. It is possible, of course, that my analysis misrepresents the tone

of this passage. But I can't avoid the feeling that the B-poet is actually uncertain about the seriousness of the *reductio ad absurdum* in A 11.250–84, and therefore protects himself with a *reductio* of his own (the position of Adam's figleaf). Such an interpretation, of course, carries with it the implication that A and B are different men. But I have no other explanation for Imaginatif's wary manner in this passage.

21. I fail to see that conscience is represented as dependent on reason, as Robertson and Huppé suggest (*Piers Plowman and Scriptural Tradition,* p. 159, n. 3; cf. also pp. 61, 158); at least the poet does not seem to stress its fallibility. Conscience should accord with Holy Church's teachings, but then if conscience and Holy Church do not agree, conscience must depart from Holy Church (B 20.378 ff.), as Robertson and Huppé observe (p. 8). All that can be said (based on the poem) is that conscience should be refined and enriched, in its ability to make decisions, with the aid of learning (B 13.202–4).

22. Frank, *Piers Plowman and the Scheme of Salvation,* p. 75.

23. Cf. Skeat's observations on the use of *Piers the Plowman* and *Do-wel,* etc., in John Balle's letter to the commons of Essex (*Parallel Texts,* II, lv). Skeat of course believed that the B-text had been completed by this time; but if, as there is good reason to believe, the B-text was not completed until 1382, then John Balle's allusions are to the A-text only. Concerning the B-poet's emphasis on patient poverty it should also be said that he is preparing the reader for the exposure of the friars' theoretical poverty at the end of the poem.

24. Cf. Stella Maguire, "The Significance of Haukyn, *Activa Vita,* in *Piers Plowman,*" RES, XXV (1949), 97–109. This is a remarkably good study, the only one I know that attempts to demonstrate in a systematic way the intimate connections of the *Visio* and the B-continuation, though it is of course limited to an analysis of Haukyn. To the point is Miss Maguire's observation that the Haukyn episode is a commentary on the *Visio* (p. 105). But I cannot accept the idea that Haukyn can in any way throw light on the meaning of the *Visio* itself. Nor do I believe that the *Visio* exhibits a failure to communicate the inadequacy of the good folk of the field. If such appears to be the case, it is because the A-text simply does not represent them as inadequate; if the Haukyn passage calls attention to the inadequacy of the good folk of the field, it is because this is the B-poet's purpose in writing it. For the real opinion of the good folk in the A-text, lucidly expressed, see the ringing conclusion of the *Vita* (A 11.299–303). But Miss Maguire has

finely stated Haukyn's allegorical function in the B-continuation (p. 99): "For Haukyn does not merely *belong* to the world of the *Visio* rather than to the more abstract world presented in the rest of Dowel; he is, in his own person, the *embodiment* of that world." (Italics are the author's).

25. Cf. Luke 14:8–14. And compare the poet's contrasting description of the heavenly feast (B 12.198–209). But A 11.38–71 seems to be the immediate reason for the B-poet's frequent recurrence to this subject. The scene depicted by Dame Study in A appears to have hit him hard. Cf. B 11.184–90.

26. This is one of those cases where it could be argued that the poet is simply using the Bible (here the parable of Dives and Lazarus, Luke 16:19–31). Now both of these passages, in A and B, are undoubtedly derived therefrom; but the pattern of B's allusions throughout the banquet scene (which must be viewed as a whole) clearly reveals the poet's indebtedness to the A-text. E.g., compare B 13.58 with A 11.24–37.

27. *Conte del Graal*, 3280–3314.

28. It has been plausibly suggested that the model for this portrait of the Doctor was the controversial Friar William Jordan. The poet seems to pun on the name in B 13.83: "I shal Iangle to this Iurdan with his Iust wombe." See Mildred E. Marcett, *Uhtred de Boldon, Friar William Jordan, and "Piers Plowman,"* New York, 1938.

29. There is a hint of satire in the condescension of B 13.115–17.

30. Cf. R. W. Frank, Jr. (*Piers Plowman and the Scheme of Salvation*, pp. 69 f.): "Piers says that Dowel and Dobet are two infinites which, with a faith, find Dobest, which shall save man's soul. This last is apparently meant to be unintelligible, for Conscience says he does not understand it. Any doctrine which comes from Piers has authority, however; of that we can be certain." Robertson and Huppé (*Piers Plowman and Scriptural Tradition*, p. 164) interpret this passage to mean that "the earthly church does not perfectly reflect its heavenly counterpart," citing B 5.614–17. I am afraid that this interpretation strays too far from the context of Clergy's remarks; it certainly seems to ignore their literary form (prophecy), and fails to take into account the dramatic role of Clergy in the banquet scene.

31. To be sure, Matt. 22:37–39 is incorporated in Piers's allegorical directions for finding St. Truth (A 6.50–52).

32. Cf. A 11.152–61; 11.236; 3.219; 8.46 (and B 2.38).

33. *Parallel Texts*, II, xxiv f.

34. That the B-poet acknowledges "Piers's" denunciation of learning is a tribute to his integrity. But this admission is strategically placed in the context of the banquet scene, where the learned Doctor is satirized, and, most important, it is coupled with love, which is to be far more extensively treated in the B-continuation than it was in A.

35. In J. Q. Adams (ed.), *Chief Pre-Shakespearean Dramas* (Boston, 1924), p. 92, lines 123 ff.

36. H. Deimling (ed.), *The Chester Plays* (London, 1893 [EETS ES 62]), I, 38 f., lines 437 ff.

37. Needless to say, the use of these terms here bears no relation whatsoever to their function in the A-*Vita* (commons, clergy, and bishops). Note also that in my interpretation of Piers's prophecy I refer to the use of Do-wel, Do-bet, and Do-best as titles of sections of the B-text, and not the exploitation of the triad as a device. Do-wel, Do-bet, and Do-best are faith, hope, and charity (B 12.30–32); they are also contrition, confession, and satisfaction (B 14.16–21). This function of Do-wel, Do-bet, and Do-best is independent of their significance as indicators of the poem's main divisions.

38. *Parallel Texts,* II, 197.

39. B 13.158–63. Cf. Romans 8:35–39, with perhaps added details from 2 Cor. 11:23–27.

40. Skeat indicates a change of speakers here, though it is entirely possible that Patience holds out the packet with the instruction, "Undo it."

41. The text represented in most of the B-MSS at this point suggests clerks that know Holy Writ as the sole alternative to "harlots." There is, however, an addition of eighteen lines in which the poet develops the idea that there are three kinds of minstrels: professionals (kings' minstrels), beggars (God's minstrels), and learned men (clerks that know Holy Writ). These lines occur only in MSS R and F. Donaldson ("MSS R and F in the B-Tradition of Piers Plowman," p. 206 and n. 66) considers this passage a part of the original B-text, accidentally omitted by the scribe responsible for the exemplar from which the other B-MSS are derived. The reason for this long leap (eighteen lines), according to Donaldson, was the scribe's use of the paragraph sign as a place marker. I doubt this. Like many of the RF passages, the present one has all the earmarks of an afterthought of the poet. He first recommended clerks that know Holy Writ as the only legitimate kind of "minstrel," and the text presents this view without a hitch if we block out the added lines (B 13.422–36, 455–57).

This makes good sense, if, as we have reason to believe, the poet is himself a learned man, a priest. But he then apparently remembered that he had said nothing of the poor who cry at the gate, and hence he added beggars, God's minstrels, as another group that should find a place at the table of lords and ladies. We have already seen the frequency of the poet's recurrence to this theme (e.g., B 11.184–90). Very curious is his addition of kings' minstrels, who are welcomed by clerks and knights, and listened to at feasts for love of the lord (B 13.437–38). This picture of the aristocratic life accords well with the poet's evident respect for wealthy lords.

42. In A, Conscience preaches a sermon (A 5.24–42) in which the commons and clergy are criticised, Repentance exhorts Envy (A 5.102–3), and *Vigilate* encourages Sloth (A 5.215–20). But the "spiritual counsel" which B emphasizes is a different thing. This is particularly evident in the B-revision of A's confession scene (see chapter 6).

43. Cf. R. W. Frank, Jr., *Piers Plowman and the Scheme of Salvation*, pp. 31 ff.

44. The poet's transition from one audience in passus 14 (the poor) to another in passus 15 (the rich) reveals a rhetorical strategy similar to that of St. Paul in his letter to the Romans. Rom. 1:18–32 deals with the sins of the gentiles; Rom. 2:1 ff. begins a transition in which Paul turns his attention to the shortcomings of the Jews. As is the case with Romans, it is difficult for the reader of *Piers the Plowman* to grasp its meaning without an awareness of the audience that the poet is addressing in a given passage.

45. Here I agree with Robertson and Huppé (*Piers Plowman and Scriptural Tradition*, p. 183): "Christ established the power of apostolic discernment into the hearts of men. This function of his divinity he transmitted to Peter, and through him to his successors. As a part of the apostolic tradition, it is a function of Piers Plowman; in so far as Christ and Piers share this power, they are the same."

46. See Knott and Fowler, *Piers the Plowman. A Critical Edition of the A-Version*, pp. 156 f., note to line 88 f. It is possible that the A-poet refers also to an allegorical interpretation of Genesis 3:22, *And the Lord God said, Behold, the man is become as one of us. . . .* Much of the medieval allegorization of Genesis is an elaboration of correspondences suggested by St. Paul, such as that one of 1 Cor. 15:22, *For as in Adam all die, even so in Christ shall all be made alive.* Thus in the Old Law man is denied the right to become like God; in the New Law he is

shown how to become "lyk to oure Lord." Cf. also Robertson and Huppé, *Piers Plowman and Scriptural Tradition,* p. 43, n. 50.

CHAPTER FOUR

1. Treatments of the literal story of the Fall do not necessitate a distinction between the tree of the knowledge of good and evil and the tree of life, e.g., *York Plays,* ed. Lucy T. Smith (Oxford, 1885), pp. 20 f., lines 50–99.

2. Cf. D. W. Robertson, Jr., and B. F. Huppé, *Piers Plowman and Scriptural Tradition* (Princeton, 1951), pp. 1–6, 191–96. As I have already indicated, I am very much indebted to these scholars for my understanding of scriptural tradition. Nevertheless, I believe their exposition of our poet's treatment of the Fall has two limitations: first, they seem unwilling to grant the poet much freedom in his handling of traditional materials; and second, they try to read Piers into the allegory (see chapter 2 above, under the *Estoire de Piers*). The result is that their analysis tends to obscure what is most striking in this passage on the Fall, namely, the simultaneous dramatization of the narrative on four levels.

3. In the preceding note I have indicated what seem to me the general limitations of Robertson and Huppé's analysis of the Fall. Their explanation of the tree is a specific illustration (p. 191): "In speaking of charity, Anima recurs to a figure suggested by Holy Church [B 1.146, 150] and used in her [Anima's] own description of inadequate priests [B 15.90–108]. . . . The tree of charity, the *lignum vitae* of Scripture, represents Christ or the Cross anagogically, the just allegorically, and the individual Christian tropologically." They then go on to explain that tropologically the tree may be good or evil, that is, a tree of virtues or a tree of vices. In a review of Robertson and Huppé (*Speculum,* XXVII [1952], 245–49), Morton W. Bloomfield offers the following criticism (pp. 246 f.): "On pp. 191 ff. the authors confuse the concept of the trees of virtues and vices . . . with the *Lignum Vitae* and the tree of charity, the genera to which the tree in Passus XVI certainly belongs." Concerning this disagreement my comment would be, first, that in terms of the B-continuation's biblical structure, Anima does not "recur to a figure," but rather introduces the reader to the Tree of Genesis; and, second, that this Tree does not belong to any "genera," but instead is the Tree which figures in the Fall, viewed literally, tropologically, allegorically, and anagogically, and depicted with agricultural imagery appropriate to the introduction of Piers into the poem.

[227]

The earlier figure of the tree employed by the poet (B 15.90–100) comes from Matt. 21 as elaborated in Pseudo-Chrysostom on Matthew, Hom. 38 f.; later quoted *in extensio* (B 15.115).

4. Tropologically, this means that the Dreamer wishes not only to know charity, but also to attain eternal life. Cf. Robertson and Huppé, p. 192, n. 35. Note also my reference to Gen. 3:22 (chapter 3, n. 46, above), and compare a similar use of the bread of life in John 6:51. The hermit teaches Perceval this same lesson in his explanation of the Grail question ("cui l'an sert") in the *Conte del Graal,* 6417–31, where the reference is clearly to John 6:51.

5. Robertson and Huppé (p. 193) offer the following valuable comment: "This slumber, which Will enters 'al for pure ioye,' should be contrasted sharply with his spiritual sleep which he began in Passus XI, in 'a wynkyng wratth.'"

6. Of course it should be understood that this imagery will reveal the poet's consciousness of allegorical levels in the narrative. Free Will, for example, must "pick and weed" the Garden. The thorns and thistles that result from God's curse (Gen. 3:18) are the sins of mankind after the Fall.

7. An exposition of the Trinity at the beginning of Genesis is of course quite common in the literature of biblical tradition. Cf. *Cursor Mundi,* 271–322; cycle plays, *passim.*

8. The poet's originality lies in his use of them as tree props, thus developing the agricultural imagery.

9. The poet does not want to use this legend, except to dramatize the Dreamer's foolishness. But certain details of the description suggest that he has it in mind. Compare B 16.22, for example, with *Cursor Mundi,* 1340–48.

10. Note how well the action of the Fall is integrated with Piers's exposition of the three props of the Tree. R. W. Frank, Jr., *Piers Plowman and the Scheme of Salvation. An Interpretation of Dowel, Dobet and Dobest* (New Haven, 1957), p. 87, finds the latter passage "confusing." But if we avoid reading Piers into the allegory, and if we understand the poet's use of the Trinity to emphasize Grace, there is no problem.

11. In the Cornish *Origo Mundi,* the devils carry off Abel and Adam to Hell (541–70, 881–916). The Cornish cycle also includes the legendary material, e.g., Seth's journey to Paradise, similar to that found in the *Cursor Mundi.*

12. *Cursor Mundi,* 1355–62; Cornish *Origo Mundi,* 809–18; Chester *Creation,* 437–72; Norwich *Creation,* 123–43.

13. Cf. Robertson and Huppé, pp. 204–8; R. W. Frank, Jr., *Piers Plowman and the Scheme of Salvation,* pp. 89 f.

14. This is of course merely a generalization designed to emphasize the change here. The Dreamer *is* taught more, and does not actually learn his final lesson until passus 20.

15. *The Ancient Cornish Drama* (ed. Norris), p. 109. I have corrected Norris' translation by consulting the unpublished edition of the *Ordinalia* (cf. chapter 3, note 7 above). Cf. also the *York Plays* (ed. Lucy T. Smith), p. 76, and the *Towneley Plays* (ed. Pollard), p. 69. The latter is evidently derived from the York play.

16. Cf. *Cursor Mundi,* 2073 ff. In the Chester *Sacrifice of Isaac,* the *Nuntius* informs the audience that this play is in honor of the Trinity.

17. R. W. Frank, Jr., *Piers Plowman and the Scheme of Salvation* (p. 87), referring to the role of grace and the Holy Ghost in defeating the World, the Flesh, and the Devil, says: "This is rather strange doctrine." (Cf. also his comment on the Samaritan's teaching of the Trinity, p. 91, n. 6.) The doctrine may be strange, but it is clearly what the poet wants us to learn. His development of the role of grace reaches a dramatic climax in the coming of *spiritus paraclitus* in passus 19 (note that Conscience himself kneels, B 19.202), and the poem ends with a cry for grace (B 20.384).

18. This is very striking. Robertson and Huppé (pp. 199 f. and n. 46) cite Bede (PL 92, 290) to the effect that Christ's exclamation is a sign of his humanity, as the poem suggests ("creatour wex creature"). But I will be surprised if anyone finds in the Fathers this identification of Christ with the widow. The poet seems quite conscious of his daring (214): "The sone, if I it durst seye. . . ."

19. Cf. J. A. Bryant, Jr., "Chester's Sermon for Catechumens," *JEGP,* 53 (1954), 399–402.

20. *The Story of the Grail,* trans. R. W. Linker, p. 144; *Conte del Graal,* 6481–91. See David C. Fowler, *Prowess and Charity in the Perceval of Chrétien de Troyes* (Seattle, 1959), p. 56.

21. Frank, *Piers Plowman and the Scheme of Salvation,* pp. 89 f.

22. *Ibid.,* p. 90, n. 4.

23. *Ibid.,* p. 91 and n. 7.

24. *Ibid.,* pp. 106 ff.

25. Plunderers in war should be required to make restitution, ac-

cording to the *Memoriale Presbyterorum* (1344). Cf. Frank, p. 107, n. 2, though Frank does not apply this to the poem. The modern reader should not be surprised to find that the Samaritan's teaching about the Trinity (frequently associated with theological hairsplitting: cf. A 11.38 ff.) actually contains a powerful emotional appeal for peace on earth. It was ever thus. Dispassionate analysis of doctrine, even in theological treatises, is very rare. In poetry, at least in my experience, it does not exist. The same is true of the most refined intellectual activity in modern times. A perfect parallel to the Samaritan's discussion of the Trinity is Kenneth Burke's *A Rhetoric of Motives* (New York, 1950). This book is an admirable example of what might be called twentieth-century "secular theology." It abounds with religious "metaphors," and seems to be concerned solely with the construction of an elaborate analytical system, far removed from the realities of modern life. But such is not the case. In the midst of the most abstract kind of analysis Burke at times reveals his passionate involvement in the contemporary crisis (p. 264): "On every hand, we find men, in their quarrels over property, preparing themselves for the slaughter, even to the extent of manipulating the profoundest grammatical, rhetorical, and symbolic resources of human thought to this end. Hence, insofar as one can do so without closing his eyes to the realities, it is relevant to attempt analyzing the tricky ways of thought that now work to complete the devotion of killing." This is an exact modern equivalent of the Samaritan's discussion of murder.

26. *Chester Plays,* p. 257; *Cornish Drama,* II, 239 ff.; *York Plays,* p. 209; *Ludus Coventriae,* ed. K. S. Block (London, 1922), p. 241. Of course it is difficult to say whether the poet is recalling the traditional Palm Sunday procession as portrayed in the cycle plays, or as actually practiced by the Church. Cf. R. Chambers, *Book of Days* (London, [1869]), I, 395–98.

27. I need scarcely point out what should be obvious by now, namely, that the "meaning" of Piers never changes. Here, as elsewhere, he is the ideal representative of humanity. Piers never "is" Christ.

28. *Towneley Plays* (ed. George England), p. 261.

29. Edited by W. H. Hulme (London, 1907), p. 62.

30. *Towneley Plays* (ed. George England), p. 276; *Ludus Coventriae,* p. 308.

31. *Ludus Coventriae,* pp. 293 f.

32. Cf. Hope Traver, *The Four Daughters of God* (Philadelphia, 1907).

33. "Book" would seem to be the Bible, but why does he say he will be "brent" (B 18.252)? For an excellent discussion of the Book passage see R. E. Kaske, "The Speech of 'Book' in Piers Plowman," *Anglia,* 77 (1959), 117–44. Kaske suggests that the poet's reference to the burning of Book alludes to the prophecies of Joachim of Flora, who envisioned a third world-age (of the Holy Ghost) in which the letter of both the Old and New Testaments would be consumed by the spiritual understanding of the "Eternal Gospel," inaugurating a universal reign of Love and Peace. Joachism was not widespread in England, but it did make itself felt at Oxford University, which is where John Wyclif seems to have picked up his information (cf. H. B. Workman, *John Wyclif,* II, 99 f.). Concerning the burning of Book, it is interesting to note that Wyclif speaks of "codices of the Law of God being burnt" (*Polemical Works,* II, 700, 711), though whether this has a Joachimite context I do not know. Forshall and Madden, editors of the Wycliffite Bible, seem to have thought that passages like this referred to suppression of the Wycliffite translation (Preface, p. xxxiii).

34. Discussed in chapter 1, above.

35. "Quo incepto, una pulsantur omnia signa." This is from the *Regularis Concordia* of St. Ethelwold, in *Chief Pre-Shakespearean Dramas,* ed. J. Q. Adams (Boston, 1924), p. 10.

36. Obviously I quite agree with Robertson and Huppé (pp. 213–16) that the wife and daughter are literary creations. But I am not sure that the poet intended for them to have as elaborate an allegorical significance as Robertson and Huppé suggest. On the other hand, I do believe that the names of the Dreamer's wife and daughter are revealing. J. M. Manly long ago pointed out that the names "Kitte" and "Kalote" are used as typical names of lewd women (who would live, of course, in unsavory districts like Cornhill). Thus the climax to passus XVIII reveals to us another use of the poet's Dummlingsmotiv: the Fool reverences God's resurrection in the company of prostitutes. To be sure, modern notions of piety may obscure this point for some readers, unaccustomed to "sincere" juxtaposition of the comic and the sublime. But more to the point, the reader must be aware of the fact that the Dreamer's foolishness is now undergoing a subtle but profound change, and is destined to emerge as the "foolishness" of God at the end of the poem. Hence our attitude toward women of ill repute in this passage must be conditioned by the teaching of Holy Writ (e.g., Hosea 3:1–3, Luke 7:36–50), which shows them to be capable of the highest acts of faith (B 11.210–12). The technique here is not unlike

that of James Joyce, who, although of necessity on the defensive, and hence driven to emphasize the bathetic, nevertheless presents a comparable juxtaposition of the comic and the sublime in his "epiphanies."

CHAPTER FIVE

1. *The Ancient Cornish Drama,* II, 188–93; lines 2499–2522, 2535–40. Both text and translation of Norris' edition have been corrected with the aid of the collations and the unpublished edition of the *Ordinalia* (cf. chapter 3, note 7, above). The Cornish original reads as follows:

III⁵ ANGELUS

p'ywa thueth a'n beys ruth
avel gos pen ha duscouth
  garrow ha treys
marth thy'm a'n densys yma
mar vskys del thueth omma
  el vyth ny neys

IV⁵ ANGELUS

henna a edom re thueth
the vyl deaul mar ny wruk vth
  marth yv gyne
rak me a dyp bos hemma
an keth map eth alemma
  yw myghtern a lowene

V⁵ ANGELUS

pyv a ylta gy bones
pan yw mar ruth the thylles
  yn gulascor nef
rak me a wor lour denses
marnes dre an luen dvses
  omma ny sef

IHC.

me yv myghtern re wruk cas
ol rag dry adam ha'y has
  a tebel stuth
myghtern of a lowene

ha'n victory eth gyne
yn arvow ruth

. . . .

ruth y couth thy'mmo bones
ow hobersen a fue gures
tev y*n* dar bol
heys ol ow croghen scorgyys
dovn y'm kyc maytho tellys
lyes myl tol

Line 2537 (tev y[n] dar bol) presents difficulties, and Norris was unable to do anything but guess at the meaning. For an ingenious (and probably correct) solution of the problem, see R. Morton Nance, "New Light on Cornish," *Old Cornwall,* vol. V, no. 2 (Summer, 1952), 59–60.

2. *Chester Plays,* p. 368. I have quoted only a part of the dialogue.

3. *A Stanzaic Life of Christ,* ed. F. A. Foster (EETS OS 166; London, 1936). See Foster's introduction, and also Hardin Craig, *English Religious Drama of the Middle Ages* (Oxford, 1955), pp. 196–98.

4. Cf. *The Golden Legend,* ed. F. S. Ellis (Temple Classics), I, 113 ff.

5. The association of Isaiah 63:1–3 with the Ascension may have arisen from the symbolic representation of Christ in Revelation 5:6, *And I beheld, and, lo, in the midst of the throne and of the four beasts, and in the midst of the elders, stood a Lamb as it had been slain. . . .* Observe the following comment by the author of *A Stanzaic Life of Christ* on the angels' second question (8997–9006):

> this ilk questioun askeden thai
> for his body was blody,
> whiche blode he keppet wel alway
> that from his body went none bye,
>
> and blody stremes he loket aye,
> as Bede sais, I schal telle whi,
> fyue causes in gode fay
> him nedet to kepe hit skilfully,

> *Beda: Cicatrices dominus seruauit & in iudicio seruaturus est, vt fidem resurectionis astruat, vt pro omnibus hominibus supplicando eas patri representet, vt boni, quam misericorditer sint redempti, agnoscant, vt per-*

petue victorie sue certum triumphum deferant, vt re-
probi, quam iuste sint dampnati, videant.

> Euer til the day of dome schal be
> and therto shewe hom openly.

The author then goes on, following Bede, to explain that the blood was
to confirm the resurrection, to intercede with the Father, to show the
mercy of the Redemption, to proclaim the victory over the devil, and to
remind wicked men of damnation. The *Pearl* poet seems to have this
whole tradition of the blood of the resurrected Christ in mind in his
description of the Lamb (1135–37):

> Bot a wounde ful wyde and weete con wyse
> Anende hys hert, þurȝ hyde torente.
> Of his quyte syde his blod outsprent.

6. *The Golden Legend* (Temple Classics), pp. 120 f. Cf. also *Stanzaic
Life of Christ*, 9445–80.

7. Norris' erroneous reading *deusys* for *densys* (line 2502) tends to
obscure the fact that the Cornish text does indeed stress the humanity
of Christ at the Ascension. The angels are not questioning Christ's
divinity (Norris: "Wonder to me if this is the Godhead!"); rather they
are expressing amazement at his *human* appearance: "Marth thym a'n
densys yma!"

8. Edited by A. J. Perry (EETS OS 167; London, 1925), pp. 6–8.

9. Cf. R. W. Frank, Jr., *Piers Plowman and the Scheme of Salvation.
An Interpretation of Dowel, Dobet and Dobest* (New Haven, 1957),
pp. 108 f.

10. It is important to distinguish between the power of the clergy in
enforcing *redde quod debes,* which the poet approves, and the power
of "possessioun" (B 15.519–29), which he condemns.

11. In addition to 1 Cor. 12:4 ff., the poet may also be alluding to 1
Cor. 6:1 ff., especially in B 19.239–41. Foluyles lawes (Fool-ville's laws?)
may refer to the ideal Christian way of settling disputes, as opposed to
the alternative which Paul deplores (1 Cor. 6:7): *Now therefore there
is utterly a fault among you, because ye go to law one with another.
Why do ye not rather take wrong? why do ye not rather suffer yourselves to be defrauded?* In this (Pauline) sense, Christian society is
"Foolville" (cf. B 20.73 ff.).

12. Cf. W. A. Nitze, *"Sans et matière,"* Rom., XLIV (1915), 14–36;

D. W. Robertson, Jr., "Some Medieval Literary Terminology with Special Reference to Chrétien de Troyes," *SP*, XLVIII (1951), 669–92.

13. *Morte D'Arthur*, XIII, 15–16, in *The Works of Sir Thomas Malory*, ed. Vinaver (Oxford, 1954), pp. 647–51. The Old French *Perlesvaus*, a baroque Perceval romance, is full of similar prefabricated allegorical narratives.

14. Piers and Grace are now inseparable and, indeed, virtually indistinguishable. Piers is man in a state of grace.

15. *Parallel Texts*, II, 283 f.

16. The Sins here are elaborated from hints in Rev. 9:20–21; 18; 21:8; etc.

17. Skeat apparently did not perceive this. Cf. *Parallel Texts*, II, 280, note to line 167. Observe also that the presence of evil churchmen in the army of Sins does *not* mean that we have to do with a different army (R. W. Frank, Jr., *Piers Plowman and the Scheme of Salvation*, p. 112). Antichrist's army gains recruits as it marches through time.

18. The vicar speaks to Conscience of "Grace, that thou gredest so of," expressing the wish that it might be the guide of all clerks. This is the poet's oblique acknowledgment of his emphasis on grace (B 19.423).

19. The poet's use of Revelation in Passus 19 and 20 is perfectly clear once we perceive his use of extra-biblical tradition and his adaptation of the apocalyptic cast of characters to contemporary conditions. True, Dobest is not a vision of the Last Judgment (Frank, p. 112), if by that statement we merely wish to deny that the poet was a Joachimite. On the other hand, there is no escaping the fact that the Last Judgment is writ large in the final scenes of the B-continuation.

20. Frank, *Piers Plowman and the Scheme of Salvation*, pp. 112 ff.

21. *Ibid.*, pp. 114 ff.

22. Conscience admits the friars because the Church had, in fact, done this (Frank, p. 111, n. 8). The poet wants us to be painfully aware of the harsh reality.

23. Of course the evidences of old age are common knowledge. But both the passage in Piers and the passage in Ecclesiastes have a somewhat distinctive, seriocomic treatment of the theme, and both stand in the context of "Remember now thy Creator." The meaning of Ecclesiastes 12:5 as it appears in the Vulgate may not have been clear, especially the words *impinguabitur locusta, et dissipabitur capparis.* But the idea of the sacred writer ("desire shall fail") is certainly represented in *Piers* (B 20.194–97).

1. See chapter 1, note 3.

2. Edited by Thomas A. Knott and David C. Fowler.

3. See my article, "The Relationship of the Three Texts of *Piers the Plowman*," *MP*, L (1952), 5–22. Exception has been taken to the conclusions reached in the above study. Cf. E. T. Donaldson, "The Texts of *Piers Plowman*: Scribes and Poets," *MP*, L (1953), 269–73; A. G. Mitchell and G. H. Russell, "The Three Texts of *Piers the Plowman*," *JEGP*, LII (1953), 445–56. The passages in the B-revision which I have excluded as primarily scribal errors are as follows: 1.98–104; 2.74–106 (includes considerable revision); 2.202–7; 3.154–64; 5.114–17; 5.544–56; 6.9–21; 6.136–53; 6.180–85; 6.194–99; 7.143–50, 167–68; 8.62–63; 8.98–106; 9.54–58. The following lines of the A-text seem to have been omitted accidentally: 1.110; 2.165–66; 3.240; 3.271; 4.10; 5.74–75; 5.153; 5.177; 5.187; 5.240–41; 5.253; 8.112; 9.45; 9.71; 10.25. A few A-lines seem out of place in B: B 4.62 (A 4.67); B 4.115 (A 4.106); B 5.44 (A 4.108); B 5.120 (A 5.71).

4. B. F. Huppé, "The Date of the B-Text of *Piers Plowman*," *SP*, XXXVIII (1941), 34–44; "The Date of the B-Text Reconsidered," *SP*, XLVI (1949), 6–13. J. A. W. Bennett, "The Date of the B-Text of *Piers Plowman*," *Medium Aevum*, XII (1943), 55–64. A. Gwynn, S.J., "The Date of the B-Text of Piers Plowman," *RES*, XIX (1943), 1–24. Father Gwynn's suggestion of an earlier date for the B-text seems not to have been generally accepted, nor do I think that he is correct. On the other hand, he points out (p. 1) that the antimendicant views of the B-text are not to be found in A, and this is certainly true. Huppé tries to refute this in his second article, but I do not believe that he succeeds.

5. *Medium Aevum*, XII (1943), 63–64. Italics are the author's.

6. In "The Date of the B-Text of Piers Plowman" (see note 4 above), p. 64, n. 4, Bennett refers to R. W. Chambers' speculation concerning a later date for the B-text in his Introduction to A. H. Bright, *New Light on "Piers Plowman,"* (Oxford, 1928), p. 15: "The last passus closes in horror and despair at the state of things produced by the Great Schism. This would seem to place it in the last months of 1378 or perhaps some years later, for what particularly horrifies our poet, as it horrified Wyclif, is that the pope should be hiring men to levy war. It is difficult not to see in this an allusion to the crusade on behalf of the pope against the antipope, which was preached in England in 1382 and carried out in Flanders in 1383. On the other hand, as you [Mr. Bright] have pointed

out to me, had the B-text been in process of composition during the Peasants' Revolt of 1381, and finished a year or two afterwards, it is difficult to believe that the events of that year would not in some way have left a clearly visible mark upon it."

7. Of course "murder" and "kill" are by no means eliminated from the poet's vocabulary, but his use of them is usually metaphoric, as in Covetousness' attitude toward poor men who need to borrow money (B 5.257–59). Compare the figurative language of Micah 3:1–3.

8. Cf. B 15.513–31. And note the skill of the B-poet in revising the Dreamer's ironic comment on the lordly religious in A (A 11.216–20). "'Thanne is Dowel and Dobet,' quod I, *'dominus* and kniȝthode'" (B 10.331). That is, since the secular power will (according to the prophecy) amend the religious, then these secular lords must be Do-wel, etc. The irony is gone, but the statement is quite pertinent, to say the least.

9. G. R. Owst first suggested that the "angel" of the B-prologue (128) was Bishop Brunton (also spelled "Brinton"), whose sermon in May, 1376, was probably addressed to the ecclesiastical Convocation which met in connection with the Good Parliament. Cf. Gasquet, *Old English Bible and Other Essays* (London, 1908) (chapter on "A Forgotten English Preacher"); G. R. Owst, "The 'Angel' and the 'Goliardeys' of Langland's Prologue," *MLR*, XX (1925), 270 ff.; Eleanor H. Kellogg, "Bishop Brunton and the Fable of the Rats," *PMLA*, L (1935), 57–68; Sister Mary Aquinas Devlin, "The Chronology of Bishop Brunton's Sermons," *PMLA*, LI (1936), 300–2; also Devlin, "Bishop Brunton and His Sermons," *Speculum*, XIV (1939), 324–44; and, finally, see the valuable critique by E. T. Donaldson, *Piers Plowman: The C-Text and Its Poet* (New Haven, 1949), pp. 112–18. The B-poet has many ideas and allusions in common with Bishop Brunton. Both allude to the murder of Archbishop Sudbury, Brunton condemning those who were involved (Sermon 99), and the B-poet praising the Archbishop himself (B 15.556). Both are concerned with absolution in its application to those who participated in the Peasants' Revolt (Sermon 99; B-text, *redde quod debes*). Brunton blames certain rich men for showing less pity for the poor than do the Saracens and Jews (Sermon 44), while the B-poet blames *bishops* for the same thing (B 9.79–93), and suggests that these bishops get to work and convert the heathen (B 15.532–601), teaching them the Creed *litlum and lytlum* (B 15.599; cf. Isaiah 28:10, and observe the use of the same passage from Isaiah in Brunton's Sermon 17). But these few points of contact merely scratch the surface. A thorough study of the

relationship of the B-text of *Piers the Plowman* and the sermons of Bishop Brunton is urgently needed. Such a study should allow the possibility that the B-text may include references to sermons as late as 1382–83. It should also be alert to the possibility that the B-poet was not dependent on "reports" (*PMLA*, L [1935], 67), circulating perhaps in Cornhill, and that he may have been, at times, among the clergy who heard the sermons of Brunton not designed for a popular audience. Cf. Sister Mary Aquinas Devlin (ed.), *The Sermons of Thomas Brinton, Bishop of Rochester (1373–1389)*, Camden Third Series, vols. LXXXV–LXXXVI (2 vols., London, 1954). With the poet's reference to bishops as "doumbe houndes" (B X, 287), compare *Chronicon Angliae* (Rolls Series, v. 64), p. 104, "ut canes muti non valentes latrare," and the English version in *Archaeologia*, XXII (1829), 242, which has "dume dogs." With the poet's general use of the blind leading the blind (B 10.256–79), compare *Select English Works of Wyclif* (ed. Arnold), I, 11–12 (Sermon iv).

10. As quoted by Sister Mary Aquinas Devlin, *PMLA*, LI (1936), 301.

11. See note 9 above. The relationship between Brunton's sermons and the B-text suggests an argument between men who have much in common, yet who disagree passionately on important controversial issues.

12. Sister Mary Aquinas Devlin reviews Bishop Brunton's role as an opponent of Wyclif, in *Speculum*, XIV (1939), 339–43.

13. The original text, containing a criticism of bishops, consists of lines B 15.535–38, 557–67 (lines 564b–567a, preserved only in *RF*, appear to have been accidentally omitted from the original of all the other B-MSS). The lines added in revision are B 15.539–56. E. T. Donaldson ("MSS R and F in the B-Tradition of Piers Plowman," *Transactions of the Connecticut Academy of Arts and Sciences*, XXXIX [1955], 206) believes that these lines were accidentally omitted and do not represent a revision at all. I cannot agree. MSS *RF* do contain passages accidentally skipped in the exemplar of the other B-MSS (e.g., B 15.564–67, mentioned above), but such does not appear to be the case with lines B 15.539–56. Note especially the awkward juncture of lines 556–57, created by the sudden transition from the praise of bishops who bear the name of Syria to the criticism of bishops who "hippe aboute in Engelonde." And observe also how the C-poet improves the juncture (C 18.279).

14. Cf. Skeat, *Parallel Texts*, II, 234, note to 278. For the life of Archbishop Sudbury by Walter F. Hook, see *Lives of the Archbishops of Canterbury* (London, 1865), IV, chapter 15, 244–314. Sudbury's life

makes fascinating reading alongside *Piers the Plowman*. It is easy to see why the B-poet may have admired him, even though his comments on bishops in the poem are generally unflattering. For an earlier attempt to identify the person alluded to in this passage, see M. E. Richardson, "The Characters in *Piers Plowman:* The Bishop of Bethlehem," *Notes and Queries,* clxxx (1941), 116 f. Richardson takes "Surrye" to be a punning reference to William, Bishop of Bethlehem, who was appointed in 1386 to the See of Llandaff, and who seems to have come from Caerleon-on-Usk, where the de Warrenne family (which bore, among others, the title of Surrey) had held manors. This is ingenious but, I think, based on a misreading of the passage. Richardson takes line B 15.556 to be an "admonition" to the bishop of "Surrye" (Bethlehem), that is, a *criticism* of the bishop. But surely this line is a compliment: whoever it is that bears the name of Surrye *has followed* the example of St. Thomas à Becket, in contrast to those who "hippe aboute in Engelonde," as is made clear by the transition in C 18.279, "And nat in Engelonde to huppe abowte . . ." (a transition which appears in MS R, though Skeat did not make it a part of his B-text). For an explicit comparison of St. Thomas and Archbishop Sudbury, see John Gower, *Vox Clamantis,* 1001–1162 (ed. G. C. Macaulay, *The Complete Works of John Gower* [4 vols.; Oxford, 1899–1902]; in *The Latin Works,* vol. IV). On the other hand, I do not know of any connection between Sudbury and Surrye.

15. Nevill K. Coghill, "The Pardon of *Piers Plowman*" (Sir Israel Gollancz Memorial Lecture), *British Academy Proceedings,* XXXI (1945), especially 29–37.

16. The critical text of A has the second person pronoun, as attested by the *y* family of MSS. The *x* family (MSS VH) is divided, and MS V, which Skeat used, has the third person pronoun. But the reading of H, the other *x* MS, confirms the critical text.

> Curatures þat schulde ȝou kepe clene in ȝoure soules
> Þei ben a combred wiþ care þei con not oute krepe
> So hard þei ben wiþ auaryce haspid to gydre

In spite of the "improved," proclerical readings of the second and third lines, H retains the original second person pronoun of the first line in this passage.

17. Particularly interesting is the B-revision of A 11.285–92 (B 10.442–51), mentioned briefly above in chapter 1, note 49. The B-poet refuses to concede that learning was *never* commended by Christ (cp. B

12.72–98), and he even implies that the help of the Holy Ghost (A 11.292) will not be available to those who merely wish to quarrel ungraciously with priests (B 10.448–51). On the other hand, it is possible that what I have called "minor revisions" (e.g., B 10.69), are simply scribal changes. But it seems to me that caution should be exercised before we conclude that these little changes are corruptions, especially where they undergo further alteration in the C-text (C 12.52). If such alterations can be explained in terms of scribal practice, well and good; if not, every effort should be made to understand them in relation to the purposes of the author.

18. D. W. Robertson, Jr., and B. F. Huppé *Piers Plowman and Scriptural Tradition* (Princeton, 1951), p. 111, n. 22, suggest Luke 9:2, where Jesus charges the disciples with the task of healing the sick, to explain the poet's reference to Luke. But the gospels were freely exploited by the antifeminists. I cannot cite chapter and verse, but I suspect this is because the meaning of the biblical text was so often distorted in converting it into ammunition for the war against women. One would have to read the literature of the controversy, keeping on the lookout for antifeminist applications of gospel texts.

19. The same idea is presented more fully in B 15.316–34.

CHAPTER SEVEN

1. "Chaucer the Pilgrim," *PMLA*, LXIX (1954), 928–36. His discussion of the "fallible first person singular" is on p. 934.

2. See my discussion of the biographical critics in chapter 1. Dunning, Robertson and Huppé, and R. W. Frank, Jr., have wisely avoided a biographical interpretation of the Dreamer's character.

3. The best account of Trevisa's life is that by Aaron J. Perry, in his Introduction to *Dialogus inter Militem et Clericum, Richard FitzRalph's Sermon: 'Defensio Curatorum' and Methodius: 'Þe Bygynnyng of þe World and þe Ende of Worldes' by John Trevisa*, London, 1925 (EETS OS 167), pp. lv–lxxv. See also H. J. Wilkins, *Was John Wycliffe a Negligent Pluralist? Also John de Trevisa, His Life and Work*, London, 1915. There has been much speculation about the date of Trevisa's birth, but no real evidence has turned up so far. The early dates frequently cited (1322, 1326) are guesses based on Caxton's erroneous date for the completion of Trevisa's translation of the *Polychronicon*. Caxton dates it 1357, whereas the correct year is 1387. The effect of this error can be seen in the speculations of Thomas Fuller, *The Church History of Britain*, London, 1655, bk. IV, p. 151. The date 1342 for Trevisa's birth

is equally groundless, and may have arisen from a misreading of John Bale, *Scriptorum Illustrium . . . Catalogus,* Basileæ, 1557, p. 518. Bale there (erroneously) describes Trevisa's continuation of the *Polychronicon* as extending "ab anno a Christi incarnatione 1342, usque ad annum eiusdem 1397." Later, Joannes Albertus Fabricius, *Bibliotheca Latina Mediæ et infimæ Ætatis,* Hamburg, 1734–36, t. 4 (1735), who cites Bale, begins his entry on Trevisa as follows (p. 450): "JOANNES *Trevisa* Cornubiensis Anglus circa A. 1342. Sacerdos & vicarius, apud Dominum suum Thomam de Barkeley gratiosus circa An. 1399." Next John J. Rogers, in the *Journal of the Royal Institution of Cornwall,* vol. III, no. xi (April, 1870), 147–54, says flatly that Trevisa was "born in the year 1342" (p. 148), without citing any authority; but Rogers consulted Fabricius (p. 149). In spite of this comedy of errors, however, 1342 is probably as close as we can come in the absence of further documentation. The earliest certain date for Trevisa that we have is the year of his matriculation in Exeter College (1362). It was probably for this reason that C. W. Boase, in his *Registrum Collegii Exoniensis* (Oxford Historical Society, XXVII), Oxford, 1894, p. 11, gives "about 1342" as the date of Trevisa's birth. Such, at least, is the supposition of H. J. Wilkins (*Was John Wycliffe a Negligent Pluralist?* p. 72, n. 1). Wilkins' own argument for an early date is circular, depending ultimately on the conjectures of Thomas Fuller (see above).

4. Perry, *ibid.,* pp. lxi ff.

5. *Ibid.* Some of the dates that I give differ from Perry's. I have recently collected further evidence concerning Trevisa at Oxford, and hope to publish the results of this research in the near future.

6. *Ibid.,* pp. lxv ff. Perry (p. lxvi) quotes John Smyth, *Lives of the Berkeleys,* ed. Sir John MacLean (3 vols.; Gloucester, 1883–85), I, 338, to the effect that Trevisa was chaplain to Thomas III (1326–61). But Smyth thought that Trevisa completed his translation of the Polychronicon in 1357, as Perry points out (p. lxxxiv), whereas we know that the translation was not completed until 1387. Hence, just as Smyth was consistent in his dates (Perry, p. lxxxiv), so he was consistent in his lords. We have no independent evidence that Trevisa was chaplain to Thomas III (d. 1361), or even to Maurice IV (1361–68). Trevisa did not enter Oxford until Lent, 1362, as we have seen.

7. *Reg. Sudbury, London* (Canterbury and York Society), II, 87. Cited by A. B. Emden, *A Biographical Register of the University of Oxford to A. D. 1500* (3 vols.; Oxford, 1957–59), III, 1903 f.

8. Perry, pp. lxvii ff. Westbury-on-Trym is now a part of Bristol. John

Trevisa is depicted in (modern) stained glass in the west window of Westbury-on-Trym parish church.

9. *Ibid.,* pp. ciii ff.; text, pp. 39 ff.

10. Cf. R. W. Frank, Jr., *Piers Plowman and the Scheme of Salvation* (New Haven, 1957), pp. 115 ff.

11. Perry, pp. c ff.; text, pp. 1 ff.

12. Perry, pp. xci ff.; cf. also W. H. Hulme (ed.), *The Middle English Harrowing of Hell and Gospel of Nicodemus* (London, 1907) (EETS ES 100), Introduction, pp. xl–xlvi. Shirley's ascription reads in part as follows: "Maistre Iohan Trevysa haþe here in mynde þat some tyme þe Greekes maden Ioustes and tournamentes. . . ." (MS. Add. 16165, f. 94b). Neither Hulme nor Perry seems to have noted the resemblance of this note to Trevisa's discussion of the Olympiad, inserted in his translation of the *Polychronicon,* lib. IV, cap. i (Rolls Series, IV, pp. 253–55).

13. Perry, pp. lxxxiv ff.

14. Perry, pp. cxv ff. Reference should also be made to the doubtful translations, *De Re Militari,* and Methodius, *Þe bygynnyng of þe world and þe Ende of Worldes.* For Trevisa's original writings, cf. Perry, pp. cxxvii ff. I refer to and quote from the Epistle to Lord Berkeley below. For additional consideration of the problem of Trevisa's translation of the Bible, see my article, "John Trevisa and the English Bible," *Modern Philology,* LVIII (1960), 81–98.

15. Perry, p. lxiv. But for further information on this controversy, see "John Trevisa and the English Bible" (in *Modern Philology*), mentioned in the preceding note.

16. The possible Oxford background of the B-poet raises interesting questions. Who were the "wise teachers" wounded by Hypocrisy (B 20.299–301)? Cf. also B. 15.365–77.

17. I have suggested that the B-poet alludes to the murder of Archbishop Sudbury (B 15.556). Of possible interest in this connection is the following item in Smyth's *Lives of the Berkeleys* (see note 6 above), II, 24: "In the fifth of Richard the second [1381] were three severall Comissions directed to this lord [Thomas IV] and others to represse those mischeevous persons, who in hostile manner had taken and put to death the Arch-bishop of Canterbury [Sudbury], lord Chancellor, and others, without any fault by them committed; In which service this lord was imployed into divers other Countyes."

18. Perry, p. lxv; *Polychronicon,* II, 61.

19. Cf. Morton W. Bloomfield, "The Pardons of Pamplona and the

Pardoner of Rounceval: *Piers Plowman* B XVII 252 (C XX 218)," *Philological Quarterly,* XXXV (1956), 60–68. Note especially p. 66: "However, it seems to me that the assumption that he [Langland] was referring to the Charing Cross Hospital is the only one that makes sense. There is no other London-Pamplona connection that I know of." In other words, there *must* be a London-Pamplona connection. On the other hand, I should add that I think Professor Bloomfield has indeed made a good case for St. Mary's Rounceval as the object of the B-poet's satire in this passage. If parts of the B-text can be dated as late as 1382, then the scandal of 1382 (Bloomfield, p. 62) would make the reference even more pointed.

20. It is perhaps worth observing that the B-poet's interest in astronomy finds its parallel in Trevisa's additions to the *Polychronicon:* cf. *Polych.* I, 329; II, 207–9; III, 133–35; III, 259–61; VI, 107; VI, 135. I have not attempted any systematic comparison of the facts of Trevisa's life with the B-text, since this sort of thing can never be decisive. Still, such a comparison might prove interesting. The reader of *Piers the Plowman* will recall that toward the end of the poem, Grace tells Piers to build a barn (B 19.314–25), which is allegorically described in some detail, including its timber (316), mortar (321), foundation (322), wattled walls (323), and roof (324). In the bursar's accounts of Exeter College for the year 1363–4 we find that 12d was spent "for hiring two horses when the Rector and John Trevise were at West Wittenham to arrange with the *firmarii* for the building of a barn" (cf. Perry, p. lxii).

21. See note 12 above. I have not been able to consult the unprinted MSS of Trevisa's translation of the Gospel of Nicodemus. Trevisa's works are badly in need of editing. The late Professor Perry had contemplated an edition of the translation of *De Regimine Principum,* from Bodleian MS Digby 233, ff. 1–182b, with an introduction by Professor Herbert E. Childs (Research in Progress, *PMLA,* LXVII [1952], item 1143a). I hope to complete this project in the near future. Professor A. L. Binns is reported to be preparing an edition and study of the *Dialogue upon Translation* (Research in Progress, *PMLA,* LXVII [1952], item 1142). Professor R. W. Mitchner is editing Trevisa's translation of Bartholomaeus Anglicus' *De Proprietatibus Rerum* (Research in Progress, *PMLA,* LXXI [1956], item 408).

22. Any educated person in the Middle Ages, of course, would have had a knowledge of the Bible. A distinction has to be made, however, between the extent and kind of knowledge gained from professional training, and the extent and kind of knowledge gained from the rare

experience of translating the Bible itself. My impression is that the author of the B-continuation of *Piers the Plowman* exhibits both kinds of knowledge. But this sort of thing is difficult to prove. Perhaps a detailed study of the poet's explicit biblical references would provide a better point of departure. E.g., compare the earlier Wycliffite version of Luke 2:7 with the B-text, 12.147–8. Cf. above, chapter 3, note 17.

23. I give volume and page numbers of the Rolls Series edition. Studies of Trevisa's translation of the *Polychronicon* have been largely confined to its language. One of these is the unpublished dissertation of Berte Leroy Kinkade, The English Translations of Higden's Polychronicon, University of Illinois, Urbana, 1934. Chapter 3 of this dissertation reviews the facts of Trevisa's life and works. Another study is that of Arthur Clare Cawley, A Study of the Language of the Various Texts of Trevisa's Translation of Higden's *Polychronicon,* University of London, 1938 (unpublished M.A. thesis). Portions of this have been published in *London Mediaeval Studies:* A. C. Cawley, "Punctuation in the Early Versions of Trevisa," *LMS,* I, 1 (1937), 116–33; and "Relationships of the Trevisa Manuscripts and Caxton's *Polycronycon,*" *LMS,* I, 3 ([1939], 1948), 463–82.

24. Cf. W. A. Pantin, *The English Church in the Fourteenth Century,* Cambridge, 1955, p. 148, where reference is made to the Franciscan, John of Wales, who would describe Diogenes or Socrates as a model friar, thus invoking classical tradition in support of the fraternal orders. Trevisa turns the tables on them with his satiric application of the story of the two Roman philosophers.

25. At least one MS of Trevisa's translation (Additional 24,194) reads "awngel of hevyn." Cf. Rolls Series edition, V, 131, note 12.

26. Cf. Frank, *Piers Plowman and the Scheme of Salvation,* p. 65 and n. 3.

27. This deduction is confirmed by Trevisa's discussion of the two Hells, in response to Higden's assertion that the soul of King Edwin was delivered out of Hell by the prayers of St. Dunstan. See below.

28. Lines 154–64 are in RF only. Professor Donaldson ("MSS R and F in the B-Tradition of Piers Plowman," p. 206 and n. 66) considers this an accidental omission. Again I must say that the passage looks to me like a revision. It gives the impression that the poet may be still in the process of formulating his own interpretation of the story. Notice his direct appeal to "men of holy cherche," and the possible admission that his version of the Trajan story does not include all the points taken

up in the *Legenda Sanctorum* (154–55). It is almost as if this revision exhibits one side of a running debate on the subject of the righteous heathen between the poet and certain men of Holy Church not named. Lines 161–64 in particular seem designed as a direct reply to an argument offered by the opposition.

29. R. W. Chambers, *Man's Unconquerable Mind* (London, 1939), pp. 145 ff.

30. T. P. Dunning, "Langland and the Salvation of the Heathen." *Medium Aevum*, XII (1943), 45–54. R. W. Frank, Jr. (*Piers Plowman and the Scheme of Salvation*, p. 65, n. 3), favors Chambers' view, and speaks of Imaginatif's "daring hope." My own view would be that as long as the poet's position is that of a "hope" (and I think it is), then orthodox medieval theologians would not regard it as particularly daring. What I find most striking is the poet's ethical (rather than sacramental) emphasis. It should be understood that my use of the word "sacramental" here is metaphoric. Furthermore, any distinction between the ethical and sacramental is bound to involve oversimplification. Perhaps it would be better to distinguish two "aids" to salvation of the heathen: one is the imprecatory power of prayer; the other is the righteousness ("pure truth") of the man himself. Both Trevisa's note and the B-text of *Piers* seem to deny the first, and affirm the second. This strikes at the very heart of the problem, and reveals a skeptical view of "trentals" analogous to the cautious attitude toward pardons in the A-text. The shadow of Lady Meed rests on chantries as well as indulgences.

31. That is, the poet chooses "boon," meaning "request," since he wants a word that lacks the sacramental connotations of "prayer."

32. The whole of Trajan's statement is given a certain detachment by making it the allegation of a pope (B 11.136). The ambiguity of terms is perhaps best illustrated by the poet's use of "pyne" and "bitter peyne," which of course can be applied either to Purgatory or to Hell.

33. Mildred E. Marcett, *Uhtred de Boldon, Friar William Jordan, and Piers Plowman* (New York, 1938), pp. 57–64. Cf. A. Gwynn, S.J., "The Date of the B-Text of Piers Plowman," *RES*, XIX (1943), 1–24, especially 19–24.

34. Of course "Malkyn" is a common name for a country wench, but its use here is unusual, so much so that Skeat misunderstood the line (*Parallel Texts*, II, 29, note to line 181). Cf. *MLN*, LXIII (1948), 52–53, and Thomas A. Knott and D. C. Fowler, *Piers the Plowman*.

A Critical Edition of the A-Version (Baltimore, 1952), p. 157, note to line 158; I know of no other occurrence of this particular use of Malkyn, much less in alliterative form.

35. A. J. Perry (EETS OS 167), pp. 6–7.

36. Smyth, *Lives of the Berkeleys* (cf. note 6 above), I, 343–44.

37. *Cambridge History of English Literature,* Vol. II, chapter III: "The Beginnings of English Prose," by Alice D. Greenwood, p. 89 (1933 reprint).

38. *Polychronicon,* Rolls Series, IX, vii ff. The editor (Lumby) quotes the assertion of Pits that John Malvern wrote *Piers Plowman* (on p. x). Where did Pits find this attribution? Was it noted in a MS of the *Polychronicon?* He mentions the Corpus Christi MS (which Lumby prints), but I assume that if this MS contained such a note, Lumby would have referred to it. It may be that Pits got his information from John Stowe, *The Annales of England,* London, 1605, p. 373: "This year [1342!] John Malverne, Fellow of Orial College in Oxford, made and finished his book entitled, The Visions of Pierce Plowman." But where did Stowe get this idea? It is strange that he would date the poem 1342, especially since elsewhere (*A Survey of London,* ed. Kingsford, Oxford, 1908, I, p. 157) he quotes a passage from the poem (B XIII, 266–71) containing a clear allusion to the famine of 1370, while in the margin he *again* dates the poem 1342 and attributes it to John Malverne. And who was John Malverne? A. B. Emden, *A Biographical Register* (note 7, above), II, 1210 f., lists two John Malvernes, and a John Malvesore who was fellow of Oriel College from 1389 to 1394. There seems to have been some confusion here, and Emden does not attempt to decide who was responsible for the *Polychronicon* continuation. The most likely candidate is probably the John Malverne who had been a scholar at Gloucester College (1355–6), but who spent most of his life as a Benedictine monk in Worcester Cathedral priory. He died in 1410. Cf. also J. Armitage Robinson, "An Unrecognized Westminster Chronicler, 1381–1394," *Proceedings of the British Academy,* III (1907), 61–92.

39. Cf. *Polychronicon,* I, liii, and VIII, 359. Nevertheless it may well be, as has been suggested, that "Willelmus W." is simply derived from the poem—the name of the Dreamer plus "W" for "Wycliffite." I have already suggested, in discussing the criticism of bishops (chapter 6, above), that the B-poet, while not a blind follower of Wyclif, seems to have been defending him against "correctors" in B 10.284, and that the influence of some of Wyclif's teachings can be seen in the B-text. This aspect of the poem has been neglected in recent years, and needs

further study. A. C. Hamilton, in an interesting and valuable comparative study, "Spenser and Langland," *SP*, LV (1958), 533–48, makes this incisive statement (p. 535): "In reading the poem, he [Spenser] was not distracted by the multiple authorship of modern Langland criticism, and he lacked that modern historical perspective which reduces the poem to an expression of orthodox beliefs. . . . It was interpreted [in Spenser's age] as a bitter satire against the Church of Rome, and its author honored as a Protestant and prophet." This does not imply, of course, that Spenser would read the poem merely as a "Reformation tract." And we would do well, I think, to hesitate before concluding that Spenser's view of the poem suffers from a bias of which the modern critic is fortunately free.

40. "The *Piers Plowman* Manuscripts in Trinity College, Dublin," *The Library,* 5th Series, VI (December, 1951), 141–53.

41. *Ibid.,* p. 146.

42. I refer to the text as represented by MS E, on which the Rolls Series edition is based. But in fairness to Brooks it should be observed that correspondences between the Dublin annals and events in the *Brut* are often very striking. Possibly the scribe's text was a *Brut*-continuation supplemented by the *Polychronicon*. The problem of the affinities of late medieval chronicles and their continuations is extremely complex, and needs further study. See note 45 below.

43. Brooks, *ibid.,* p. 147.

44. Noted by Kinkade (English Translations of Higden's *Polychronicon,* p. 15). Cf. *Polychronicon,* VIII, 325.

45. Perry (EETS OS 167, p. lxxviii) mentions a manuscript attributed to Trevisa in Trinity College, Dublin (no. 506, E. 54, a folio of the 15th century). But he adds that the Librarian of Trinity College examined the MS (in 1915), and found that it did not correspond to Trevisa's version. Unfortunately, study of the numerous Latin texts of the *Polychronicon* seems not to have progressed much since the publication of the Rolls Series edition. But see the recent article by V. H. Galbraith, "An Autograph MS of Ranulph Higden's *Polychronicon,*" *Huntington Library Quarterly,* XXIII (1959), 1–18, which clearly demonstrates, I think, that Huntington MS HM 132 represents the final recension of the *Polychronicon* (to 1352) in the handwriting of Higden himself. Moreover, a study of the *Polychronicon* continuations by John Taylor, of the University of Leeds, is scheduled to appear shortly. Mr. Taylor's view of the "John Malvern" continuation is that it is a relatively late one (i.e., not written before the 1380's), and that it is based on what he

calls "the main Polychronicon continuation" and extracts from Walsingham's history.

46. The Dreamer is here speaking for the author. See my comments on the flexibility of the Dreamer's function at the beginning of this chapter.

47. There is no room here for a discussion of Trevisa's language. Suffice it to say that his dialect agrees surprisingly well with what has been deduced about the archetypal dialect of the B-text of *Piers the Plowman*. For the most accessible discussion of Trevisa's language, see Perry (EETS OS 167), pp. cxxxiii ff. Most of the earlier studies, which Perry cites, deal with the language of individual manuscripts, and are not concerned with distinguishing the author's own dialect from that of the intervening scribes. Yet Perry concludes, rightly I think, that Trevisa's dialect was "West Southern." The most recent and informed conclusions about the B-text of *Piers the Plowman* are to be found in the article (to which I have referred) by E. T. Donaldson, "MSS R and F in the B-Tradition of Piers Plowman," *Transactions of the Connecticut Academy of Arts and Sciences,* 39 (1955), 177–212. In this article Donaldson, speaking of the hypothetical archetype of the B-MSS ("Copy 1"), says that "the dialect was probably predominantly southwestern" (p. 185), and that recessive dialect features of the other MS groups support this conclusion (pp. 186–7, 190, 200–1). Of course it should be recognized that the dialect of an archetype is not necessarily that of the author himself. But the convergence of the dialect evidence is of interest in light of the present authorship hypothesis. No doubt a detailed dialect study of all *Piers Plowman* MSS (which I understand is forthcoming) will provide additional evidence, but it will be useful mainly in revealing patterns of MS dissemination, rather than in determining the dialect of the author. One further point made by Donaldson in the article cited above is that there is an occasional *e*-reflex of OE *y* (as in *kende*) in "Copy 3," and that this may have been a feature of the archetype (p. 186). Such a form may not be significant (p. 186, n. 22); but if it is, then it is worth noting that the same phenomenon appears in MSS of Trevisa's works (Perry, p. cxxxviii f.).

In view of the somewhat fragile nature of dialect evidence, I would suggest that a detailed study of the vocabulary of *Piers the Plowman* might provide valuable supplementary information about the author's language. An example is the word "goky" (B 11.299 f.):

> The gome that gloseth so chartres for a goky is holden.
> So is it a goky, by god, that in his gospel failleth . . .

W. W. Skeat, in his glossary, cites modern English "gawky," but, the phonological difficulty aside, "gawky" does not, according to the *OED,* appear in English before the eighteenth century. The *OED* lists "goky," but apparently the editors could find no occurrence of it outside *Piers the Plowman.* The files of the new Middle English Dictionary at Ann Arbor, Michigan, disclose one other certain use of the word in *Mum and the Sothsegger,* line 1582 (EETS OS 199, London, 1936, p. 73), a work remarkably influenced by our poem, as pointed out by the editors, who cite, as an example of this influence, "the occurrence of the rare word 'goky'" (p. xiv). This word, however, is "rare" only if we overlook the text of the Cornish *Ordinalia,* where it occurs, in one form or another, no less than twenty-seven times. In its unmutated form it appears as *goky, gocky, gokky,* and (plu.) *gockyes, gok* (O.M. 173, 489, 2655; P.C. 1149, 1662, 1781, 2043, 2890, 2897; R.D. 87, 972, 983, 1043, 1136, 1273, 1454, 1464, 1465, 1565). The word seems to function at times as a noun (e.g., P.C. 1149, 1781) and at times as an adjective (e.g., R.D. 1454). In its mutated form it appears as *woky* and *wokky* (P.C. 1290; R.D. 989, 1105, 1513). There is also a noun in Cornish formed from this word: *gokyneth,* meaning "foolishness." This occurs unmutated in O.M. 1512, and mutated in O.M. 473, P.C. 1808, 1989 (*wokyneth*).

But what is the origin of the word? Robert Williams, in his *Lexicon Cornu-Britannicum,* Llandovery, 1865, derives it from the adjective *cok,* "empty," "foolish," having the Welsh cognate *coeg,* both descended from the Indo-European root represented by Latin *caecus,* "blind," and Gothic *haihs,* "one-eyed." (Cf. Henry Lewis and Holger Pedersen, *A Concise Comparative Celtic Grammar,* Gottingen, 1937, p. 9.) R. M. Nance, on the other hand, in his *New Cornish-English Dictionary,* St. Ives, 1938 (and in the rev. ed., 1955), lists it as a borrowing from Middle English, in spite of the fact that earlier, in "A Glossary of Celtic Words in Cornish Dialect" (*Royal Cornwall Polytechnic Society,* 1923, p. 14), he had listed "*Gooky, Gucky.* A fool (St. Just). *Cok,* foolish, from *cok,* empty. W. *coeg.*" But Nance undoubtedly changed his mind because he subsequently found the word in the *OED,* where, as we have seen, the entry is based on a single occurrence in the B-text of *Piers the Plowman,* the native English authorship of which is at best presumptive. Hence the argument for *goky* as a borrowing from English is circular. In the absence of other evidence, therefore, I conclude that the frequency of occurrence of this word in Cornish, combined with its rarity in English, is linguistically significant, and that it is therefore of Cornish rather than Middle English origin, whatever its earlier history may have been. It is worth noting that the word is used with flexibility and ease in the Cornish text, whereas it is actually used in *Piers* only once (line 300), preceded by an explanation of its meaning (line 299).

A careful study by a qualified Celtic scholar of unusual or doubtful words in *Piers the Plowman* should be helpful. A few possibilities suggest themselves: *tryne* (C 21.87, glossed as "taste" in B 18.84); *decorreth* (B 14.193); *brockes* (B 6.31); *kex* (B 17.219); *troiled* (C 21.321, 334, though B 18.296 has *trolled forth*); and *vore* (C 7.118). There may well be others.

48. The question of the style and diction of the A and B versions needs investigating, for most of the observations that have been made on this topic suffer from authorship polemics. By far the best and most sensitive criticism of the poetic language of *Piers the Plowman* yet written is to be found, I think, in an article by J. A. Burrow, "The Audience of *Piers Plowman*," *Anglia,* 75 (1957), 373–84. Burrow's point is that *Piers* differs sharply from the other poems of the revival in the economy of its use of alliterative poetic diction. Furthermore, "where we do find 'characteristically alliterative' words used in *Piers Plowman,* it is in a new way—for secondary, ironical effects" (p. 381). The examples given (A 3.9–14; 11.35; prol. 7–10) provide striking support for this observation. All of these passages, however, are from the A-text. Perhaps this is merely fortuitous; but if so, what are the examples that might have been cited from B? As far as I can see, they do not exist. The function of the ten visions in the B-text, mentioned parenthetically (p. 383), is a matter of structure, and not style.

The poetic language of the B version is quite a different thing from that of A, and, I might add, lacks the technical skill evident in A's "secondary, ironical effects." On the basis of the passages cited from the A-text, Burrow concludes that the poet was "on the edge of the alliterative tradition" (p. 382). Using the styles of the A and B versions as a basis, I would prefer to say that the A-poet stands *above* the tradition (in the sense that his art springs from it, as Gollancz perceived, but goes beyond it, as Burrow points out), while it is the B-poet who stands "on the edge." The art of the B-text stands in a significant relation to that of A, and has its own high quality, but it is different. Where did the B-poet acquire his art? He learned it, I think, from the A-text itself. In our study of the literary relations of the two texts we have seen with what frequency the reader of the B-continuation encounters passages, especially in B passus 11–15, which seem to have been "generated" by passages or scenes in the A-text. Some of these are mere rebuttals (e.g., B 11.103–310); but others are directly inspired by the A-text (B 12.141–55, cp. A 11.297–303; B 13.21–178, cp. A 11.38–85; etc.). In fact the entire section of the B-continuation which deals with the "A-text revisited" theme—and which in some ways makes great demands on the reader—provides valuable evidence of "the poet's progress" in matters of both style and structure. Beginning with B passus 16, however, if not before, the apprenticeship is complete, and the poem asserts itself, begins to move with its own power.

Burrow also discusses the audience of *Piers* with considerable penetration (pp. 373–9). It seems to me that the A-poet's audience is best defined by Holy Church, when she says (A 1.125): "Lerith it this lewide men, for lettrid it knowith . . ." True, the poet addresses "lettrid" and "riche" men on occasion, but his tone is usually angry and uncompromising, and he thus surrenders any serious hope of converting them to his point of view. The B-poet, however, though he makes every effort to "hold" the audience of the A-text, also addresses those groups in society not reached by the earlier poem: the learned, the wealthy, and the powerful. As we have seen, the contrast between the two audiences of the B-continuation can best be observed in a comparison of B passus 14 and 15.

A final point about the position of *Piers the Plowman* in the alliterative revival needs to be made. Some years ago J. R. Hulbert, in a valuable study entitled "A Hypothesis Concerning the Alliterative Revival," *MP*, XXVIII (1931), 405–22, suggested that the language, sophistication, and deliberately archaic form of the alliterative poetry is best explained on the assumption that it was cultivated by the baronial opposition, a "group of nobles standing in opposition to the royal court, and seeking to foster a form of literature more truly 'English' than that prevailing in London" (p. 406). Needless to say, the Trevisa hypothesis fits these conditions very well (cf. Hulbert, *ibid.*, 422, n. 1).

49. I have carefully avoided any consideration of the C-text. The literary relations of the A and B texts are sufficiently complicated to discourage a simultaneous, synoptic reading of all three versions. Yet this will have to be done, and I can only hope that the present study will make the task a little less difficult. I do not believe that any of the versions of *Piers the Plowman* can be regarded as "historical accidents, haphazard milestones in the history of a poem that was begun but never finished," as Donaldson tentatively suggests (*Transactions of the Connecticut Academy of Arts and Sciences*, XXXIX [1955], 211; with Bloomfield concurring, *Anglia*, 76 [1958], 228 and n. 1), although I too

have experienced that wave of wanhope that inevitably comes from detailed study of MSS of the poem. The C-text will be found, I think, to contain two basic types of revision. The first comprises those revisions that result from dissatisfaction with the style or structure of B, and the second (equally if not more important) those revisions that result from changes in the poet's own ideas and attitudes (e.g., his attitude toward bishops). The latter type of revision will need to be analyzed in the light of historical events and the changing atmosphere in England from 1383 to near the end of the century (in the absence of any clear *terminus ad quem* for the C-text). This analysis should produce interesting results, analogous to, though not identical with, those achieved so brilliantly by V. H. Galbraith in his essay, "Thomas Walsingham and the Saint Albans Chronicle, 1272–1422," *English Historical Review*, XLVII (1932), 12–30.

As for authorship of the C-text, due weight will have to be given to R. W. Chamber's suggestion (*Man's Unconquerable Mind*, p. 167): "I have sometimes thought that the poet may have died, leaving his work of addition unfinished, and that some friend may have taken great liberties in issuing the C-text." On the other hand, it may be that the B and C versions are the work of one man. As far as the Trevisa hypothesis is concerned, the important works to consult would be Trevisa's translation of the *De Regimine Principum* of Ægidius Romanus, and his translation of Bartholomæus Anglicus, *De Proprietatibus Rerum*. Unfortunately, neither of these texts has been edited (see note 21, above). Some valuable studies, however, have been made. One of these is Herbert E. Childs, A Study of the Unique Middle English Translation of the De Regimine Principum of Ægidius Romanus (MS Digby 233), unpublished Ph.D. thesis, University of Washington, 1932. Another is Elizabeth J. Brockhurst, Bartholomew Anglicus: "De Proprietatibus Rerum," unpublished Ph.D. thesis, University of London, 1952. Robert W. Mitchner, who is editing the *De Proprietatibus Rerum*, has published a manuscript study, "Wynkyn de Worde's Use of the Plimpton Manuscript of *De Proprietatibus Rerum*," *The Library*, 5th series, Vol. VI, No. 1, June, 1951, pp. 7–18. My impression from reading these studies is that Trevisa's later translations lack the frequent, idiosyncratic notes of the type found in the *Polychronicon*, which were written in the "heat" of the 1380's, and it may be that his later works will have little to offer for comparison with the C-text. It is possible, however, that they will exhibit a congruence of interests. In the *De Regimine Principum*, for example (in bk. III, pt. iii), we find a thorough discussion of military tactics, including methods of besieging a fortress with missiles, mines, engines, rams, etc. (H. E. Childs, A Study of the Unique Middle English Translation, pp. 67, 302 ff.), a subject which seems to have engaged the attention of the C-poet (C 21.283–96).

At what time Trevisa first read the *De Proprietatibus Rerum* we do not know; he completed his translation of it (as he tells us) on 6 February, 1398. It is possible that he had become familiar with it much earlier at Oxford. R. W. Frank, Jr., uses it (without claiming that it was a specific source) in his study of the B-text (*Piers Plowman and the Scheme of Salvation,* esp. p. 46 and n. 2). Trevisa does insert occasional comments of his own in the translation, but they are not as revealing as the *Polychronicon* notes, and indeed are often quite pedantic. For instance, in bk. II, ch. ii of the *De Proprietatibus Rerum* he inserts a note in which he tries to elucidate a grammatical point (I am indebted to Prof. Mitchner for sending me this passage transcribed from the Plimpton MS): "As if a childe knoweþ þat if þe nominatif caas and þe verbe discordeþ in persoun and in nombre, þen resoun is incongrue, as in þis maner: *puer sumus bonus.* Þanne tak for on premis no resoun is congrue in þe which þe nominatif caase and þe verbe discordeþ in nombre and in persoun, and tak for oþer premis in þis resoun: *puer sumus bonus.* Þe nominatif caas and þe verbe discordeþ in number and in persoun; and mak þi conclusioun in þis manere. *Ergo:* þis resoun is not congrue: *puer sumus bonus.* Þanne if he knoweþ þe forsayde tweye premisses he knoweþ þe conclusioun by þe premisses for he concludeþ þat on of þat oþer." Just what this explanation means is not entirely clear; but it seems possible to me that the man responsible for it might also be capable of writing lines like the following from the C-text of *Piers the Plowman* (C 4.335–40, 407–9):

> Thus ys mede and mercede as two manere relacions,
> Rect and indyrect, rennynge bothe
> On a sad and a syker, semblable to hym-selve—
> As adiectif and substantyf vnite asken,
> Acordaunce in kynde, in cas and in numbre,
> And ayther ys otheres help—of hem cometh retribucion. . . .
> Thus is man and mankynde in manere of a substantif,
> As *hic et hec homo,* askyng an adiectif
> Of thre trewe termysons, *trinitas unus deus;*
> > *Nominativo, pater et filius et spiritus sanctus.*

50. Especially valuable here is E. T. Donaldson, *Piers Plowman: The C-Text and Its Poet* (New Haven, 1949), in particular chapter IV, "The Politics of the C-Reviser." In my opinion Donaldson clearly demonstrates the essential conservatism of the B and C texts. The A-text is another matter altogether. True, the occasional "prescriptive" passages in A (e.g., the plowing of the half acre, Thought's definition of the triad) are orthodox enough. But A's radicalism is a matter of tone, rather than direct statement, and can be seen especially in his sweeping denunciations of the learned and the wealthy, and his praise of the fundamental spirituality of the commons. This basic opposition between A and B-C will explain the cleavage of opinion among the critics as to the political views expressed in *Piers the Plowman,* to which Donaldson calls attention (p. 85). Those whose impressions of the poem are derived primarily from the A-text (whether directly or from the A-text as preserved in the first part of B) call the poet radical; those whose impressions come mainly from B (or C) call him conservative. A close study of the critics cited by Donaldson would, I think, bear this out, to the extent that it is possible to detect the basis of their impressions. The opposition between A and B-C will also resolve the "paradox" (Donaldson, *ibid.,* p. 110) of the association of *Piers the Plowman* with the Peasants' Revolt. As I have already suggested, John Ball invoked the A-text; the B-text had not yet appeared, and was probably not completed until late in 1382.

51. E. M. W. Tillyard, *The English Epic and Its Background* (Oxford University Press, 1954), p. 171: "I conclude, therefore, that *Piers Plowman* emerges as the undoubted, if imperfect, English epic of the Middle Ages." Tillyard's entire critique (pp. 151–71) should be read; I particularly admire the honesty of his analysis in dealing with the difficulties as well as the felicities of the poem. Although he relies on the work of Chambers, Coghill, and Wells, he does not pass lightly over the problems which their theory of the poem's structure creates. On the other hand, while it may be difficult to say whether a poem is perfect, I believe that most, if not all, of the imperfections which critics have seen in *Piers the Plowman* will turn out to be defects of criticism rather than defects in the poem itself. *Mea culpa!*

INDEX

Adams, J. Q., 225, 231

Ægidius Romanus, 188, 252

Allegory: in the A-text, 16–18; in scriptural exegesis, 44, 120–26, 134–35; in B-continuation, 57–58, 155–56. *See also* Bible

Arimathea, Joseph of, 56

Arnold, T., 238

Arthurian romance. *See* Romance literature

Athanasian Creed, 12, 16

Babington, Churchill, 218, 221

Bale, John, 241

Ball, John, 205, 223, 254

Bartholomew Anglicus, 188, 243, 252

Becket, St. Thomas à, Archbishop of Canterbury, 174, 239

Bennett, J. A. W., 167–68, 236

Berkeley, Maurice IV, Lord, 241

Berkeley, Thomas III, Lord, 241

Berkeley, Thomas IV, Lord, 186–88, 190, 200–1, 241–42

Berkeley castle, 188, 203

Bible: in B-continuation, 43–47; allegorical interpretation, 44, 120–26, 134–35; translated by John Trevisa, 188–90, 242; Wycliffite translation, 190, 222, 231, 243–44

— *Genesis:* as a whole, 30, 56, 66, 68, 70, 90, 121–29; *1:28*, 133; *1:31*, 71; *2:19–20*, 67; *3:18*, 228; *3:22*, 226, 228; *6:5* ff., 177; *18:1* ff., 131, 133

— *Exodus: 4:1*, 131; *14:21–30*, 120

— *1 Samuel: 6:19*, 77; *13:8–14*, 77

— *2 Samuel: 6:6–7*, 77

— *Job: 42:5–6*, 13–14, 211

— *Psalms: 15*, 88; *23*, 13; *23:4*, 26; *24:10*, 152; *42:3*, 86; *85:10*, 142; *133:1*, 35, 144; *145:9*, 61

— *Ecclesiastes: 12*, 163–64; *12:5*, 235

— *Isaiah: 1:3*, 70; *2:1–8*, 215; *5:22*, 86; *6:1–5*, 211; *6:11*, 134; *11:2–5*, 76, 113; *11:6*, 67; *28:10*, 118, 237; *63:1–3*, 150–51, 233

— *Hosea: 3:1–3*, 231

— *Micah: 3:1–3*, 237

— *Matthew: 5:13*, 116; *6:25–26*, 15; *9:4*, 76, 113–14; *21*, 228; *22:5*, 116; *22:14*, 61, 63; *22:37–39*, 88, 224; *23:1–12*, 214, 217; *23:2*, 37, 177

— *Mark: 4:8*, 124; *13:9–11*, 41, 218; *15:34*, 133; *16:15*, 117, 156; *16:17–18*, 94

— *Luke: 2:7*, 222, 244; *7:36–50*, 231; *9:2*, 240; *11:17*, 76; *14:11*, 214; *14:12*, 64; *16:9*, 23; *16:19–31*, 134, 224; *18:22–23*, 64

— *John: 3:8–11*, 76; *3:13*, 39; *6:51*, 228; *19:34*, 140

Index